2014

APPROACHING ENGLISH GRAMMAR ANALYTICALLY: A STUDENT GUIDE

ERIC B. DREWRY

APPROACHING ENGLISH GRAMMAR ANALYTICALLY: A STUDENT GUIDE

ERIC B. DREWRY

First published in 2014 in Champaign, Illinois, USA
by Common Ground Publishing LLC
as part of The Learner book series

Library of Congress Cataloging-in-Publication Data

Drewry, Eric B.
  Approaching English grammar analytically : a student guide / Eric B. Drewry.
    p. cm. -- (The Learner Book Series)
  Includes bibliographical references and index.
  ISBN 978-1-61229-542-8 (pbk : alk. paper) -- ISBN 978-1-61229-543-5 (pdf : alk. paper)
  1. English language--Grammar. 2. English language--Grammar--Problems, exercises, etc. I. Title.

PE1112.D74 2014
425--dc23

2014024618

Table of Contents

Chapter 4: Phrasal Categories, Phrasal Roles, and Phrase Structure   69

Chapter 5: Types of Clauses: Main and Dependent (Adjectival, Adverbial, and Nominal)   107

Chapter 6: Non-finite Clauses   127

Chapter 7: Movement, Transformations, and Empty Categories — 142

Chapter 8: Phrase Structure Tree Diagramming — 162

Chapter 9: Reed-Kellogg Diagramming — 198

Acknowledgements

Others have invested time and energy into the revising of this text, most especially ten semesters' of students who took the Approaches to Grammar course at Azusa Pacific University ("APU"). My thanks to them for their many comments, and to the anonymous reviewer whose comments boosted it over several final humps. An expression of gratitude is also due to three present or former students at APU who helped by creating many of the sentences in the practice exercises, redoing diagrams, paginating the index, and putting the text into the proper format: Eric Catanzaro, Nick Philips, and Joshua Drewry. Thank you. My thanks also to the administrators at APU for providing both the stimulus and the reserved time for me to write, to my colleagues in the English department for their support, and to my wife for providing consistent and necessary encouragement.

It also matters greatly that the authors listed in the Works Cited section published their findings for others to learn from. This text is merely a shadow of what they produced, and it is a grateful shadow.

List of Tables

List of Abbreviations

A	adjective
AAE	African American English
Adv	adverb
AdvP	adverb phrase
AP	adjective phrase
Aux	auxiliary
C	complementizer
c:	complement (in phrase structure)
CCP	coordinating/correlative conjunction phrase
Conj	conjunction
CP	complementizer phrase
CP(A)	adjectival complementizer phrase
CP(Adv)	adverbial complementizer phrase
CP(Aux2)	auxiliary second complementizer phrase
CP(N)	nominal complementizer phrase
CP(Q)	question; interrogatory sentence
DO	direct object
DRRRIIIPPP	mnemonic for the subcategories of pronouns (demonstrative, reciprocal, reflexive, relative, indefinite, intensive, interrogative, personal object, personal possessive, personal subject
e	empty category
fanboys	mnemonic for the coordinating conjunctions (for, and, nor, but, or, yet, so)
h:	head (in phrase structure)
Int	intensifier
IO	indirect object
IP	inflected phrase
m:	modifier (in phrase structure)
ModP	modal phrase
N	noun

NEG	negative particle
NP	noun phrase
P	preposition
PerfP	perfect phrase
PP	prepositional phrase
PPRAIID	mnemonic for the subcategories of determiner (personal, possessive, relative, article, interrogative, indefinite, and demonstrative)
Prn	pronoun
ProgP	progressive phrase
PS	phrase structure
Qual	qualifier
Q	quantifier
s:	specifier (in phrase structure)
SAE	Standard American English
V	verb
V2	verb second
VP	verb phrase
Vpart	verb particle
wh-	interrogatory word or relative marker (who, what, where, when, why, whose, which, and how)
XP	unspecified phrase
?	marked or marginally acceptable
*	grammatically unacceptable

List of Symbols

Reed-Kellogg symbol for a PP, IO, Adjectival Complement Clause or NP used adverbially

Reed-Kellogg symbol for a subject and predicate

Reed-Kellogg symbol for a clause with something modifying the subject (adjective, determiner, gerundive, or clause, but not a noun)

Reed-Kellogg symbol for a clause with something modifying the verb

Reed-Kellogg symbol for a modifier which is itself being modified

Reed-Kellogg symbol for a clause with an introductory 'that' or 'whether'

Reed-Kellogg symbol for a verb with a direct object

Reed-Kellogg symbol for a (linking) verb with a subject complement

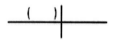

Reed-Kellogg symbol for a subject with an appositive

Reed-Kellogg symbol for the position of a nominal clause or a PP subject complement

Reed-Kellogg symbol for a (verb+ing) gerund

Chapter 1: Approaching Grammar

About Approaching Grammar

In the past there have been many different ways to approach grammar, some better than others. The most famous early grammarian is the Hindi scholar Pāṇini, whose description of Sanskrit in about the fifth century B.C. (or B.C.E.) is still considered excellent work. We won't be using his work as our model, however, since Sanskrit grammar is not similar enough to help us approach English grammar well.

More surprising, perhaps, is that this Guide rejects the approach championed in latter eighteenth century England by a group called the Grammarians, including Joseph Priestly ("Rudiments of English Grammar" in 1761), Robert Lowth ("Short Introduction to English Grammar" in 1762) and Lindley Murray ("English Grammar" in 1794) and for very similar reasons (Crystal 2-3). It's not that the English of two and a half centuries or so ago was so different from modern English, because the two really are very similar. The approach used by the Grammarians, however, was based on Latin as the 'perfect' language. During that time, which was the time of the English Renaissance, everything Greek and Latin was idolized. Fancy buildings were built with Greek or Roman columns, and parks got classical-style statues. This fad created a basic error in terms of grammatical analysis, though, since Latin grammar does not give us a useful model for analyzing English grammar. English comes from Anglo-Saxon, and not from Latin. The Grammarians did their best to fit the square English peg into the heptagonal Latin hole, though.

Echoes from the work done by the Grammarians can still be heard in many primary and secondary school systems today. One echo from that period that this approach to grammar takes issue with or aims to clarify is primarily the following: English has eight or nine parts of speech (=lexical categories), and they are nouns, pronouns, verbs, adverbs, adjectives, prepositions, conjunctions, and interjections. The ninth category would sometimes be articles, but these are then usually considered 'adjectives'. Why object to that - isn't it true? Yes, it's true in the same way that's it's true to say you have two sisters when you really have three: it's true, but it isn't complete. It is more useful for our list of lexical categories to be both true and complete. English having eight or nine lexical categories is true, but twelve is both true and more complete, at least for our discussions here and now.

Here is a more complete and useful list: nouns, determiners, pronouns, verbs, verb particles, auxiliaries, adverbs, qualifiers, quantifiers, adjectives, prepositions, and conjunctions. And interjections are not even needed in the 'complete' category, since they are complete expressions, by themselves, unrelated to the structure of the sentence they're in (or used as noun phrases, so not in need of a category of their own). How, then, do we go from nine (or eight, now that we've deleted interjections) to twelve? By understanding that English is a Germanic language which has not developed from Latin in the way that French, Italian or Portuguese have. Some categories in Germanic languages, such as English, are not represented in Latin-based languages. When the Grammarians adopted Latin grammar as a model, they had about nine categories to fit the all twelve Germanic lexical categories into. So they had to use some categories, such as adjectives and adverbs, as catch-all categories to throw in the lexical items that didn't conveniently fit any other category. We'll pick up that strand of the discussion very soon.

What we noticed in our historical overview is also true presently: we need to recognize that approaches to language vary over time. That is what was intended by the comment above about a list of twelve lexical categories being 'more complete, at least for here and now.' Only for 'now' and not forever? Well, sort of. The two approaches discussed in this book will probably be adequate for the rest of our lives and an entire career of teaching in primary or secondary schools. But we'll still do our best to be true and complete without claiming that no other approach is ever going to be more complete.

Many approaches are possible, and this book has adopted only two major approaches – the main approach is a modern one based on Noam Chomsky's twentieth-century research paradigms (called 'transformational-generative theory' in the version we'll look at); the secondary approach is a more traditional one, still used in school systems in parts of the U.S. (Hoffman), and based on the work of two teachers at Brooklyn Polytechnic Institute in the latter half of the nineteenth century. Their names are Alonzo Reed and Brainerd Kellogg, and their approach is called the 'Reed-Kellogg' approach.

For some students the idea of 'approaching' grammar is a comfort, since it's possible to approach a mountain range, for example, without ever arriving there. Similarly, it's possible to approach grammar without ever claiming that one certain approach really arrives at the complete truth. If professional linguists are still debating how best to describe the sentence structure of English, we can adopt a similarly modest view that no single approach is the only true one. So the two approaches to grammar in this Guide aim to be true and basically complete without claiming that some other approach may not be even better in some ways. There is a great advantage to be gained by not opting for the slightly more complete versions, however, because a small gain in completeness usually drags along a much more complex theory with it. We can be glad not to need the larger number of theoretical details involved in a number of modern syntactic approaches which are even more complete and much more complex. In observing and absorbing two approaches to grammar, we will also need, on occasion, to recognize two different technical terms for a given grammatical structure, so a glossary at the end of the book will help clarify the relevant terminology. Several sections in chapter one have further commentary about echoes from the Grammarian movement.

About Explicit Grammar Teaching and this Guide

Grammar is best learned in a context, either writing or speaking. Children learn their first grammar entirely in context without any formal instruction, and they learn it perfectly. Here we mean 'grammar' as a mental construct, not a system of rules about correct writing. Grammar, in our first language, is innate, and much of this Guide will simply make explicit what native speakers all know implicitly. In the 1960's, when this innateness became widely known and accepted, schools in the U.S. (but not elsewhere in the English-speaking world) stopped teaching grammar as a subject by itself, and integrated it into the reading, writing, and speaking parts of the language arts curricula. An entire generation later, scholars and researchers noticed that many students from that era cannot express themselves about grammatical notions. So the pedagogical pendulum swung back, and many elementary and secondary programs began again teaching grammar explicitly.

Research in the late 1970's showed that explicit grammar teaching in the context of a writing course does not necessarily improve a student's writing (MacQuade 29; Hillocks and Smith 248). The lack of effect on student writing doesn't mean that grammar needn't be taught explicitly, only that the purpose of such teaching needs to be made clear and kept clear. The approach to grammar in this Guide is designed to help future teachers, tutors, and other speakers of the English language better explain and discuss the systematic nature of English grammar. This Guide, in chapters one to eight, uses insights from the research movement spear-headed by Noam Chomsky in the second half of the twentieth century and attempts to express these insights in accurate, but less technical modern terminology. In addition, chapter nine discusses the same range of grammatical patterns from the modern perspective but in the traditional vocabulary and graphics of early twentieth century grammar.

Outlining this Guide's approach to English grammar can be done quite easily and briefly. It discusses English grammar in terms of words, phrases, and clauses of varying types. That's all the parts that a sentence has. We will learn to distinguish and name the different kind of words, phrases and clauses. Phrases and clauses have a structure, and within clauses, words and phrases are sometimes moved or deleted. These movements and deletions have important consequences for sentence structure. That's all there is to explain. And the order of the material in this book follows that brief overview: chapters two and three discuss types of words; chapter four discusses types and structures of phrases; chapters five and six discuss types and structures of clauses; chapter seven discusses the movement and deletion of words and phrases; chapters eight and nine show two ways to display this information in the form of diagrams, and chapter ten explores some analytical tools to consider writing style. All the information in this Guide should be arranged according to this outline. If a given piece of information seems out of context or not immediately relevant, it's probably good to ask ourselves why it's there. It may turn out to be more useful than we thought, or it may have gotten into a context where it doesn't really belong.

About Choosing which Grammar Rules to Memorize

At the beginning of the term, one of the most common questions that students ask in my advanced English grammar courses is "Do we have to memorize that?" When you think that English probably has a half million nouns, it's clear that the question "Is that a noun?" can't be answered by memorizing all the nouns. Even worse is the question, "Is this an adjectival clause or an adverbial clause?" The number of possible clauses in English is infinite, so even the world's greatest memorizers could not prepare to answer such a question by memorizing clauses.

The best way to answer these questions is to know how to recognize a noun or a certain kind of clause, in a way similar to how doctors diagnose diseases. Nouns have certain 'symptoms,' as do adverbial clauses. Grammar students need to know what questions to ask so that an accurate grammatical 'diagnosis' can be made. The process is called 'syntactic testing.' Syntactic testing of lexical categories, such as nouns and verbs does not require very much memorization, nor does syntactic testing of adverbial or adjectival clauses. Generally, students find that an analytical approach beats a mnemonic (memory-based) approach. Nonetheless, memorizing certain diagnostic questions is actually useful after all, since they allow us to answer many questions about English grammar by just accessing our implicit, native-speaker, mental grammars.

Another point where memorizing is useful concerns the sub-categories of each lexical category, and we'll see some mnemonic tricks to help in that process. So memorizing is not the biggest part of discussing grammar as this Guide approaches it. The scope of this Guide is intended to include a solid background in what a high school teacher may want to know to be able answer any grammar question that an advanced English class may ask. For teachers of younger students, the information and the approach are still useful, but more effort is needed to translate the concepts into understandable language and examples.

Approaching Grammar with Style

Sometimes, especially in elementary school, it's not convenient to explain how complex some grammatical or stylistic considerations are since the pupils would only be confused by all the details. At that level, we choose to give them short bits of wisdom which they can implement easily. Since this guide is meant for mature students and future tutors or teachers, it should be all right to talk in greater detail with complexity and abstraction about some of those elementary bits of wisdom. Again, this Guide is not about rules of correct writing (prescriptive grammar). Instead, it's about the mental construct of English that all native speakers absorb as toddlers (descriptive grammar). But the two sometimes intersect, and when they do, it's good to try to make sense of whatever conflict or complementarity may arise.

Don't Use Double Negatives

Are double negatives grammatically unacceptable or simply stylistically weak? In thinking about that question, we should probably start by saying there are different ways of negating an idea - syntactically, morphologically, and semantically. Syntactic negation uses 'n' words a lot – 'no' and 'not' are the main ones. They also combine with other worlds in a sort of morphological way, creating 'never' (not ever), 'nobody', 'nothing,' and 'none,' among others. Standard morphological derivation uses prefixes like 'dis-,' 'un-,' 'im-,' 'il-,' 'ir-,' and 'non-' to create negative forms. Semantic negation is found in words like 'neglect,' 'fast,' 'forget,' 'refuse,' and numerous others. The main objection to double negation in modern usage is to double syntactic negation, such as, 'I don't have no time for that.' This sort of double syntactic negation, and even triple syntactic negation, are generally seen as more emphatic than single negation in many non-standard dialects. Objecting to syntactic double negation is part of an attempt to help students who speak non-standard dialects of English learn to master the grammar (in this case the syntax) of one of the standard dialects (British, American, Australian, or others).

Nonetheless, syntactic double negation is sometimes perfectly acceptable in standard dialects as well. In a news story about the great emotional value that soldiers in war zones put on the dogs that they adopt there, the spokesperson for American Dog Rescue emphasized the dogs' value this way: "There wasn't one of the soldiers – male or female – who did not cry when they saw their dog" (Benjamin). Here we see the negative particle 'not' twice in one sentence, and yet the sentence is perfectly grammatical. We could remove the double negation to express the same thought: "Every soldier – male and female – cried when they saw their dog."

As in non-standard dialects, the double syntactic negation helps to emphasize a point. The only difference between the two is that standard dialects require that the two negators be in different clauses. In this case, the two 'nots' are in different clauses separated by the subordinating conjunction 'when.' Another example will show two 'nots' in even closer proximity. The context would be a conversation about a pushy boss who is putting a lot of pressure on an employee to go to a conference instead of letting the employee go on a family vacation. "We have to reschedule the vacation," the employee says sadly, "I can't not go to the conference." Here the two negators are right next to each other in the same clause. This is an exception to the general rule about double negation in standard English dialects, but it shows that elementary school wisdom about double negation requires further consideration when we become old enough to work with more details and variables.

There is another objection to double negation that is not related to differences between standard and non-standard dialects. It is purely a stylistic choice within the standard dialects. Mixing morphological and semantic negation has virtually no grammatical limit. Instead, the limit is one of consideration for the reader or the hearer. After you read the following sentence, which contains multiple semantic negation, notice how long it takes you to answer the question immediately after it. "She refuses to neglect to avoid her vegan eating habits." So does she eat meat or not? Vegans don't eat meat. Avoiding those habits would mean eating meat. Neglecting to avoid them would mean not eating meat.

Refusing to neglect to avoid them would mean eating meat. So she eats meat. This is not about the idea of neglecting to avoid something, which does sound very odd, but about the availability of semantic negation in long strings.

Besides that, we could introduce a morphologically derived negative, such as 'disregard' ('not regard') and extend the string to quintuple negation. Even without that, the original sentence is an example of grammatical quadruple semantic negation. It isn't a very pretty sentence, and no one would expect to use it in any normal discourse, but it is grammatical. However, this sort of writing or speaking is very inconsiderate to the listener or reader. Each negation has to be processed separately to make a positive from two negatives and a negative from a third negation, and so on. Multiple semantic or morphological negation fails not because of its grammar, but because of the burden it puts on the reader or listener to process the negating of other earlier negations. A descriptive view of grammar (as a mental construct) takes into account the various grammatical possibilities and helps us explain the differences between style and grammar more clearly.

Don't End a Sentence with a Preposition

Winston Church famously responded to this admonition in one of the following ways, depending on the accuracy of the source: "Ending a sentence with a preposition is something up with which I will not put ("Churchill"), or "The rule which forbids ending a sentence with a preposition is the kind of nonsense up with which I will not put" ("Preposition"). Both quotations or paraphrases preserve the main point at the end of the sentence, which is "up with which I will not put" instead of the more natural "which I will not put up with." Churchill was in favor of the more natural syntax. Should we agree? Again, this turns out not to be a rule of grammar, but a rule of style. Both Churchill's convoluted rule-bound syntax and the more natural syntax are equally acceptable grammatically.

 Stylistically, however, not all acceptable sentences are equal. Being able to create the more convoluted sentence is a sign of a certain mastery of English grammar, which is useful to show off in special situations, such as recommending oneself as a grammar teacher. A person applying for a job as a highly-qualified grammar teacher could say the same thing in several ways: "Your students have exactly the profile that my training deals most successfully with," or "Your students have exactly the profile that my training deals with most successfully," or "Your students have exactly the profile with which my training deals most successfully." The choice is a matter of style, which in this case translates to a choice of the type of impression that one is trying to make. The preposition rule is not about grammar in the descriptive sense, but in a prescriptive (style) sense.

Verb Forms

When we talk about grammar, verbs seldom get the attention they deserve. There are a couple of ways to remedy that. This guide invests quite a bit of chapter two discussing verb types as a basis for distinguishing seven different types of simple sentence. Before getting to that, as a kind of warm-up, let's talk about verb tenses for a couple of paragraphs. If you ask any linguist, she or he could tell you that English verbs only have two tenses (present and past) and that would be correct.

But it might not be too helpful, since many people talk about verb aspect and time and voice as the same as tenses, such as the present perfect progressive 'tense'. So let's look at the many different forms that a single verb can have and which many perfectly wonderful people continue to refer to as verb tenses.

We'll use the verb 'draw' because it shows several forms very clearly, and we'll use the pronoun 'she' as our subject, since third person singular pronouns show more different verb forms than the plural pronouns or singular 'I' and 'you' forms. Since 'draw' is generally transitive, only some of the entries in the chart seem like full sentences. For this reason, the chart will dispense with capital letters and periods. Our chart has three time designations across the top: present, past (our tenses) and future (not a tense really, but a time). There are four rows down the side of the chart: simple forms, progressive forms, perfect forms, and perfect progressive forms. The final three are all technically verbal aspects, rather than tenses. The first chart shows the verb forms in the active voice.

Table 1: English verb tenses and aspects in the active voice

	past	present	Future
Simple tenses and forms	she drew	she draws	she will draw
Progressive aspect	she was drawing	she is drawing	she will be drawing
Perfect aspect	she had drawn	she has drawn	she will have drawn
Progressive Perfect aspect	she had been drawing	she has been drawing	she will have been drawing

Without slowing down to catch a breath, let's move on to a parallel set of verb forms representing the passive voice. The following table is almost a mirror image of the first one. The main difference is that passive verb forms have an extra form of the auxiliary verb 'be' and the main verb 'draw' always uses its past participle form 'drawn.'

Table 2: English verb tenses and aspects in the passive voice

	past	present	Future
Simple tenses and forms	she was drawn	she is drawn	she will be drawn
Progressive aspect	she was being drawn	she is being drawn	she will be being drawn
Perfect aspect	she had been drawn	she has been drawn	she will have been drawn
Progressive Perfect aspect	she had been being drawn	she has been being drawn	she will have been being drawn

We can, with a little bit of effort, imagine a context where almost any of the above verb forms could be used. The passive forms are often frowned on for stylistic reasons, since they are a little longer, more indirect, less active, and likely to create uncertainty as to who or what main actor in the sentence is.

Summary

There are numerous ways to approach grammar, with a major division between a descriptive (or cognitive) approach and a prescriptive (or writer's) approach. This Guide discusses two descriptive approaches and de-emphasizes stylistic considerations, but without abandoning stylistic discussions entirely. Where possible, a link is made between the description and prescription to show the reasoning and cognition behind some of the stylistic rules for formal writing. The Guide's purpose is to help future tutors, teachers, and language users explain more clearly the systematic nature of English grammar and what makes certain sentences acceptable in speech or writing and other sentences unacceptable to native speakers under any circumstances.

Practice Exercises

1. Should future teachers allow students to use double negatives?

2. Is it acceptable to end a sentence with a preposition in English?

3. How many tenses do verbs have in English? How many aspects?

Chapter 2: Testing for Lexical Categories

What Difference Do Lexical Categories Make?

This chapter introduces the four biggest lexical categories of English – adjectives, adverbs, nouns and verbs. Right at the start, though, let's ask a rather fundamental question – why should we care if we're able to identify a given word's lexical category? Let's call it my job to give each of us some reasons why we should care. That way, if there's ever a need to tell anyone else a reason to care about this part of grammar, we'll have some evidence in our favor. Here are a couple of famous examples, which we can find on the web with an electronic search engine under 'funny headlines' in numerous places. These were found on the web site http://www.plain-language.gov/examples/humor/ head-lines.cfm, but there are also other such sites:

1) British Left Waffles on Falkland Islands

2) Teacher Strikes Idle Kids

The source of the humor here is that one word in English may sometimes be a noun, while in another context the same word may be a verb, or an adjective. It turns out that we don't really consider them to be the same word, but different words with the same spelling, or homonyms. So even before we start our discussion of verbs and nouns, we need to recognize how each of the above sentences has two distinct meanings, one of which is unintended. In the first example, the newspaper wanted to say that the liberal politicians (the 'left') in England changed their mind ('waffled') about something. The unintended, funny meaning is that some British people forgot ('left') some fried food ('waffles') somewhere. 'Left' is an adjective (used as a noun) in the intended meaning, but it also has a homonym, which is the past tense of the verb 'leave.' 'Waffle,' which is a verb in the intended meaning, also has a homonym which is a noun. Both 'strikes' and 'idle' also have homonyms in the second example sentence above. It's a worthy challenge for us to look for the two meanings of the second by ourselves, both the intended meaning and the funny one.

So the parts of speech (= lexical categories = **syntactic categories** = **grammatical categories**) of words matter at least for this one type of humor. Is that enough of a reason to care? Maybe not. So let's look at another reason. If one of us has a chance to help non-native speakers (say, Chinese speakers) learn English, we may run into this kind of sentence in their English: *"I very want to help you," meaning "I sincerely want to help you." One 'adverb' ('sincerely') works and another word ('very') doesn't – why? Suppose we can prove that 'sincerely' is an adverb, but 'very' is not? Then, if the two words 'very' and 'sincerely' are considered to belong to different lexical categories, it's more logical to have them work differently in sentences. We will soon show that 'very' is actually not an adverb at all. This ability to distinguish lexical categories gives us a pretty good explanation for the difference in grammar. Other reasons will (gradually) become clear as we continue, so let's continue to build on our knowledge of adverbs a little bit more.

About Adjectives and Adverbs

We'll soon discover that there are several kinds of adjectives, so it will be important to have a way of distinguishing the various kinds of adjectives and ways of distinguishing adjectives from other words thrown into the adjective pot by the Grammarians. Looking at typical examples is usually a helpful way to start.

Color terms are considered one of the most typical examples of adjectives. Here are two typical ways that adjectives are used.

3) The jacket is green.

Here the adjective is at the end of a sentence after a form of the verb 'be.' This position is called 'predicative.' The adjective is in the part of the sentence called the predicate. This term is very traditional and will be discussed when we get to Reed-Kellogg sentence diagramming.

4) This is a green jacket.

Here the adjective is before the noun "jacket." This position is called an 'attributive' use of the adjective. It describes an attribute or characteristic of the noun. There'll be time to discuss nouns soon, too; for now, please take it on faith (or from what the second- or third-grade teacher said about nouns) that 'jacket' is a noun.

Learning words like 'attributive' and 'predicative' will help as the discussion of grammar continues and builds. Memory cards for this kind of learning may actually be helpful as we continue to add new vocabulary.

Building up some more example sentences (used as data) will show several of the characteristics, or 'diagnostics' of adjectives.

5) This jacket is greener than that one; it's the greenest one I've ever seen.

Here we see that adjectives can form comparatives (forms ending in '–er' meaning 'more,') and superlatives (forms ending in '-est' meaning 'most,'). Both forms can be used for comparisons. For longer adjectives, like 'beautiful,' the comparative and superlative suffixes '–er' and '–est' are not acceptable, so we use the words 'more' and 'most' before longer adjectives. For each new concept, there is often more technical vocabulary to note. It may help to note at this point this Guide will continue to use the relevant terminology for each grammatical concept that is discussed. So please take time to learn the technical terms as they appear. It's good to notice again that definitions of technical terms are in the glossary at the end of the book. Here is a sentence with a series of adjectives.

> 6) I see you have an attractive, new, green, imported jacket.

Here we see that adjectives can follow one another in a series, which is sometimes called stacking. The exact order of the adjectives is not random, but those details are more appropriate for a TESOL text (designed for 'Teaching English to Speakers of Other Languages') than for this more general text.

Summary: as the above example sentences show, adjectives have comparative and superlative forms, and they can be stacked. What else? In the first two example sentences, we saw that they may occupy a position (attributive) between words like 'this,' 'a/n', 'the' and a noun, or they may occupy a position (predicative) at the end of a sentence after some form of the verb 'be'. There are a few other verbs like 'be' in this respect, called 'linking verbs' and we'll get to them when we talk about types of verbs. Now comes the rub: even though the above is true, what if it's not complete? If adverbs and verbs and all manner of other words have the same diagnostics or characteristics, such as comparative forms and stacking, we have been exercising our grammatical diagnostic skills without identifying the diagnostic tests that are going to be most useful in understanding sentences.

And, so we see, to our chagrin, in this next sentence, that adverbs can also have comparative and superlative forms. As we recall – with some suspicion – the elementary school definition of an adverb is a word that modifies a verb, an adjective, or another adverb. They, too, can have –er and –est forms, as we see from an example which has been carefully chosen:

> 7) Jo and Li typed faster than we did; in fact, they typed the fastest of the whole group.

So here we have an adverb that looks just like an adjective in its morphology with its comparative and superlative suffixes. This was carefully chosen because very few adverbs have only one syllable and the ability to accept the –er or –est endings. In many linguistics descriptions, these endings are discussed as 'inflections.' Typical adverbs have the ending '-ly' as in 'beautifully', which becomes unacceptable if we use the form *'beautifullier' as a comparative. In fact, *'beautifullier' gets underlined in red as unacceptable by grammar checkers in our word processing programs. Note that the asterisk '*' before a data example means that it is unacceptable to native speakers of Standard American English. The form 'more beautifully' is the acceptable comparative form. And we see that adverbs, like adjectives, can also be stacked, as we see in the next sentence.

> 8) "We worked slowly, methodically, and carefully until deep in the night."

So we see that the attributive and predicative qualities of adjectives are unique, but the tests of stacking and suffixing do not distinguish adverbs from adjectives. We also note that there is a diagnostic test which only adjectives and adverbs can pass. No other lexical category (noun, verb, preposition, conjunction, ...) has comparative or superlative forms. We should all be able to think of examples impossible suffixing for comparative and superlative nouns, verbs, prepositions or conjunctions: *'car-er,' *'write-est,' *'with-er,' *'but-er'. Some other lexical categories such as nouns, verbs, and prepositions can be stacked, however: 'trees, bushes, and shrubs,' or 'jumps, runs, and hides,' or 'on, under, and behind the car.'

When an Adjective is Not an Adjective

Not everything traditionally called 'adjective' is still considered one in modern approaches to grammar. The eighteenth-century Grammarians had a limited number of options to choose from when they were dividing English words into Latin-based parts of speech. The articles 'a, an, the' and words such as 'my,' 'your,' 'his,' 'her,' 'our,' and 'their,' and a few others slowed them down a bit. But they noticed that these words, like adjectives, modify nouns, so the choice was obvious – call them adjectives.

This labeling of articles, for example, as adjectives is still preserved in some modern grammar books for correct writing such as *The New McGraw-Hill Handbook,* which says 'they function as adjectives" (Maimon *et alia* 541) and *The Little-Brown Compact Handbook,* which calls them "special kinds of adjectives" (Aaron 237). For purposes of prescriptive grammar and correct usage, more accurate distinctions are sometimes not needed. The problem is that the articles and other quasi-adjectives don't act like ('pattern like') adjectives when we approach them descriptively or cognitively. Has anyone ever heard of comparative or superlative forms, like *'the-er' and *'the-est'? I thought so. How about stacking a number of **articles** or similar words, as in this sentence?

9) *We saw your the expensive red carpet.

So we can say with some confidence that articles and the so-called possessive adjectives (my, your,...) do not pass the diagnostic tests for adjectives. They need their own category, which is called '**determiners**.' The determiner category also provides a place for some of the other words that the Grammarians could not categorize well, such as the **demonstratives**, 'this,' 'that,' 'these,' 'those,' and 'yon' (this final item is included for completeness). From now on, we'll call this group of five items '**demonstrative determiners**.' Articles are still called **articles**, and are considered a sub-category of determiners, which are not related to adjectives. And 'possessive adjectives,' such as 'my' and 'your' will henceforth be knighted '**possessive determiners**.' There's actually a couple of other groups of determiners, and we will postpone talking about them until we have developed a little more background information.

When an Adverb is Not an Adverb

We know that adverbs can be tested the same way as adjectives, in that they also have comparatives and superlatives. They can also be stacked, as shown ("slowly, methodically, and carefully") in the example sentence above. And we've noted that attributive and predicative distinctions can be used to distinguish adverbs from adjectives.

We have just seen that the determiners were classified as a type of adjective by the Grammarians. So now let's look at some of the words that the Grammarians threw into the 'adverb' box that really don't pass the diagnostic tests for adverbs. How about 'very' or 'somewhat,' and 'rather' ? Can they become comparative and superlative, such as *'verier' *'veriest,' *'somewhater' or *'more very' or *'most very' or *'most somewhat'? Will they stack? Well, we can say "He is very, very careful," so maybe it is an adverb after all. But how about * "He is very, somewhat careful."

If we look at real adverbs, we see that they can also repeat themselves identically, but we wouldn't call it stacking, since there is really only a single meaning, which is somewhat intensified: "We worked slowly, slowly until deep in the night." If we stack two different adverbs, it works fine, as in the example sentence above, but if we try to stack 'very and 'somewhat,' or 'rather' none of the combinations is acceptable.

What do we conclude then? That we need another category, called '**qualifiers**' or, in some texts '**intensifiers,**' for these items with no comparatives and no stackability. Although it may be useful to prefer the word 'intensifier' in order to avoid confusion between the words 'qualifier' and 'quantifier,' this Guide will generally use the term 'qualifier' because some qualifiers, such as 'rather' and 'quite' don't really intensify the meaning of the adjective or adverb that they are modifying. Instead, rather they diminish its intensity. The term 'qualifier' seems to remind us better of this spectrum of possible meanings. The other term 'quantifier' will be introduced after we get used to qualifiers a little more.

So now we have added determiners and qualifiers/intensifiers to our list of lexical categories, both based on their unique morphological (no –er/-est forms) and syntactic (inability to stack) characteristics. A full list of lexical categories is seen in the headings of the table of contents. It would be a good exercise at this point to list the diagnostics that we have discussed up to this point and what they do.

Adjectives can occupy the position between an article and a noun, and they can be stacked. This combination is unique to them. They share with adverbs, and nothing else, the possibility of comparative and superlative forms.

Since both adjectives and adverbs have comparative and superlative forms, we cannot use that as a way to identify adverbs uniquely. Even though we have the attributive and predicative qualities of adjectives to help us, we will soon see that there are additional ways to distinguish these two categories.

Determiners can occupy the same position as an article, and they cannot be stacked. Articles are a sub-category or determiners, and there are several more, which we will also need to discuss in more detail.

Intensifiers can occupy the position between an article and an adjective, or directly before an adverb, and they cannot be stacked.

Practice Recognizing Adjectives, Qualifiers, and Determiners

Here's an opportunity to distinguish adjectives, qualifiers and determiners (we'll save adverbs for the next set of exercises). Decide if any of the underlined words belong to any of the three categories. If it's not one of our three target categories, please don't worry about figuring out at this stage what it might be.

1. It was <u>quite</u> <u>a</u> <u>balmy</u> <u>summer</u> evening when <u>our</u> <u>bright</u> hero emerged <u>from</u> <u>the</u> darkness.

2. Spreading <u>his</u> <u>white</u> light across the bumpy path in front of him, he tried to move <u>a</u> <u>bit</u> to his <u>left</u>.

3. The chains binding his ankles prevented <u>much</u> movement, but he rode on <u>fairly</u> <u>well</u> till the darkness began to lift and <u>his</u> <u>own</u> <u>light</u> paled in that of <u>the</u> <u>sun</u>.

4. It was a <u>great</u> price he had paid to go into the darkness but <u>one</u> <u>that</u> he felt was <u>worth</u> the expense.

5. <u>No</u> stopping, no falling, <u>never</u> turning to the left; he continued along <u>the</u> <u>rock</u> path.

6. From a great distance, his father saw him <u>several</u> times during <u>his</u> <u>upward</u> climb.

Breaking New Ground—The Need for Syntactic Diagnostic Tests

What we have noticed from our overview of adjectives and adverbs is that their comparative and superlative forms help us distinguish them from other parts of speech, such as determiners and qualifiers/intensifiers, but not always from each other. This inconvenient characteristic of overlapping –er and –est endings is symptomatic of a more general problem with English words: some endings (suffixes) serve several purposes and are not ideal as diagnostics. If we look at the '–er' suffix, we soon notice 'speak-er', which is an entirely different use of '–er,' meaning a person who does something, or 'New York-er,' meaning a person from a certain place.

Another typical example is the final '-s' on words. Sometimes the final '-s' is attached to a noun to make it plural, such as in the example 'one pen – several pens.' Or the final '-s' can mean the third person singular form of a present-tense verb, such as in the example 'to write – he, she, it writes.' It's also important to mention the possessive '-s' in 'hers,' 'its,' 'ours,' and 'Jeff's'. We can conclude is that English word morphology is a help in identifying lexical categories, but it does not provide the best diagnostics for identifying a word's lexical category. Better yet, we can use morphology, as in suffixation, to tell if a given word does

NOT belong to a certain category, such as 'very' failing to be an adverb, but even after a word passes the morphological diagnostics, we still need another kind of test, which turns out to be a syntactic one. We've introduced stacking as one kind of diagnostic test which is syntactic, and we'll add several more pretty soon.

About Style and Language Change

If we have an opportunity to help others learn or refine their English, sometimes we will enter the area called **prescriptive grammar**. There is some overlap between this book's emphasis on descriptive grammar and the area of prescriptive grammar. As the occasion arises, that overlap will be mentioned. Prescriptive grammar emphasizes that 'some ideas should be written this way' and **descriptive grammar** emphasizes that 'some ideas are expressed this way' without making any judgment. For example, students sometimes write a sentence like the following one, which made their junior and senior high English teachers blanch and try to reform their habits to adopt a more prescriptive mind-set. This may be considered a grammar error, or it may be considered a matter of style.

> 10) ? Jo and Li walked slower than we did; they even walked the slowest of the whole group. ('?' means questionable - marginally acceptable)

Our grammar teachers probably told us to use 'more slowly' and 'most slowly' in such a sentence. If we write a letter asking for a job interview with someone who cares about standard grammar, it really could matter which form we use. Those who use the forms in the example sentence above may not get invited for an interview if the job requires careful use of written conventions.

This raises the problem of language change and language history. English has its roots in Anglo-Saxon, one of a number of Germanic dialects of the first millennium A.D. (or C.E., depending on one's preference). Germanic languages did not then, and modern German and Dutch and other typical Germanic languages still do not, now, have any ending like 'ly' to indicate adverbness. The Anglo-Saxon speakers of Old English seem to have gotten the idea from the speakers of Norman French after William of Normandy conquered Britain in 1066 and established Norman French as the language of court and of prestige. So the usage in the example sentence above is non-standard, but it reflects the situation of English grammar in its most original Germanic form.

From about 1200 A.D. up into the late twentieth century, the '-ly' form was more formal and high-class than the Germanic form, but languages change continually. This change usually begins at the spoken level and gradually becomes acceptable for the written level (or not, depending on many factors). Perhaps the English language is now changing to make such Germanic adverbial forms as 'slow' acceptable again. At a typical rate of change, though, it will be our children or grandchildren who can use the comparative forms for words like 'slow' and still get invited to a job interview for a grammar teaching position. For now, we will probably stick with the frenchified adverbial suffix -ly for the next few decades. Or until the official grammar mavens publish an *ex cathedra* change in policy. Or until one of us applies for job where this kind of thing doesn't matter.

Another, more modern example of this area called prescriptive grammar is the use of genderless pronouns and related forms. In the mid-twentieth century, the following sentence was considered perfectly normal:

11) Everyone should do his best.

During the latter half of the twentieth century, this became unacceptable, since 'his' was interpreted to no longer include women. It is now normal to hear, but not to write, sentences such as this one:

12) Everyone should do their best. (again marginal, but in this case we mean only in a formal, written style).

Again, if one of us writes this, we may not get an interview with a person who is up to date on prescriptive grammar. We need to change the subject to a plural form, such as 'All students should do their best,' or change the determiner to the stylistically weaker 'his or her,' or perhaps even 'her or his' in some environments. Either the plural subject 'all students' or the double singular determiners 'his or her' is grammatically correct, in contrast to the example sentence above which is not yet grammatically acceptable. The only difference between the two correct versions (one using singular forms and one using plural forms) is that one is better writing style than the other.

Grammar analysis may occasionally touch on matters of style, but these are basically outside of the scope of descriptive grammar, because the main distinction is descriptive grammar is what is grammatical and what is not and to try to explain the reasons for such differences. The approach to grammar adopted in this book accepts language change as inevitable and style variation as a tangentially related, but different, subject. This descriptive approach encourages an attitude that is non-judgmental, and seeks to focus on the structures involved, whatever their form might be. We can now move on to the next revelation, which is a rather sobering one – that our elementary school teachers were passing on incomplete or incorrect grammatical ideas to us. This may feel like telling elementary students that there is no Santa Claus, but it's important for older students.

About the Things We All Learned in Elementary School

In hundreds or thousands of first grade classrooms each year, teachers tell their students the following: "A noun is the name of a person, place, or thing." So the children are happy for a couple of years naming everything inside and outside the classroom a noun. And then, in the third or fourth grade, the teacher springs a couple of new examples on the children, asking them something like this: "Well, what about a word like 'honesty'? Is it a person, place or thing? Why of course not... " And it turns out that words like 'honesty,' 'ethics,' and 'patriotism' are also nouns. So the definition has to be expanded, and the fourth graders feel much superior to the first and second graders, because they know that a noun is really about "a person, place, thing, or idea."

Similarly, in the lower elementary grades, teachers also help their little charges become sensitive to verbs by telling them that "a verb describes an action." So they jump and shout to their heart's content for a year or two, knowing that 'jump' and 'shout' are verbs. Then comes the sobering day in fourth grade (or so) when the teacher asks, "What about a word like 'am' ? Is there no verb in the sentence, 'I am happy'?" So the fourth graders learn an expanded definition and can again look down their collective noses at the lower grades, recognizing wisely that "a verb describes an action or a state of being." These two tales of gradual revelation are meant to help us prepare for still another level of sophistication. There is more to learn, so let's prepare for the next questions and try to avoid the temptation to later scoff at those who are still locked into those old definitions, comforting as they were.

Here's a sentence similar to what Noam Chomsky, and many others since him, enjoyed using as an example to rid us of some of our mental clutter:

13) The destruction of the city was heart-wrenching.

What is 'destruction,' an idea (noun-like), or an action (verb-like)? It does not seem to be an abstract idea like 'honesty', but rather a decisive, appalling action. Yet the word is a noun. Let's take some time to show that diagnosis as clearly as possible. Remember, we now know a reason or two for caring what part of speech a given word is. Continuing the diagnostic approach that first looks at morphological endings and then moves on to syntactic diagnostic tests, let's ask what endings distinguish nouns and verbs.

The '-s' suffix was mentioned above and now deserves some attention. 'Waffles' can mean more than one waffle (plural), or something which some she, he, or it does (or a **third person singular** subject' does in grammatical terminology) on occasion. But 'destructions' sounds a little odd, so we'll introduce the 'other s,' namely the possessive one, as in 'its,' 'ours,' 'hers,' and 'Jeff's.' It can appear with this handful of pronouns, and it can appear with most nouns, but never with verbs, adverbs or adjectives, or prepositions (try it). So it will help us set up another diagnostic test for nouns. With nouns, it needs an apostrophe, so we ask to what extent we like the word 'destruction's'? If it's acceptable, the word 'destruction' passes one morphological test for nounhood (or nounness) and we can move on to a syntactic one. If not, we need to re-think our position. Here's a sentence to check the possessive diagnostic, "The destruction's path through the city was long and narrow." So now we can move the word 'destruction' out of the 'verbs-indicate-action' category and move it into the 'nouns-can-be-possessive' category.

Here we won't worry about the critique that the sentence is acceptable grammatically, but weak stylistically, since "The path of destruction through the city was long and narrow" sounds so much better. We're just looking at grammar, and not style, so we'll give 'destruction' a passing grade as probably a noun according to the 'possessive –s' diagnostic. We won't worry either about the fact that the plural '-s' diagnostic did not work well. That's not a deal-breaker, as we'll see when we discuss different types of nouns, so please just wait a little for the rest of that discussion. The diagnosis moves forward nicely when we notice the way the third person singular present tense '-s' diagnostic for verbs is completely unimaginable for 'destruction,' as in *'He destructions the city.' This is a clear indication that the word is not a verb. So morphology, carefully used, has helped us out. But we can also see that the syntactic (sentence-based) diagnostic tests are also needed.

Now, what's wrong with thinking of nouns as names of people, places, things, or ideas? For one, nouns like 'destruction' get miscategorized. That's because nounhood shows itself most clearly not in a meaning, like 'the name of a place' but more so in how a word functions in a sentence. The best way to see this is to dissect a sentence full of words that we don't know the meanings of. How about this one?

14) The ghecky hengst in the hoek vrat the hooi gulzigly.

The only English words in the sentence are 'the' and 'in,' but we can still take a good guess (or call it a 'hypothesis' if you like) about the lexical category of each nonsense word simply by its role in the sentence. Since they're nonsense words, they have no meaning, so we're clearly not using meaning to judge what lexical categories they belong to. I've added familiar suffixes to two of these words to provide a first guess as to lexical category. The '-y' on 'ghecky' and the '-ly' on 'gulzigly' suggest that the first is an adjective with an ending like 'whacky,' and the second is an adverb, like 'slowly.'

We would further guess that the three words that begin with 'h' are all nouns because of the word 'the' which introduces them, and we would want to test that hypothesis, too. We would probably want to test the word 'vrat' for its verbness, since a sentence of the form "The thing vrat the thing (easily)" most likely has a verb between the two 'things,' like 'The boy ate the hotdogs hastily." The adverbness of 'gulzigly' as a hypothesis or theory to test would lead us to use the diagnostics that we discussed above of comparative form and stacking.

How about using 'and' as part of our stacking, as in the sentence "The gely hengst in the hoek vrat the hooi gulzigly and carefully." Even though we have never heard of 'gulzigly' and doubt that it's a word in English, we can still judge the form with 'and' (called the **coordinate structure**) form easily, because coordinate conjunctions, properly used, only connect words of the same lexical or phrasal category. So we can say that 'gulzigly' is the same part of speech as 'carefully,' which makes it an adverb. But, at a certain point, we do need to know something like the meaning of a word, or at least how it's used, in order to diagnose its part of speech. This is because much of the diagnosis that works best relies on a native-speaker's unconscious mental grammar. For this, we need to move back into English in order to call on our native-speakers' judgments about grammaticality.

Summing up, looking at meanings and morphological endings are two ways that we can take a reasonable guess at the part of speech of a certain word. And even if we don't know the meaning of a word, we can still come up with a reasonable hypothesis about what its part of speech is based on its apparent role in a sentence. What remains to be done now is to show that there is a more conclusive type of diagnosis than either the word's meaning or its morphological endings. The best way of all is to use syntactic diagnostics and to test words in the framework of a sentence. Not just any sentence will do; however, we need carefully designed sentences with 'test frames' that filter out everything but one lexical category.

Frame Sentences and Syntactic Diagnostics

Didn't we all hear in elementary school that "An adjective modifies a noun," and that "An adverb modifies an adjective, verb or another adverb"? These are primary school mantras, and they're more useful than the ones for verbs and nouns because they're about sentence usage and not about the possible meanings of the words. That's a much better start than the traditional meaning-based definitions of nouns and verbs. Their main shortcoming is that these definitions don't recognize that some sentences work really well as diagnostic filters while others only create confusion. We want sentences where only one lexical category will work and every other category will be filtered out. As we have seen above in connection with sentence,"* We saw you're the expensive red carpet", determiners modify nouns in a rather un-adjectival way, and we discussed how qualifiers/intensifiers modify adjectives and verbs in a sort of un-adverbial way.

If we simply ask whether one of the determiners 'a/an' or 'the' can immediately precede a word, that is one good test for a noun. But, in a given, random sentence which has not been carefully designed, we may see adjectives and determiners, and perhaps some other things modifying nouns, and we may also see adverbs and qualifiers/intensifiers and perhaps some other things modify verbs and adjectives (and adverbs). So, for a second diagnostic test, we want to focus on the most useful frame sentences that have been developed by syntacticians.

Noun Frame Sentences

For nouns, one of the most useful frame sentences has the form "They have no _____" This sentence is useful because it will allow singular and plural nouns, like 'home' or 'furniture' or 'pens' and irregular plurals like 'sheep' or plurals without singular forms like 'pants,' or even abstract nouns like 'honesty' and 'patriotism.' In order to test a deceptive noun like 'destruction,' or other **abstract nouns** such as 'honesty' and 'patriotism,' we may want to tweak the sentence a little to make it "They have no _____ to speak of." For words with a negative meaning, like 'destruction,' we can also make one more optional addition, giving us a sentence with a number of variations:

> "They have (suffered) no _____." Examples: 'They have no interest/fame/furniture/dogs.' Filtered out: 'They have no *it/*there/*insist/*yet.

Here the parentheses indicate an optional part of the sentence – to be used if needed in order to get an acceptable frame for the meaning as well as the grammar. Now we have an approved frame sentence for nouns. For other lexical categories, there are other sentences, which work similarly. Here is an opportunity to practice identifying nouns.

Practice Testing for Nouns

Which of the following are acceptable in the frame sentence for nouns?
    1. singer

    2. lettuce

    3. stupendous

    4. buying

    5. advertising

    6. craving

    7. acquaintance

    8. countess

    9. joyfulness

    10. solo

Answers to the first several questions are at the end of the book

A Frame Sentence for Adjectives

The most useful kind of sentence that accepts adjectives and rejects all other lexical categories is this type:

> 15) "The (_____) noun is (very) (_____)." Example: 'The interesting course is very interesting.' Filtered out: 'The *go/*and/*slowly course is (very) ...'

This sentence incorporates the characteristics of adjectives that were mentioned in sentences 1) and 2) that we started with above: they can be used next to a noun (attributively) or after a verb like 'be' (predicatively). Different nouns work well for various adjectives, depending on whether the meanings are compatible. For most adjectives, both positions work, as in the sentence, "The old man is (very) old," or "The good performance was (very) good." It is worth noting that the word 'very' is sometime helpful and sometimes not, so it is in parentheses. That discussion will come in the next chapter regarding different types of adjectives.

    At this point, we should some adjectives are only predicative and others are only attributive. Since there are not very many, a list of them may be the most helpful. The following adjectives can only be used attributively before a noun: chief, main, principle, sheer, entire, utter, and outright. We may discover others, but probably not too many of them. The complementary situation is the group of adjectives which can only be used after a linking verb, like 'be': asleep, awake, afloat, aglow, alone, afraid, alive, and aghast. They all begin with 'a,' but there may be another one or two that will break that mold. Here is a demonstration of the **attributive-only** and **predicative-only** nature of typical examples from the lists just given.

16)
a) The principle negotiator is (very) *principle.

b) That negotiator over there is *principle/tired.
    (notice that 'tired' is acceptable).

c) The *afloat sticks remained afloat.

We have just identified several types of adjectives: those that can only be attributive, those that can only be predicative, and those (by far the largest group) which can be either. In the next chapter under the heading 'types of adjectives', we'll subdivide this latter group into two and have four basic types of adjectives.

Practice Testing for Adjectives

a) Which of the following words pass the frame sentence diagnostic for adjectives?

1. glossy

2. absent

3. umbilical

4. plastic

5. arbitrary

6. absorbent

7. hemp

8. psychedelic

9. gearing

b) Identify the nouns and adjectives in the following sentence:

> The helpful foreigner standing near the bicycle accident gave his unused blanket to a homeless beggar among a group of others who all belonged to the poorest of the poor.

Answers to selected practice words are at the end of the book.

How Many Frame Sentences are Needed?

Now we have frame sentences for nouns and adjectives. What about verbs and adverbs? And are there useful frame sentences for still other lexical categories? The short answer to the first question is yes, there are useful frame sentences for these two categories. The short answer for the second question is no, we don't need specially designed sentences for other parts of speech. We'll learn to test for them by analogy, that is, we recognize the most common several and see if others work the same way.

In English, we have about 21,000 verbs according to Henry Burger, the publisher of *The Wordtree - a reverse dictionary*. This is clearly too big a number to memorize, so it's good to have an easy way to recognize whether a word is a verb or not. The same is true of nouns, adjectives, and adverbs.

But it's not true of the other lexical categories, which usually have only a dozen to several dozen or so entries. We don't want to memorize long lists of the words in these other categories, but we do not really need a diagnostic test for each. We need a familiarity with the most important ones, so that we can compare other words to them. This is the main focus of chapter 3 below.

Adverb Frame Sentences

When we look for frame sentences for adverbs, we run into something of a contradiction: the frame sentences that are commonly used only diagnose one kind of adverb. Here is what the standard answer looks like, and we have a choice, depending on the meaning of the word:

> 17) They told the story (very) _____ .

> Examples: ... (very) movingly/clearly/subjectively

> (or)

> They handled the matter (very) _____ .

> Examples: ... (very) carefully/wisely/quickly

These two sentences test adverbs with different kinds of meanings. The problem that arises immediately, though, and that is that this test works mainly for the most common kinds of adverbs, called **manner adverbs** which **modify** (describe) how the verb's action is done, such as 'slowly' or 'carefully.' There are other adverbs, called **sentential adverbs** such as 'actually,' and 'fortunately' that modify entire sentences. If we test either 'actually' or 'fortunately' in the frame sentences above, they don't seem to fit, or they change meaning from the sentential one to a manner one. So we need to look further into the syntax of adverbs to find a better way to test for them. Section 3.3. below introduces this other syntactic characteristic of adverbs, namely that they can move to several different positions within the sentence. This is a unique characteristic of adverbs and can also be used as a diagnostic test.

Another type of adverb resists this diagnostic test, though, too. These have to do with negation, such as 'hardly.' This brings us full circle to the idea that perhaps, in the case of adverbs, it may help us along if we used a semantic criterion in addition to all the syntactic ones. As we noticed with nouns and verbs, there is often a semantic criterion which gives us a hypothesis that we can test in other ways. This same idea may help us with adverbs. Semantically, most words which answer the questions 'when,' 'where,' 'how,' or 'why' are likely candidates for adverb status. It's worth noting that manner adverbs answer 'how' for the verb they're modifying. Words like 'sometimes,' and 'always' answer the question 'when,' so we would want to test them to see if they're adverbs, too. 'Here' and 'there' talk about 'where,' so they deserve to be tested for adverb status as well.

Practice Testing for Adverbs

Which of the following words pass the frame sentence diagnostic for adverbs or the movement test for adverbs?

1. rarely

2. excellently

3. elderly

4. nervously

5. very

6. friendly

7. softly

8. yearly

9. savagely

10. hardly

Answers to several of the practice words are at the end of the book.

Frame Sentences for Verbs

Morphologically, verbs have the richest number of inflections of any part of speech in English: '-ing,' '-ed,' '-(e)n,' and '-(e)s.' A couple of examples will help us see that morphology alone is insufficient for a conclusive determination of a word's lexical category: 'interesting' has a verbal inflection, but is almost always an adjective (test: 'the interesting book is very interesting.'); 'greeting' also looks verbal in the same way as 'interesting,' but it is more often a noun, as in 'season's greetings.' For words like 'interesting' and 'greetings', we need to use the frame sentences for adjectives and nouns. Now we can continue on to syntactic testing. For verbs, we also have two possible frame sentences, depending on the type of verb.

18) They should/may/can _____ (something). (or)

19) (The) <u>noun</u> _____ <u>adjective</u>; such as 'The music sounds good,' or 'The patient looks healthy.'

We first notice that the verb+ing and verb+n forms of the verb does not work in these frame sentences. The first one also rejects the verb+ed and verb+s forms. So we need to shear verb candidates of these inflectional suffixes in order to test them with the first (and sometimes the second) frame sentence.

The reason that we need two frame sentences, is not for differing meanings of verbs, such as for the differing meanings of adverbs in sentence 18) above. Here we need two for differing types of verbs. The second sentence can only be used to test the so-called **linking verbs** (like 'be'). So clearly we need to spend some time learning about the various kinds of verbs. And while we're doing that, we should also notice that there are also different kinds of adverbs, nouns, adjectives, and other lexical categories. And so we will soon begin a tour of the various types (or subcategories) of lexical categories. We will discover as we walk through each of the lexical categories that many are easy to identify as we become familiar with their subcategories, so we won't need any other frame sentences. Or we can make up our own as we go.

Practice Testing for Verbs

a) Which of the following words pass the frame sentence diagnostic for verbs?

1.   revelation

2.   landscape

3.   repeat

4.   shot

5.   revolve

6.   pull

7.   soliloquy

8.   create

9.   shiny

b) Recognize all the adverbs and verbs in the following sentence:
After they had been working hard all day, the laborers could not easily suppress their longing for a refreshing change of pace.

Answers to several of the practice words are at the end of the book.

Chapter Summary and Conclusion

In the introductory chapter to this Guide, we learned that English has twelve basic parts of speech, as listed there and repeated here: **nouns, determiners, pronouns, verbs, verb particles, auxiliaries, adverbs, qualifiers, quantifiers, adjectives, prepositions,** and **conjunctions**. Our discussion here on frame sentences only covered the four so-called '**open categories,**' which are open in the sense that new words can always be added by borrowing from other languages or creation within English itself: nouns, verbs, adjectives and adverbs. At the beginning of this chapter, we talked about the way the adjective and adverb categories were used by the Grammarians as sort of catch-all categories, and we separated out the determiners from the adjectives and the qualifiers from the adverbs, because neither of these removed categories can stack the way adjectives and adverbs do, in addition to their lack of normal comparative morphology or syntax. That's six of the twelve categories that we have learned to identify and distinguish from all other parts of speech. What about the other six? We'll learn how to identify them at the same time that we discuss their sub-categories in chapter three.

Our conclusion here is that no matter how many lexical categories English has, we will only have to learn to use frame sentences (and perhaps morphological tests for an initial impression) for four of them: nouns, verbs, adjectives, and adverbs. For the other categories, making up our own sentences by using a basic example will allow us to identify them accurately.

The frame sentences can be recapitulated as follows.

For **nouns**, one of the most useful frame sentences has the form "They have no _____." In order to include nouns with a negative connotation, we might want to expand it sometimes to "They have (suffered) no _____ (to speak of)." Examples: 'They have no interest/fame/furniture/dogs.' Filtered out: They have no *it/*there/*insist/*yet.

The most useful kind of sentence that accepts **adjectives** and rejects all other lexical categories looks like this, "The (_____) noun is very (_____)." Example: 'The interesting course is very interesting.' Filtered out: 'The *go/*and/*slowly course is very ..'

We need two sentences to test **manner adverbs** with different kinds of meanings: "They told the story (very) _____ (movingly/clearly/subjectively)," or "They handled the matter (very) _____ (very carefully/wisely/quickly)". Other types of adverbs show syntactic movement, and it may help to check the semantic property of answering the questions 'where,' and 'when.'

Similarly, for **verbs**, we also need two possible sentences, depending on the type of verb: "They should/may/can _____," or (The) <u>noun</u> _____ <u>adjective</u>; such as "The music sounds good," or "The patient looks healthy (not *'healthily')."

Chapter 3: Types within Each Category

Seven Types of Verbs

Let's start by introducing the whole line-up by name with an example sentence for each. Their names are also in the table of contents above, and we'll repeat them here as a way of getting warmed up to discuss them: (a) **linking,** (b) **intransitive,** (c) **transitive,** (d) **prepositional,** (e) **ditransitive,** (f) **transitive prepositional,** and (g) **complex transitive**. The verbs in each example sentence below are typical of that verb type, so it's good to notice these verbs especially. It's also helpful to start making connections right away between the name of the verb type ('a' through 'g' above) and the underlined words and phrases following the verb in the predicate. These underlined items are typical of each specific verb type. The technical names of the predicate words and phrases are noted in parentheses. This is a lot of information in one dose, so please look through it slowly enough to make some connections. These technical terms are important to start keeping track of. Remember, definitions are in the glossary at the end of the book.

1) (a)(i) That patient is becoming healthier. (an **adjective complement)**

(a)(ii)That patient is becoming a journalist.(a **noun complement**)

(b) Sam's parents are sleeping. **(no complement or object)**

(c) She has read her history assignment. (a **direct object**)

(d) They are living in Phoenix (an **obligatory prepositional phrase)**

(e) He is writing her a letter (an **indirect object** and a direct object)

(f) Please put your shoes in the corner (a noun-phrase object and an obligatory prepositional phrase)

(g)(i) They considered the course easy (a direct object with an adjective complement)

(g)(ii) They considered <u>the course</u> <u>a challenge</u>. (a direct object with a noun
complement)

Linking Verbs and the Uniqueness of 'Be'

One characteristic of some (but not all) linking verbs (and complex transitives) is
that they can have either an **adjective complement** or a **noun complement** in
their predicates, as shown by the difference between (a) (i) and (ii) and between
g) (i) and (ii) above. Don't worry about getting linking verbs confused with
complex transitive ones, since their predicates look quite different. The more
important identifying characteristic of linking verbs, shared only by the complex
transitive verbs (g) is that they may be followed by a predicate adjective but not
by a predicate adverb. Linking verbs best can be identified by putting an adverb
in the predicate position, where it is unacceptable, as in (a) below. The verbs of
perception (look, feel, smell, taste, and sound) have a different meaning when
used with an adverb in the predicate position, as contrasted in (b) and (c) below.
Only the adjectival predicate in (b) is indicative of the verb being a linking verb.

Another good way to identify linking verbs is to ask if the adjective in the
predicate modifies the subject noun phrase. If it does, you have a linking verb.
Notice in (b) below the adjective 'rough' describes the subject "the fabric." In
contrast, the adverb 'roughly' in (c) below describes not the merchant, but how
she or he handled fabric. The adverb 'roughly' modifies the verb "feel" in (c)
below.

If the last four sentences of explanation didn't register, it's important to go
through that diagnostic process again with the examples. This is key in being able
to make up ingenious, original sample sentences for review later. If the predicate
of the linking verb is a noun, as in (a)(ii) above, the diagnostic test is whether the
noun in the subject refers to the same person or object as the noun in the
predicate. If so, you're dealing with a linking verb. In (a)(ii) above, the noun
'patient' and the noun 'journalist' both refer to the same person. This is in
contrast to (c) below where the noun 'merchant' in the subject does not refer to
the same person or object as the noun 'fabric' in the predicate. This shows that (c)
below does not have a linking verb.

2) (a)*That patient remained /is /stayed /appears /seems healthily.

(b) The fabric felt rough to the merchant.

(c) The merchant felt the fabric roughly.

Although meanings do not give us enough accuracy to identify lexical categories
or sub-categories, it may help us remember the scope of linking verbs by looking
at their meanings. Their meanings cover two main areas: 1) present condition (be,
seem, appear, remain, stay, prove, look, sound, taste, smell, feel; and 2) change to
a new condition (become, get, grow (both meaning 'become'), run (as in 'run
wild'), and turn (as in 'turn sour').

An interesting wrinkle in the linking verbs relates to 'be,' which can function
in all of the ways the other linking verbs can, plus one other way unique to itself.

This is demonstrated in the following sentence and contrasted with 'seem' and 'become,' which are 'be's closest relatives.

3) (a) They are here/there/in condition/on the porch.

(b) They seem/have become *here/*there/?in condition/*on the porch.

So the verb 'be' can not only have predicate complements that are adjectives and nouns, like other linking verbs, but it can also have predicate complements that are adverbs of place and prepositional phrases with various meanings. This is the first way we have seen that 'be' is unique among the verbs in English. The second is that it has eight different forms. Here's a list of the forms of 'be': be, being, am, is, are, was, were, and been. That's all of them: eight forms. Other verbs have at most five: draw, drawing, draws, drew, and drawn. Most only have four forms: play, playing, plays, and played. Some few only have three forms: cut, cuts, and cutting. That was a short installment about the uniqueness of the verb 'be'. So we shouldn't get depressed to discover that it can have four different types of predicate complements while other linking verbs only have two possible types of predicate complements.

Intransitive Verbs and Adjuncts

The predicate of intransitive verbs sometimes looks as simple as those of linking verbs, but the predicate of an intransitive verb has no noun or adjective as seen in (b), repeated here for convenience:(b) Sam's parents are sleeping. This is the simplest of all predicates, lacking any kind of object. Perhaps now is a good time to mention that the particular form of the verb is not relevant to its classification as to verb type. So the verb 'sleep' is intransitive no matter whether its form in the sentence is 'was sleeping,' 'has slept,' 'sleeps,' 'had slept,' 'has been sleeping,' or 'had been sleeping.' This variation is irrelevant to diagnosis in terms of verb type. The presence or absence of auxiliary verbs before 'sleep' is also irrelevant, as in 'can sleep,' 'could sleep,' 'should sleep,' or other auxiliaries. The verb 'sleep' is still intransitive in all these forms.

Another point in avoiding confusion is that any number of optional modifiers (technically called '**adjuncts**') could be added without changing the analysis of the verb type. So the verb in this sentence is still intransitive: "Sam's tennis improves more on Saturday mornings because of his trainer's good advice than during the rest of the week without that advice." All of the extra prepositional phrases in the predicate are optional in the sense that they could be dropped without changing the meaning of the verb and without rendering the sentence unacceptable.

As soon as the verb has a **direct object** though, it is no longer intransitive, but transitive, which is the next category.

Transitive Verbs and Homonymy

Our model sentence here is (c) 'She has read her history assignment.' We should ask 'read what' or 'read whom' and the answer to that question, if there is one, is the verb's **direct object**, which is a complement. Verbs with a direct object are always considered transitive. Many English verbs have both transitive and intransitive forms. One familiar example is the verb 'read.' If the question is 'what's she doing?' the answer might be 'She's reading,' where the verb is intransitive, or it might be 'She's reading her book,' where the verb is transitive. While it may seem inconvenient to discover this fact about English verbs, as in "Why can't the verbs clearly belong to a single category?" this flexibility is actually one of the reasons that the English language is so expressive and useful.

So, can we go back to the model intransitive sentence about Sam's tennis and turn the verb into a transitive one? Native speakers can usually judge the grammatical acceptability of any sentence they hear. So does this sentence sound acceptable or not? 'Sam improved his serve dramatically in the past year.' My native speaker feeling is that the sentence is acceptable grammatically, so I would say 'improve' could be either transitive or intransitive. That's an example of a quick analysis of a verb's type.

Our conclusion here is that some verbs belong to either of two categories depending on how they are used in a sentence. Intellectually, this may be easiest to pigeon-hole and process if we say that it's similar to the more familiar homonymy where a word can be either a noun or a verb or another lexical category depending on the way it's used in a sentence, as in these sentences showing homonyms of the word 'equal.

4) (a) No one in the class is her equal (noun).

(b) We used equal amounts of sugar and water (adjective).

(c) Five plus six equals eleven (verb).

Calling the two forms of 'read' homonyms of each other, rather than considering the verb 'read' to have a split personality (technically called '**bivalent**'), will help us make better sense of the idea of complements, which is introduced in the next section. In other words, the two forms of the verb 'read' are considered to be two different verbs which are **homonyms**, just as the various forms of 'equal' in 23) above are considered different words which are homonyms of each other. The transitive form of the verb 'read' is considered to require (technically, '**subcategorize for**') its direct object, even though the intransitive homonym does not require a direct object.

Complex Transitive Verbs

Combining the noun complement of a transitive verb with the adjective or noun complement of a linking verb will give us some idea of what to expect in the complement of a complex transitive verb: a direct object which is followed by an adjective complement or a noun complement. The following sentences give us two examples, the first with an adjectival object complement and the second with a nominal object complement. There are a rather limited number of complex transitive verbs in English, like 'find,' 'elect,' 'appoint,' 'name,' 'call,' 'label,' 'mark,' 'make,' and 'consider.'

> 5) (a) The class found the teacher friendly.

> (b) The class elected Harriet president

Ditransitive Verbs

The name 'ditransitive' suggests double transitivity, and that is exactly the case. There are two objects: one direct, which usually answers the question 'what?' and the other indirect, which usually answers the question 'to whom?' or 'for whom?' There are not many ditransitive verbs in English. We have already mentioned that 'read' is bivalent (transitive and intransitive), and now we will discover that it is actually trivalent.

> 6) (a) Dad reads his children a story every evening at bedtime.

> (b) The company gave Sam a fancy watch when he retired.

Other similar verbs are 'tell,' 'call,' 'order,' 'write,' 'paint,' 'play,' 'sing,' 'show,' 'teach,' and 'make.' Here we can slow down for a second to notice that some of the ditransitive verbs listed here are also listed in the previous section on complex transitive verbs, such as 'call' and 'make.' This gives rise to sardonic jokes like this one, "Will you call me a cab, please?" "OK, you're a cab." The request was made using 'call' as a ditransitive verb, but the response misinterpreted 'call' in its complex transitive meaning.

Prepositional Verbs and Complements

In discussing intransitive verbs, we noticed that adding any number of optional prepositional phrases (adjuncts) to the predicate is irrelevant to the verb's classification. Now we will discover that sometimes a prepositional phrase is not optional for certain verbs, but required. Parts of the predicate which the verb requires in order to be complete are called **complements**. Our model sentence for a prepositional verb is repeated here for convenience:

> 7) They are living in Phoenix.

"But," the inquiring student's mind reflects, "can't the verb 'live' be used just as well without a prepositional phrase, as in 'My parents are both still living'?" Is this homonymy again? Actually it is, and the difference between the two verbs is even clearer here, since their meanings are so different. In the sentence 'My parents are both still living,' the verb 'live' means 'to be alive.' But the homonymous prepositional verb 'live+prepositional phrase (of location)' means 'to reside (in a certain place).' This is quite a different meaning. In other Indo-

European languages, there are pairs of non-homonymous verbs for 'live' and 'reside,' such as German 'leben/wohnen' and French 'vivre/habiter'.

The verb 'reside' is also useful here. Suppose we hear the sentence, *'He is residing.' This is the same diagnostic test that is used to see if a verb is transitive. Now we see that the test tests for any complement, whether direct object or other complement. How does a native speaker judge the sentence? As grammatically unacceptable. Why? Because it's incomplete. It's missing a required part; it's missing a complement, which in this case is a prepositional phrase giving location. So we conclude that 'reside' is also a prepositional verb.

If we look at one exception, we'll discover that the name 'prepositional verb' is actually a bit of a stretch, even though it's probably the best term available. What is a native speaker's judgment of this sentence?

8) They are living here.

It's grammatically acceptable, isn't it? But it doesn't have a prepositional phrase in the predicate, does it? The word 'here' is an adverb, not a preposition at all. And the meaning 'to reside' is preserved, right? How can we explain that, except to call it an exception and move on? What's even worse is pointed out by the following sentence, "They are living at this time." In this sentence the predicate includes a prepositional phrase, but the verb's meaning is 'to be alive' and not 'to reside.' Now what? Not any prepositional phrase will do for some prepositional verbs, but only prepositional phrases with a certain meaning. In the case of 'reside,' the complement needs to state a place, which is usually done with a prepositional phrase, although 'here' and 'there' are adverbs which also indicate location and are, in this case, acceptable complements to the verb.

In summary, one of the most important parts of identifying prepositional verbs is to weed out prepositional phrases that are not complements, such as the one in 'They were reading in the library.' The fact that there is a prepositional phrase in the predicate does not make 'read' a prepositional verb. The test is whether the prepositional phrase is needed for a certain meaning of the verb, such as 'live in…' being different from 'live.'

Discussing a couple of somewhat trickier examples at this point may help sharpen our analytic skills in this area. Some typical verbs of motion like 'run' and 'walk,' as well as verbs of position like 'stand,' 'sit,' and 'lie' will give us enough grist for the mill. Is there any significant change for the native speaker between the verbs used by themselves (similar to 'live') and them used with a preposition phrase (or an adverb, perhaps) showing location (like 'live in')? Here are some sentences to compare. Of course, if the verb by itself seems incomplete, that shows that the prepositional phrase is a complement.

9) (a) They walked. They walked home.

(b) They are running. They are running
down the street.

(c) They were sitting. They were sitting on
the porch.

(d) We are still standing. We are still standing here.

(e) They enjoyed lying. They enjoyed lying on the beach

In each case, at least in my dialect, there is a significant (albeit not humongous) difference in the way the two sentences feel – the first seems either incomplete or focused only on the motion or stance, while the second is both complete and focused not on motion or stance, but on position. For other native speakers, the perception could be quite different, leading them to conclude that none or only a few of the verbs of movement and position are prepositional verbs. This is an area of grammar where some fuzziness is allowable, although it's still crucial to know what diagnostic tools are appropriate and how to use them.

Transitive Prepositional (Or Transitive Adverbial) Verbs

Transitive prepositional/adverbial verbs combine the complements of a transitive verb and a prepositional verb. There are not many verbs of this type. The best example is the verb 'put,' which is clearly incomplete without a prepositional (or adverbial) complement showing location. Other verbs with a similar meaning, such as 'set,' 'place,' 'embed,' 'fasten,' 'insert,' 'lay,' 'plop,' (perhaps 'plunk') and 'situate' also fit this category. The following examples show it as incomplete with a second complement in (a), completed with a prepositional complement of location in (b), and completed with an adverbial complement of location in (c).

10) (a) *We put the guests' coats.

(b) We put the guests' coats on the bed.

(c) We put the guests' coats there.

A word about having a second name of this sub-category. In other grammar presentations, this category is uniformly called 'transitive prepositional.' Why add the alternative name 'transitive adverbial,' if not just to burden students with excess information? After all, we noticed that prepositional verbs can also have AdvP's of location as complements and we didn't record that information in an additional name for that category. The reason is that in this case there are verbs which seem to accept only an AdvP as a second complement after the direct object. Here is an example that helps justify a broader category name, 'We always take such matters seriously.' For this meaning to come with the verb 'take,' we clearly need the AdvP. This necessity makes it a complement. In my dialect 'handle (a matter)' would also fit into this category, since 'handle a problem,' and 'handle a problem well' seem to have somewhat different meanings for the verb. Other dialects may differ without causing problems, as we noticed with verbs of motion.

A final note on the sub-category transitive adverbial verbs would be a warning that a VP like 'to set matters straight' does not belong to this group.

'Straight' is an AP here, and not an AdvP. So this VP belongs to the category of complex transitive verbs.

Practice with Verb Subcategories

Identify the sub-category of each verb (and verb form) in the following sentences.

1. Odysseus had rescued many people, and he was now enjoying a rest.

2. He was considering the wave conditions; they make the surf so dangerous sometimes.

3. "Please tell us the story of the Cyclops."

4. The man was looking at Odysseus, and he was rocking nervously.

5. Odysseus' son considered the questions repetitious, and he told the guest about the short timeline for the interview.

6. He wondered about some time in the future when this conversation would no longer appeal to his father.

7. Sometimes he got impatient when Odysseus entertained such guests for too long.

Phrasal Verbs and Verb Particles

In discussing verbs, we also discover that we need to introduce one more part of speech – the verb particle. A **phrasal verb** is a verb whose meaning has changed because it has combined with a verb particle and the meaning of the combination is not the same as the two individual meanings would indicate. Sometimes a **verb particle** looks like a preposition and sometimes it looks like an adverb, but it doesn't act like (or '**pattern like**') either one. A verb particle is the added part of a phrasal verb, such as 'by' in 'get by on (only a little income),' or 'up' in 'give up on (someone).' We notice that 'to give up' is not about 'giving' and not about 'up,' but which has a different meaning because of the combination of 'give + up.' Another, somewhat trickier, example is 'look up' when we mean we are using a dictionary. The meaning still includes the idea of 'looking,' but doesn't include any meaning related to 'up.' This is still a phrasal verb.

Our discussion up to this point has been based on a semantic definition. As we have seen before, using only semantic diagnostics leads us to look for better testing techniques, and we will discuss syntactic testing shortly. Phrasal verbs are very Germanic constructions, proliferating in Germanic languages and non-existent in Romance languages like French and Spanish. They are hard for non-native speakers of English to master because their meanings are not predictable from the two or three words that they are composed of. The meaning of each phrasal verb is idiomatic and must be memorized.

This is the reason that Benjamin Franklin's famous quotation about all of the signers of the Declaration of Independence needing to cooperate with each other is so clever:

11) We must all hang together, or assuredly we shall all hang separately (Bartlett 3949)

Both 'together' and 'separately' are originally adverbs, but in 'hang together' the verb does not mean literally 'hang' anymore. This is a stark contrast to the verb in 'hang separately,' which is not a phrasal verb, and where the verb really does mean literally 'hang.' The fact that the meaning of a phrasal verb is hard or impossible to figure out by looking at the meanings of its individual parts gives us a good way to recognize them, though. A shift in meaning that comes with the combination of a preposition or an adverb and a verb is the first indication that we may be looking at a phrasal verb. As always, a diagnosis or analysis of a word's lexical category based only on its meaning is suspect. The semantic oddity of the verb-preposition/adverb combination gives us a good hypothesis in this case, but we still need a syntactic test to confirm many of these combinations.

Three Types of Verb Particles

At first glance, the syntax of verb particles may looks a little messy, but there is a clear explanation for that. There are three types of verb particles: 1) those that must remain next to their head verb, which we'll call adjacent verb particles, 2) those that must move away from their head verb, which we'll call non-adjacent verb particles, and 3) those that have the option of staying adjacent to their verb or moving away from it, which we'll call movable verb particles. Some examples will show us more clearly which ones may not move, must move, and may move.

12) (a) I can't do without my glasses;
* I can't do my glasses <u>without</u>.
(it may not move)

(b) Please <u>do</u> this assignment <u>over</u>;
* Please do <u>over</u> this assignment (it must move, at least in my dialect)

(c) She helped me look the word <u>up</u>;
She helped me <u>look up</u> the word. (it may move)

Some otherwise marvelous grammarians have suggested that the mobility of verb particles is a useful diagnostic for recognizing phrasal verbs (for example Clark 131, Curzan and Adams 148). This only works for the optionally movable verb particles like the one in (c) in 12) above, and not for the other two types of verb particles. So what general characteristic will help us recognize any of the three types of phrasal verb? If it's not clear yet, let's make it clear now that the prepositions in prepositional verbs may never move in the way that some particles do:

13) * They are living the fifth floor on.

We would like some clear diagnostic tool to distinguish between the preposition in a prepositional verb and the verb particle in a phrasal verb. The most useful test may come from a fact about coordinate structures, which was noticed by Andrew Radford (104) among others.

It can be combined with the short answer test quite effectively.

14) (a) Q: what did he do? A: ran up the hill and up the mountain

(b) Q: what did he do? *A: rang up his sister and up his dad.

Since 'ring up' is a phrasal verb, the word 'up' cannot function as a preposition in (b) as it can in (a).

Analyzing the verb 'look at' may provide another useful example. Is this a phrasal verb or a prepositional verb? We can compare it with 'look up' (in a dictionary), which we have already identified as a phrasal verb, since its particle may move.

15) (a) Q: What is he doing? Looking at the TV and at his cards

(b) Q: What is he doing? *Looking up that new word and up its odd

abbreviation

The first answer 'at the TV' shows us that the 'at' is part of a prepositional phrase, so the verb is a prepositional verb. The second answer 'up its odd abbreviation' shows us that 'up' cannot function as part of a prepositional phrase so it must be part of a phrasal verb, which we already know to be true, since 'up' can move. Checking this diagnostic tool out with examples (a) and (b) in 30) above indicates that it can work for all three types of verbs, as seen below:

16) (a) What is he doing? *Doing over his report and over his quiz.

(b) What is he doing? *Doing without his glasses and without his

cola.

Another example may be useful in sharpening our analytical skills. How about the verb 'insist'? Is it prepositional or phrasal? Q: What's she doing? A: Insisting. The answer is clearly incomplete, so something else is needed, but what? Is it missing an obligatory prepositional phrase, the complement of a prepositional verb? Or is it missing the verb particle of a phrasal verb?

17) What is he doing?   Insisting on his place in line and on his right

to free admission.

Here we see that 'insist' passes the test as a prepositional verb. For students who would like to practice using this diagnostic tool, there is a plethora of examples in a dictionary of phrasal verbs at this web site: http://www.englishpage.com/prepositions/phrasaldictionary.html. As is almost always the case with this sort of web material, there are errors in detail in this site, so it provides us a good test of both our critical abilities and our analytic abilities. Besides that possibility, this Guide provides an opportunity to practice

Practice with Phrasal Verbs

a) Identify the phrasal verbs in the following sentences.

> 1. Molly was sick of sitting around every day; she felt like she was going to break down.
>
> 2. She didn't come up with the ideas to open the blinds or work out, but a friend brought it up in conversation.
>
> 3. Now, she's going to carry out her New Year's resolution and live up to her new commitments more consistently.
>
> 4. She's already counting on some of her new exercises to help her settle down more quickly.
>
> 5. Besides that, she's going to work up the strength to sit out her panic attacks for least several hours.
>
> 6. She's going upstairs to throw out the TV; after that, she'll feel good enough to take on a new challenge or two.

b) Identify the types of verb particles in the following sentences.

> 1. Thomas the tailor was tired of letting out people's pants.
>
> 2. He wanted a change of life-style - a chance to mix things up, and decided a trip to Paris was exactly the right solution..
>
> 3. His wife wouldn't listen to him until they had enough savings to fall back on if the trip were not to work out as they hoped.
>
> 4. Thomas decided to go her one better and get someone to fill in for him while they were gone so that their income would not fall behind their expenses.
>
> 5. His nephw Salizar was the best replacement he could come up with.
>
> 6. Salizar agreed to bear with their clients and to back them up while they were gone.

c) compare the two verbal combinations: 'get away from' and 'get away with.' What kinds of verbs are they?

Verb Typology Applied to Phrasal Verbs

Can phrasal verbs belong to all the sub-categories of verbs: linking, prepositional, intransitive, transitive, ditransitive, complex transitive, and transitive prepositional? Theoretically they could, but a brief survey of them indicates that they seem to fit most often into one of three classes: intransitive, transitive, and prepositional. Some examples, in the same order, would be 1) 'sleep in' or 'wear out', 2) 'look up (a word)' or 'sit out (the game),' and 3) 'carry on with (a project)' or 'carry on about (a pet peeve).' A very few seem to fit into a fourth category – linking verbs, with examples like these: 'my estimate turned out (or came out or ended up) very low;' or 'she somehow turned into an A-list actress.' Examples using the verb 'be' with what might be a verb particle, like 'their estimate was way off' would probably not be analyzed as phrasal verbs. Instead, the word 'off' would probably be seen as an adjective which is homonymous to the adverb 'off' and the preposition 'off.' But it's perhaps possible to think of such 'be' examples as phrasal verbs which are linking verbs.

Four Types of Adjectives

We can start our discussion here with the idea that some adjectives work find in an attributive position (before the noun), but not in a predicate position (after a verb like 'be'). We saw examples of this in the previous chapter. In one example, we saw that the word 'principle' works fine in a noun phrase like 'the principle designer,' but sounds unacceptable in a predicate like *'...was very principle.' Such adjectives are called **attributive-only adjectives**. Other adjectives, such as 'asleep,' are just the opposite, as seen in the unacceptability of *'the asleep children,' compared to the normal-sounding '...was completely asleep.' Adjectives like 'asleep' are called **predicate-only adjectives**. Attributive-only adjectives include compound (adjective + noun) adjectives such as 'last-place.' Other attributive-only adjectives relate to experience ('previous' or 'former' president), direction ('left,' 'upper,' or 'western' part), quantity ('entire' or 'only' friendship), and completeness ('utter,' 'sheer,' or 'absolute' joy). Predicate-only adjectives include those that have a prefix 'a-' such as 'asleep,' 'alive,' and 'awake,' and those that describe a lack of health, such as 'ill,' 'infirm' or 'faint.'

One other adjective phenomenon is those adjectives that cannot be either attributive or predicative directly because they must be completed ('**complemented**' in technical terms; see the glossary) by a prepositional phrase ('PP'). An example would be 'reminiscent.' Nouns have to be 'reminiscent of (something),' so neither adjective position in the sentence, *"The reminiscent man is very remniscent" is acceptable. With its PP **complement**, such adjectives can only occupy the predicative position, as in 'The staging was reminiscent of the 70's.'

For those adjectives which can be either attributive or predicative, we'll look at two sentences that will help us make one more useful distinction:

18 (a) Those children are very courteous.

(b) *Those children are very female.

Here we see a difference between an adjective like 'courteous' or 'dangerous,' which can easily accept the qualifier/intensifier 'very,' and one like 'female' or 'absent' which cannot. Adjectives like 'female' are either all or nothing, so they cannot be described in terms of 'somewhat,' 'rather,' 'extremely,' or any of the qualifiers/intensifiers that we can think of. Such an adjective has no gradations of less and more female; mammals (and some other living things) are either female or they're not. Here we also have to be careful to exclude metaphorical usages, such as the one when teachers sometimes feel that a certain student is only partially present. This is a metaphorical use of 'present' and that's a complication we hope to avoid. This type of adjective is called '**non-gradable,**' meaning it has no gradations. This is why the word 'very' was introduced in parentheses in the previous chapter: words that fail the predicative part of the frame sentence might be non-gradable or they might be attributive only, so testing without the word 'very' is important to distinguish these two possibilities.

The other type of adjective is called '**gradable,**' meaning qualifiers/intensifiers can specify the relative intensity of that characteristic, such as how winsome or dangerous something is. For a diagnostic test for gradable adjectives, asking the question "How ___ is that?" for many adjectives usually works well.

Distinguishing Non-gradable from Predicative-only Adjectives

19) (a) *The former president was very former.

(b)*The former president was former.

(c) *The nuclear reactor was very nuclear.

(d) The nuclear reactor was nuclear.

Here the presence or absence of the word 'very' helps distinguish between predicative-only adjectives and non-gradable ones. Predicative-only adjectives are equally unacceptable with or without 'very.' But non-gradable adjectives sound somewhat better – and sometimes much better - without 'very' than with 'very.' This shows the usefulness of using the frame sentence with and without very for instances where the second half of the adjective frame sentence indicates an unusual type of adjective.

Another trap to watch out for is the use of nouns in an adjectival role, since they may test similarly to non-gradable adjectives. These two sentences look superficially similar.

Distinguishing noun modification from non-gradable adjectives

20 (a) * The vertical pole was (very) vertical.

(b) * The iron pole was (very) iron.

In each case, the attributive use of 'vertical' and 'iron' is fine, but the predicative usage is not. Nonetheless, 'vertical' is a non-gradable adjective, and 'iron' is a noun. How can we prove this to ourselves? It will help to test each of the words to see if it is a noun. 'They have no iron' is a fine sentence, but *'They have no vertical' is unacceptable. In this way, we can (slowly) learn to recognize words like 'iron' as nouns which are being used adjectivally, and words like 'vertical' as a special kind of adjective.

We should note in passing that noun phrases like 'the iron pole' show that the noun 'iron' can modify the noun 'pole' without turning into an adjective. 'Iron' remains a noun in this example of stacking of nouns.

Six Types of Adverbs

One of the unique characteristics of adverbs in English is that they can occupy a number of different positions in the sentence. This is demonstrated in the two sets of sentences below. We also note that different kinds of adverbs show different degrees of mobility. The list of six types includes conjunctive, relative, interrogative, manner, predicate, and sentential adverbs ("crimps" as a mnemonic, perhaps).

Manner Adverbs, Predicate Adverbs, and Sentential Adverbs

As we have learned to expect by now, we'll discover only part of what we need to know by utilizing either of two (well-chosen) sentences where one is grammatical and the other is not, highlighting a specific grammatical category that we are discussing. In this case, we need two sets of sentences to show the necessary contrast.

21) (a) Carefully, she will open the champagne bottle.

(b) She will carefully open the champagne bottle.

(c) She will open the champagne bottle carefully.

22) (a) Fortunately, she had read the assignment.

(b) * She fortunately had read the assignment.

(c) She, fortunately, had read the assignment.

(d) *She had read the assignment fortunately.

(e) She had read the assignment, fortunately

The first set shows the various positions and relevant punctuation for the so-called **'manner' adverbs**. They describe/modify the verb, saying 'how' the verb operates. The second set is notable in that its adverb is only grammatical when set off from the rest of the sentence by commas. This is called a **'sentential' adverb** and indicates commentary by the speaker or writer about the entire sentence. It is, therefore, not really a part of the sentence, and does not modify the verb within the sentence. Here we want to take a moment to notice that the frame sentence for adverbs works well for manner adverbs ("They handled the matter carefully"), but not so well for sentence adverbs (?"They handled the matter fortunately.") As the example sentences above show, sentence adverbs in the middle and final positions in the sentence seem to change in meaning unless they are marked off by commas. Both types are mobile within the sentence, but in markedly different ways. So both the mobility of adverbs is, in this instance an even better diagnostic test than the frame sentence. Both tests, however, help us distinguish these two types of adverbs.

Earlier, we identified 'there,' 'then,' 'once,' and 'twice' as adverbs because they fit the frame sentence reasonably well. We now notice that they fit reasonably well in all the three positions of the word 'carefully' above. So does that make them manner adverbs? In TESOL contexts, the adverbs which modify the verb are often divided into a number of semantic categories: adverbs of manner (quietly, slowly, and well), degree (thoroughly, enormously), duration (briefly, temporarily), frequency (always, often), time (again, now, then, early), instrument (mathematically, hydraulically), place (abroad, locally, back, here), addition (too, also) restriction (just, only, merely, hardly, never), act-relation (expressly, knowingly), stance (rudely), and also adverbs that are hedges (sort or, kind of).

Let's ask how these semantic categories map to syntactic ones. We have already distinguished manner adverbs and sentence adverbs based on their possible positions (their "distribution") within the sentence. It appears that the stance adverb 'rudely,' the duration adverbs 'briefly' and 'temporarily,' the frequency adverb 'often' (but not 'always'), the time adverbs 'again,' 'then,' and 'now' (but not 'early'), the instrument adverbs 'mathematically' and 'hydraulically,' and the act-relation adverbs 'expressly' and 'knowingly' can all join the manner adverbs as fitting all three positions well enough, but 'well' cannot (it only has a single possible position). This does not simplify our task much, but it does show that the division of adverbs into semantic categories does not help us very much in terms of their syntax. Since these adverbs all modify the verb, we can probably still call them 'manner adverbs,' and even use one of the two frame sentences to test them.

Of the adverbs that are neither sentence adverbs or manner adverbs, we have some that only fit the sentence final position, such as 'well, early, enormously (?), abroad, locally, back, and here.' Of these, 'here' can move, as discussed in the second paragraph below.

Others seem to be acceptable only in the pre-verbal position, such as 'always, just, only, merely, hardly, never,' and the hedges (sort of, kind of). We notice in this list that only those which are restrictive in meaning can be moved to the sentence-initial position, but when they are, the auxiliary seems to follow them, displacing the subject into the post-auxiliary position.

A couple of adverbs in the previous two categories can also occupy the sentence-initial position in the sentence, but their meaning changes when they are in that position: 'only' and 'here'.

And a final group seems to be acceptable in both the sentence-final position and the pre-verbal position, but not the sentence-initial position, such as 'thoroughly, too, also, expressly.'

In order to simplify our task, we will call all of the above adverbs that are not sentence adverbs or manner adverbs **predicate adverbs**. All of them can be used in one or both of the two predicate positions (pre-verbal and sentence-final), without commas, in contrast to the sentential adverbs.

Can adverbs modify adjectives as the elementary school mantra proclaims? A couple of examples will show us that not all modifiers of adjectives are qualifiers, like 'very,' but can, indeed, be true adverbs: 'Getting to class on time can be both psychologically and economically important.' Here the words 'psychologically' and 'economically' each modify the adjective 'important' without any sense of qualifying it. These are manner adverbs modifying an adjective. They have the semantic characteristic of answering the question 'how,' and they are acceptable in the frame sentence with 'handled.'

Interrogative Adverbs

Interrogative adverbs are used in questions. We can use the word 'interrogation' to help us remember this term. Four of them ask direct questions: 'Where did you go/When did you arrive/How was the trip/Why didn't you stop by?' The questions they ask and the answers they elicit all modify the verb, as we expect from manner adverbs. They are also use in asking or state questions indirectly, such as 'I wonder where he went. As we consider indirect questions, one more interrogative adverb needs to be added to our list: whether. Notice that interrogative adverbs cannot be deleted from the sentence there are in without making it ungrammatical. Do interrogative adverbs fit either the frame sentence or the newer test of adverb mobility? No to the frame sentence, and yes to the mobility (except for 'whether').

The way we can see that they move is by imagining a police officer talking to someone who cannot walk a straight line, "You say you weren't drinking when/where?" The officer is not really asking a question, but the sentence is grammatical and shows us the position of the interrogative adverb before it moves to the front of the sentence. This movement is discussed in more detail in section 6.1. and 6.2.5. later in this Guide. Notice that there are only two positions in the sentence for interrogative adverbs, so their movement is quite restricted. The interrogative adverb 'whether' is something of an exception, but we can say that it used pattern much more like the other four in Shakespeare's time, including direct questions, such as "Whether had you rather lead mine eyes, or eye your master's heels?" (Mistress Page in The Merry Wives of Windsor, III, ii, 3). Since that time, the use of 'whether' has become restricted to indirect questions.

Relative Adverbs

We can move seamlessly from interrogative adverbs to **relative adverbs**, since there is so much overlap in what they look like and sound like. Relative adverbs are a small group of three that we can easily list: where, when, why. Notice that 'how' cannot serve as a relative adverb, even though the other three can. It's an odd lack of consistency in English that we cannot say *'The way how you did it was creative.' Examples of the three relative adverbs are here:

    23) (a) There's the test area where the rocket was launched from.

    (b) This is the week when the big decision will be made.

    (c) There is no logical reason why I should stay at home this evening.

Relative adverbs can be distinguished from **interrogative adverbs** because they are easy to delete from sentences such as those above without changing the meaning: (a) could be 'the test area the rocket was launched from;' (b) could be 'the week the big decision...', and (c) could be 'no reason I should stay...' They also aren't used to form questions. We should notice here that the preposition 'from' needs to end sentence (a) in order for the relative adverb to be deletable. If it is dropped, 'where' is not longer deletable. One other characteristics is that when a relative adverb is present in a sentence, we notice that it cannot move from its usual position in the sentence, which contrasts with most other types of adverbs. So relative adverbs are poorly behaved in a syntactic sense. But we still consider them adverbs.

Conjunctive Adverbs

Conjunctive adverbs include a rather longer list of words. They are also called **connectives** in some presentations. We need to carefully keep these separate from subordinate conjunctions, which serve a similar function in connecting clauses, but do not have the same syntactic characteristics. Since they are adverbs, conjunctive adverbs are able to move within the clause they are connecting to the main clause; subordinating conjunctions cannot move this way. The longest list on the web seems to be one with 51 items, but many are antiquated and no longer useful. The most useful list to appear is at http://www.sdstate.edu/ writingcenter/ conjunctions_ and_ conjunctive_adv1.htm. Below is that list, divided according to the meaning of the adverb for a convenient overview.

    24) (a) Time: then, meanwhile, henceforth, afterward, later, soon, sometimes...sometimes, now...then;

    (b) Addition: likewise, moreover, furthermore, besides, then too, also, partly...partly;

(c) Concession or contrast: however, nevertheless, still, instead, rather;

(d) Result: consequently, hence, then, therefore, thus, accordingly;

(e) Condition: otherwise (= if not)

One tricky aspect of this lexical category is the punctuation, which high school English teachers love to explain. Here are examples which show six acceptable options:

25) (a) They decided to go anyway; however, they arrived late.

(b) They decided to go anyway. However, they arrived late.

(c) They decided to go anyway. They,however,arrived late.

(d) They decided to go anyway; they,however, arrived late.

(e) They decided to go anyway; they arrived late, however.

(f) They decided to go anyway. They arrived late, however.

The various positions available to the conjunctive adverb 'however' in the above set of sentences give us one convenient way to distinguish conjunctive adverbs from subordinating conjunctions or other conjunctions. We can test this by showing that the subordinating conjunctions 'before,' and 'since' can only occupy the slot of 'however' in the first (a) example sentence and none of the other five. The coordinating conjunctions 'so' and 'but' can occupy only the slot of 'however' in the first two (a) and (b) sentences in the set above. In summary, we notice that several kinds of adverbs demonstrate the ability to move within the sentence: sentential adverbs, manner adverbs, interrogative adverbs, and conjunctive adverbs can move, but relative adverbs cannot. Relative adverbs, however, look very much like interrogative adverbs ('where,' 'when,' 'how,' and 'why'), so a 'red flag' for adverbness should still go up in our minds when we see them.

Qualifiers (or Intensifiers)

At the beginning of our grammar discussion in chapter one, we added determiners and **qualifiers/ intensifiers** to our list of lexical categories by showing that they didn't fit the adjective and adverb categories. Qualifier/intensifiers need a separate category because they lack comparative and superlative characteristics of adjectives and because they cannot be stacked the way adjectives can. In fact, informal English does allow stacking of qualifiers, as seen in this example: "It was kinda sorta cool." But we can still use the lack of comparative or superlative forms to recognize qualifier/intensifiers as distinct from adverbs. We do need to note that some qualifier/intensifiers have an '-ly' ending, which should lead us to wonder whether they are adverbs or not. Some examples are 'essentially,' 'actually,' 'merely,' and 'absolutely.' In some instances the word can be an adverb in one context and a qualifier in another, so we need to look twice at words ending in '-ly'. Here are two sets of contrasting sentences.

26) (a) The judge decided the controversy fairly.

(b) The umpire called the game fairly well.

(c) They handled the matter completely.

(d) The concert was completely awesome.

The first sentence (a) could be modified to say, "Of the two judges, the local one decided the controversy more fairly." But no amount of editing will allow the second to be adapted for a comparative form: *"Of the two umpires, the experienced one called the game more fairly well." This same diagnostic demonstrates that 'completely' in sentence (c) is an adverb, but in sentence (d) it is a qualifier. Thus testing for a possible comparative or superlative form is the most convenient way to distinguish the two until we find something better. When we use 'more' and 'most' to test for qualifiers, we can say that we're using a syntactic, rather than a morphological test, for instances when this distinction matters. Other examples that may be used as either adverbs or qualifiers are these 'sufficiently, 'clearly,' 'truly,' 'perfectly,' 'simply,' and 'slightly.'

Another way to see if a word ending in –ly is an adverb of a qualifier is semantic: does the word have an antonym? If it does, it's a content word (an adverb, in this case), and if it doesn't, it's a grammatical or function word (a qualifier here). Using the same sentences above shows how this would be applied:

27) (a) The judge decided the controversy unfairly. (the antonym works)

(b) *The umpire called the game unfairly well/unjustly well.

(c) They handled the matter incompletely. (the antonym works)

(d) *The concert was incompletely awesome. (unacceptable)

Since semantic testing is always somewhat suspect, it's still good to use the comparative/superlative test to corroborate the semantic test.

The category 'qualifier' is an open category, to which new items can be added. This is seen historically in the development of modern English 'very' from Middle English 'verray' meaning 'truly,' as in 'She answered truly/verily.' A modern example is 'totally,' as in, "That concert was totally awesome."

Another diagnostic is that adverbs can usually be intensified, but qualifiers cannot normally be modified by another qualifier: 'They handled the matter very completely.' Here 'completely' is an adverb. This contrasts with *'The concert was very completely awesome' where 'completely' and 'very' clash when both are used as qualifiers. Either one by itself would be grammatically acceptable as a qualifier.

We have categorized the word 'enough' as a quantifier, but there seems to be one usage where it is a qualifier, as in 'That's good enough' or 'We did that well enough.' It's somewhat odd that 'enough' follows the adjective or adverb which it is qualifying, but that also helps to distinguish this usage from its usage as a quantifier, as in 'We have enough water for the hike.' The inverted word order can be used for enough as a quantifier, but it sounds somewhat poetic, as in 'We thought we had money enough.'

A final note is that the words 'more,' 'most,' 'less,' and 'least' are themselves qualifiers when they are used to make longer adjectives comparative or superlative ('more attractive' or 'least affordable'). The four clearly cannot themselves be made comparative or superlative, similar to other qualifiers.

Practice Distinguishing Qualifiers and Various Types of Adverbs

Decide which of the underlined words is either a qualifier or adverb, and for the adverbs, which type of adverb it is.

1. Sometimes I wish that I could just go outside and jump around.

2. It's a feeling I often get very late at night when I'm typing my most challenging papers.

3. Tomorrow morning, I'm really sure that things will move along incredibly well.

4. I'll wake up, walk briskly downstairs and really enjoy that first cup of tea.

5. Perhaps I'll be patient and patiently wait for the toast to pop up.

6. But now I'm simply stressing; it's raining too hard outside now for my taste, and I feel quite trapped.

Four Types of Nouns

When talking about nouns, it's all right to start with the sub-categories that we learned in elementary school: some nouns are proper nouns, which are always written with a capital letter, and other nouns are common nouns, which don't need a capital letter except at the beginning of a sentence. That's accurate enough and gets us started well. Other types of nouns, such as non-count nouns and abstract nouns, were mentioned in passing in the discussion in chapter two above.

One pair of contrasts within the noun category is shown by this pair of sentences:

28) (a) They bought a large chair and some smaller chairs.

(b) *They bought a large furniture and some smaller furnitures.

The second sentence demonstrates the unacceptability of a determiner like 'a' in front of the noun 'furniture,' and the unacceptability of a plural form like *'furnitures.' These are the characteristics of **mass nouns**, which are also called **non-count nouns**: 1) the determiner 'a' is unacceptable before a non-count noun, and 2) such a noun does not have a plural form. The word 'chair' belongs to the subcategory of '**countable**' or **count nouns**, which can be preceded by the determiner 'a,' and which have plural forms.

Another useful distinction between types of nouns is seen in these two sentences:

29) (a) The water in the pond is important.

(b) *The liberty in our country is important.

(c) Liberty in our country is important.

The second sentence does not allow a determiner like 'the' before the noun phrase 'liberty in our country' while the first one does for 'water in the pond'. The second type of noun is labeled '**abstract**' in contrast to the first one, which is called '**concrete**.' There are a number of complications attached to the use (or not) of determiners with abstract and concrete nouns, but this short introduction should give us a good start in distinguishing them. We can use the sentence "_____ in X is (not) interesting/important" as a frame sentence. Abstract nouns are acceptable in such a sentence, while concrete ones are not. If we do not include a prepositional phrase such as 'in the pond' both sentences would be fine without 'the' So, if a common noun (one that is not capitalized) in the blank is acceptable in a singular form (not plural) without any determiner, such as the article 'the,' it could be either a non-count noun or an abstract noun. The difference can also be seen in the meanings, so this is a semantic distinction which turns out to be helpful. Non-count nouns refer to physical objects (technically, and more accurately, 'have concrete referents'), and abstract nouns do not.

Practice with Types of Nouns

a) Identify the nouns and the types of nouns in the following sentences:

1. Sam has had to make hard decisions sometimes.

2. Recently, he started out looking for a block of cheese but wound fraternizing with several workers in the deli department.

3. Yes, he'd heard about spending less of his income on fattening foods, but then he thought about all the protein in dairy products.

4. Since the nation had become so conscious of credit card and mortgage debt, his shopping habits had changed drastically.

5. His refrigerator no longer stores blocks of cheese, but quarts of milk and plastic containers of cottage cheese.

6. He recently heard a talk about honesty in communication, so he's started sharing his insight with those around him.

b) Identify the types of nouns in the following sentences (Butcher and Lang):

> Odysseus was the King of Ithaca, a small and rugged island on the western coast of Greece. When he was but recently married to Penelope, and while his only son Telemachus was still an infant, the Trojan war began.

Seven Types of Determiners

In introducing determiners as 'non-adjectives' in the discussion above, our discussion already listed three kinds of determiners: articles, possessive determiners (my, your, his, her, its, our, and their), and demonstrative determiners (this, that, these, and those). To make the list of possessive determiners complete, we should probably add 'one's,' as in 'One's home is one's castle,' even though that sounds a little overly formal to an American ear. That makes eight possessive determiners in English.

Personal Demonstrative Determiners

Personal demonstratives are easy enough to list and recognize, since they appear in sentences like the following:

> 30) They're violating the rights of <u>us</u> students; <u>we</u> students demand our rights!

Besides the 'we' and 'us' forms above, the only other possible form is 'you' in English. We can't say * "I student deserve more," or * "She student deserves better." So there are only three personal determiners in English (we/us and you).

Interrogative Determiners

That leaves three kinds of determiners to introduce: interrogative, relative, and indefinite. **Interrogative** (meaning 'question') **determiners** are used in asking questions, such as

> 31) Which house/what company/whose car are you talking about?

Those are the only those three determiners that are also question words. As is true of all determiners, they must be followed by a noun; otherwise, they are not determiners, but something else.

Relative Determiner

English has one **relative determiner**, as in this sentence,

> 32) That's the man whose house we visited yesterday.

The relative determiner 'whose' looks like a question word, but, as the marker of a relative clause ('whose house we visited yesterday'), it must follow the noun that the relative clause is about ('man').

Indefinite Determiners

Indefinite determiners have been saved until last in the hope that we have got enough background with determiners by now to work well with the biggest group of determiners. A traditional list of these includes *some, any, no, every, other, another, many, more, most, enough, few, fewer, less, much, either, neither, several, all, both, such* and *each.* Because some of these words violate one of the syntactic filters (diagnostic tests) for determiners (non stackability), we will need to separate them out in a different category. In the following examples, we see the words *half, all,* and *both* preceding the determiners which means they cannot be determiners themselves:

> 33) Half the Belgian chocolate/all those dirty windows/both my English classes.

The words *many, several,* and *few* also cannot be determiners for the same reason, as we will see in the next section. In addition, we find another group of words often listed as a type of determiner which we will likewise need to disqualify from that category:

> 34) The one exception that matters…

Happily for us, there is one category that will accommodate all these words: '**quantifier**,' and we will explore that further in the next section.

In summary, we need a list of the indefinite determiners that pass the diagnostic tests and do not stack with other determiners. They are these '*some, any, no, every, another, other, more, most, enough, less, fewer, much, either, neither, such,* and *each.*' Other, similar terms, that occur in some lists will appear in the following section on quantifiers.

Sentences like 'The more the merrier' and 'The fewer the better' can be suggested as examples showing that 'more,' 'less,' and 'fewer' can be stacked with the determiner 'the' and so should also be deleted from the list of indefinite determiners. The main reason to disagree with this point of view is to recognize that the word 'the' in these 'the…the…' structures is not functioning as a determiner at all, but rather as a conjunction, or more specifically a correlative conjunction. So 'more,' 'less,' and 'fewer' are allowed to remain on the list of indefinite determiners for that reason.

Finally, for students who want to be able to recall all six of the types of determiners, perhaps the acronym "ppraiid" will help them. Or perhaps they can discover another acronym that will work better (or perhaps 'ppiraid' or 'pipraid').

Two Types of Quantifiers

Quantifiers include cardinal numbers and six indefinite forms. They were mentioned in the previous section, and they are one of the lexical categories that we did not discuss in the previous chapters. As their name suggests, they include all ›the numbers. They also include *half, all, both, many, several,* and *few,* as we noted in the previous section. They are different from determiners and pronouns in their ability to follow a determiner. They are different from adjectives in their lack of comparative or superlative forms, such as

      35) *"They saw more several/many children."

In the sentence 'They saw two more children,' the word 'more' is not functioning as a comparative qualifier, but more like the adjective 'additional.' But there are instances where, like adjectives, they can stack with each other, as in 'The first several scoops of ice cream were delicious.'

The category includes one kind of number: **cardinal** (*one, two, three, …*). Notice that the **ordinal** numbers (*first, second, third,…*) numbers pattern like adjectives in all respects: they fit the frame sentence, "The first runners were first (by two minutes)", for example. They also have the quality of adjectives that when they are made into non-count nouns, they represent an indefinite group of people: "the first will be last" is very similar in its patterning to "the poor have no voice." The other words that we listed above are called **indefinite quantifiers**: *half, many, few, several, all,* and *both,* even though 'half' and 'both' seem rather definite in their meanings. It may help students recognize quantifiers by stacking them with determiners:

      36) "We talked about the many choices/the few opportunities/the several great courses/all the nice colleagues/both the graduation parties on Wednesday.

Stacking with determiners is the most convenient syntactic test that we have to distinguish quantifiers from determiners. This category is not included in some textbooks, perhaps because it is a little prickly. Theoretical linguists have debated about the syntax and semantics of quantifiers for decades, but we only need a basic view for our purposes here. The comforting aspect about remembering this category is that it is easy to memorize all of its two areas: cardinal numbers and six indefinites (many, few, several, all, half and both). That's all we need to remember. The hardest part of this to remember is that such a category even exists! Well, there are a couple of possible pitfalls with numbers, so let's look at them for a minute.

First, fractions (besides 'half,' which can act like a fraction or like an indefinite quantifier) do not pattern the same way as numbers or indefinite quantifiers, since they usually require the preposition 'of' after them, which helps us see that they are nouns. They also have plural forms: three-quarters. They are even nouns in a sentence such as "They have already reached the two-thirds mark," but we'll have to return to discuss nouns which function adjectively after we have finished describing the lexical categories in English.

Second, sometimes numbers can become nouns, such as when we talk about the names of playing cards or the scores we got on a test: 'I got two threes' or 'She got an eighty-five.' This happens with cash, as well, as in 'You can have both my fives.' These are examples of numbers functioning as nouns and not as quantifiers.

Pronouns—Another Elementary School Myth

Pronouns are another of the basic twelve parts of speech that we are now beginning our discussion about. How does one recognize a pronoun and distinguish it from every other lexical category? One accessible way to approach pronouns is to think back to the elementary school saying, "Pronouns replace nouns," and work further from that. This saying is sometimes true, for example, when we talk about proper nouns, abstract nouns, or plural count nouns. Notice that distinguishing types of nouns has become important to this discussion. So we can say,

37) 'Monica wept' = 'She wept'; 'Eagles fly' = 'They fly'; and 'Honesty matters'='It matters.'

Those examples exhaust the true part of the elementary school saying. But what about this next one? 'The man on the corner is selling tickets to today's game.' We recognize 'man' as a singular countable noun. For 'man' we would expect to use the pronoun 'he' as a pronoun replacement. What is the result of the replacement?

38) *'The he on the corner is selling tickets to today's game.'

Whoops! The correct sentence reads 'He is selling tickets,' and the pronoun must replace the entire noun phrase, 'the man on the corner.' The governing principle is actually quite straight forward: pronouns replace noun phrases, and only noun phrases. Proper nouns, abstract nouns, and plural count nouns all turn out to be noun phrases in addition to being individual nouns. So that will serve as our test for pronouns – they are used to refer to a noun phrase which they are replacing. That's not too far from the elementary school mantra, but the difference is significant. We'll return to this point when we talk more about phrases. It will also help our recognition of pronouns to know what all of the sub-types are, all ten of them. So let's move on to types of pronouns.

Ten Types of Pronouns

Pronouns are the most rainbow-colored of all the parts of speech, covering a wide range of uses, as seen by the list in the heading above. Each pronoun refers to another noun phrase, called its **antecedent**.

Demonstrative Pronouns

The list of demonstrative pronouns is the same as the list for demonstrative determiners: this, that, these, and those. They are included here for the sake of completeness, even though there should be some doubt about whether they function the same way as other pronouns. It is true, as we read in standard grammar descriptions, that they can stand alone, as in

39) "I'll take these."

As a pronoun 'these' needs to refer to another NP, its antecedent.

The difference between the demonstratives and other pronouns is that the non-demonstrative pronouns cannot double as determiners. Putting a noun after these forms makes them determiners, as in "I'll take these apples."

Personal Pronouns

Moving on, let's talk about personal pronouns, since they are so familiar. The familiar subject pronouns are *I, you, he, she, it, we, and they.* In addition, we need to add the word 'one,' as in

40) 'One cannot be too careful these days.'

The pronoun 'you' serves as an informal form of this general, impersonal subject pronoun. That makes a total of nine subject (personal) pronouns.

There are seven **object (personal) pronouns**: me, you, him, her, it, us, and them, with 'you' serving also as the object form of the general pronoun, as in 'If you neglect to pay taxes, they'll fine you.' In the following sentence, notice how 'one' cannot serve as both a subject and object pronoun in that sentence, even though 'you' can. 'One' can only function as a subject pronoun:

41) *'If one neglects to pay taxes, they'll fine one.'

Also notice the overlap of three forms with the **subject pronouns**, if we count 'you' twice. It may be some small comfort to harried students at this point to recall that the pronoun systems of other Indo-European languages are quite a bit more complex, with different forms for singular and plural 'you' and also for formal and informal 'you' (such as tu/vous in French or du/Sie in German or tu/usted in Spanish).

Possessive Pronouns

Possessive pronouns are sometimes mentioned in the same breath with possessive determiners, but they are not the same. There are seven of them: mine, yours, his, hers, its, ours, and theirs. The impersonal meaning of 'you' seems also to function for the possessive pronoun, although it is clearly informal: 'If you neglect to pay taxes, you'll get **yours**.' The possessive pronouns generally fit into a frame sentence like this one: "That's _____ you/they can't take it."

Only 'his' and 'its' overlap with their possessive determiners, and the other five (mine, yours, hers, ours, and theirs) are unique forms as possessive pronouns.

Indefinite Pronouns

Indefinites have been discussed as a type of determiner, so we should see which ones can also function as pronouns. The list of indefinite determiners is repeated here for reference: *some, any, no, every, another, other, more, most, enough, less, much, either, neither,* and *each.* To start with most of the indefinite determiners can also function as pronouns: *some, any, another, more, most, enough, less, much, either, neither,* and *each,* as well as all the compounds of 'some,' 'any,' 'no,' and 'every' when they combine with '–one,' '-body,' and '–thing' (namely, *someone, anyone, no one, everyone, somebody, anybody, nobody, everybody, something, anything, nothing,* and *everything*) It also includes the compounds of 'some, any, no and every' with 'other.' The inclusion of 'another' and 'others' adds two more items. Beyond that there are the lexical items 'one,' 'none,' and 'fewer.' The word 'oneself' is sometimes miscategorized here but belongs with the reflexive pronouns, which we will turn to immediately.

This is one of the longest lists we have encountered so far, so it's perhaps helpful to see if there are common threads that all these pronouns share. It includes most of the indefinite determiners and many words with –one, -body, -thing, and 'other.' That's a little shorter list. We notice that it does not include the indefinite quantifiers (*half, many, few, several, all,* and *both)* because these can follow a determiner, something that pronouns cannot do.

One pattern of the indefinite pronouns is different from that of the personal pronouns. Indefinite pronouns can be followed normally by a prepositional phrase with 'of', such as 'some of the rivers', which personal pronouns may not do.

Reflexive Pronouns

There are nine **Reflexive pronouns** (*myself, yourself, himself, herself, itself, ourselves, yourselves, themselves,* and *oneself*). This group is larger by one than the usual personal pronoun list because it has separate forms for singular and plural 'you.' The first eight in the list fit in the frame sentence,

42) '(Subject noun phrase/pronoun) looked at _____ self/ves in the mirror.'

A variation is "It is sometimes hard to look at _____ in the mirror." This second frame sentence identifies the ninth reflexive pronoun 'oneself.' We also notice that the second frame sentence could be filled with 'yourself' in its general, impersonal, universal meaning. Even though we notice that a frame sentence is possible here, the suffix '-self' is also very easy to recognize. So why bother with a frame sentence? The answer is in the following section.

Intensive or Emphatic Pronouns

Having discussed reflexive pronouns, we can easily make the transition to **intensive/emphatic pronouns**, since they look the same but function differently. They fit the frame sentence:

    43) "(Subject pronoun/noun phrase) did it _____ self/ves."

This is not like looking in a mirror and seeing oneself. This is an emphasis on who exactly did something, as in "After the pilot's heart attack, John and Sherman flew the plane themselves, with only occasional instruction from the control towers along the way." As we know, we can also add the preposition 'by,' as in 'by myself' to indicate doing something without any outside help. This use of 'by' may help students distinguish intensive/emphatic pronouns from reflexive ones. So even though the '-self' suffix makes these pronouns exceedingly easy to recognize, we still need a further diagnostic to distinguish reflexives from emphatics.

Reciprocal Pronouns

Reciprocal pronouns provide material for only a very short discussion, since there are only two of them in English: *one another* and *each other*. They help describe the mutuality of an action, such as "We/they/you need to take care of each other." Notice that the subject needs to be plural for there to be mutuality. We're not tempted to say *"He needs to take care of each other."

Interrogative Pronouns

Interrogative pronouns are pronouns that are used in questions such as:

    44) Who did you visit? Whom did you go with? What did you see?

There are three of these in English (who, whom, and what), which are quite recognizable. The object form 'whom' is great fun for English teachers to explain. An easy way to remember it as an object form is to think of the 'm' in 'whom' as the same as the 'm' in 'him' and 'them.' When looking at 'who' in a sentence, it helps to substitute 'him' or 'them' as a check to see if the position is an object one or a subject position. First, the interrogative pronoun should be put in the position it occupies for an 'echo question,' such as 'You visited who?" If 'him' or 'them' works as a subsititute for 'who,' then 'whom' should be correct in the question as well. In the above question, the substitution would be "Did you visit them?" where 'them' is correct. So 'Whom' would also be correct in "Whom did you visit?" in 41) above.

Relative Pronouns

The relative pronouns are related to the interrogative pronouns in a way similar to relative adverbs and interrogative adverbs: they look the same and sounds the same, but they function differently. Relative pronouns are also similar to relative adverbs in that they can sometimes be deleted, as in the first two of these examples:

45) (a) Those are the people (who(m)) we saw yesterday.

(b) That's the dog (that/which) we saw yesterday.

(c) Those are the people who invited us out.

(d) That's the dog that/which ran away yesterday.

What we need to notice about deleting the relative pronouns here is that they can only be deleted when they are followed by the subject of the verb in the relative clause. The word 'we' in (a) and (b) above serves as the subject of the relative clause, which is why the relative pronouns can be deleted in those two sentences. Otherwise, as in (c) and (d), where they are the subject of the verb in the relative clause, the relative pronouns cannot be deleted. This is because the verb in the relative clause must have a subject.

In terms of recalling all ten types of pronouns (counting subject and object pronouns as two types of personal pronouns), perhaps the acronym '**drrriiippp**' will help. The three 'p's are personal subject pronouns, personal object pronouns, and possessive pronouns.

Practice with Pronouns:

a) Choose the correct pronoun form in these sentences:

1. There was one person who/whom I wanted to address in the arena.

2. She was the one that/which I hoped to interview.

3. Unfortunately there was no way to find out who/whom her manager was.

4. Ms. Lin was the person that/which I was assigned to interview.

5. But Ms. Ray had just been introduced as the sculptor of an exceptional flying figure that/which I had been admiring.

6. So I introduced myself to her and told her that she was the person who's/whose work I most admired.

b) Identify the quantifiers and pronouns in the following sentences

1. It was the third fantastic morning of vacation when Draper arose from his bed and walked a couple of steps to his refrigerator.

2. As always, he listened first to his stomach and delved into the several white expanses of the appliance, searching for as many worthwhile items as possible.

3. Like most great explorers and archaeologists, he took some time to closely exam all its contents before he found a two-day-old Danish hidden behind the one container of vegetable curry he had made the night before.

4. After some milk and a few bites of the Danish, Draper willed himself to be ready for both the momentous tasks that he'd initiated two nights earlier.

5. His single desk covered with numerous clippings and several books reminded him of his first task: cleaning up.

6. His computer reminded him of the second one as it began whirring and clicking its way to life while he reread the newspaper headlines, "MAN ON TRAPEZE LOSES GRIP FOR LAST TIME".

c) Identify the types of determiners, quantifiers and pronouns in the following sentence:

That young prince, whose uncle was among the many heroes that there are in their family, had himself watched his uncle defeat two dozen armed rebels by himself by causing many of them to fight among themselves.

Three Types of Prepositions

After a list of ten kinds of pronouns, it should come as a relief to find that there are only three kinds of prepositions, and that the three are very simple to distinguish. If a preposition consists of a single word, it is a simple preposition; if it consists of more than one word, it is a phrasal preposition. Recognizing a preposition depends on its function in a sentence, since it (usually) has to have a noun phrase as a complement. Jack Lynch of Rutgers University suggests that you can recognize prepositions by putting 'he' after them. If 'he' has to become 'him', then you have either a preposition or a verb, and you just have to make sure it isn't a verb. There's a list at the bottom of this section with most of the prepositions in the language. Those two sub-types will take care of 99% of the prepositions we will ever encounter. For the simple prepositions, an elementary school mental trick that will help us get a general idea and a partial list is to ask,

47)'Where can a squirrel jump in a tree?'

This gives us a list that has everything to do with spatial relationships, which is a good place to start: 'above, across, against, along, around, behind, beside, between, beyond, close to, down, far from, in front of, into, in, inside, near, next to, opposite, out, outside, off, on, onto, over, past, through, toward(s), underneath, and up.' That's a pretty good list to start with – thirty-one out of one hundred is almost a third of the list.

One other bit of comfort may come from restating an old truism that 'prepositions form a closed class,' meaning that new ones cannot be invented or created, as can so easily be done with nouns (an ipod), verbs (to google, to blog), adjectives (brutalitarian) and adverbs (quixotically). If prepositions are a closed class, we can look at the phrasal prepositions with fresh eyes. First, they shouldn't have nouns in them. This might sound odd, but nouns can be, and have been, used to create new phrasal prepositions.

Examples of potential phrasal prepositions that we can remove from consideration for this reason include 'in preference to,' 'for the benefit of,' 'in advancement of,' 'in concert with,' and 'in relation to.' It is also easy to re-analyze such long phrases as two prepositional phrases, such as 'for the sake' plus the preposition 'of' with its own noun-phrase complement. This would remove all three- and four-word phrases from standard lists, reducing the number of phrasal prepositions to twenty. It should be some relief to reduce to some extent the list of prepositions to be familiar with.

In order to leave this topic on a high note, it is interesting to note that English also has several (lonely) **postpositions**. These are odd in that they follow their noun-phrase complements instead of preceding them. The most typical example of a postposition in English is 'ago,' which follows its noun-phrase complement, as in 'ten years ago,' rather than *'ago ten years.' The 'pre' in 'preposition' means that its position is before the noun phrase which completes it (called its **complement** or object). A language like Japanese has only postpositions and no prepositions, but other Germanic languages besides English also have postpositions, as we see in 'den Fluss entlang' ('along the river' in German; literally 'the river along') or 'de stad in' ('into the city' in Dutch; literally it's 'the city into').

So 'ago' is not such of an iconoclast as it might seem at first. Two other 'pure' postpositions in English are 'away' ('two miles away'), and 'hence' ("two months hence"). One verb form, 'excepted,' seems also to function as a postposition. A number of 'mixed' prepositions can be used both postpositionally and prepositionally: 'aside' ('these exceptions aside' or 'aside from these exceptions'), 'notwithstanding' ('that introduction notwithstanding,' or 'notwithstanding that introduction'), 'on' ('eight months on,' or 'on that day'), and 'through' ('the whole winter through,' or 'through the winter months'). That is a good enough overview, so now we can simply list the prepositions in their three categories.

Simple prepositions in English: aboard, about, above, across, after, against, along, alongside, amid(st), among(st), around, as, aside, astride, at, before, behind, below, beneath, beside, besides, between, beyond, but (meaning 'except'), by, concerning, despite, down, during, except, failing, following, for, from, given, in, inside, into, like, minus, near, of, off, on, onto, opposite, out, outside, over, past, per, plus, regarding, since, than, through, throughout, till, to, toward, towards, under, underneath, unlike, until, up, upon, versus, via, with, within, without, worth.

English speakers sometimes encounter prepositions borrowed from French (such as 'sans' and 'vis-à-vis') and Latin (such as 'qua' and 'circa'). Others have become antiquated or poetic: atop, round, save, times, and unto. And we have some that can be considered slang, such as 'barring,' and 'upside.' ("List of English Prepositions")

Phrasal prepositions in English: according to, ahead of, aside from, because of, close to, due to, except for, far from, inside of, instead of, near to, next to, out from, out of, outside of, owing to, prior to, pursuant to, regardless of, subsequent to, that of, as far as, and as well as. These last three are indeed three-word phrases, but there is no noun to allow analysis as a PP inside a PP.

A number of three-word phrases can be analyzed, as mentioned above, as a recursion or embedding of prepositional phrases, so we won't count them as single (phrasal) prepositions: in addition to, by means of, in case of, in front of, in lieu of, in place of, in spite of, on account of, on behalf of, on top of, with regard to, and in accordance with (lists adapted and modified from "A List of Prepositions").

Four Types of Conjunctions

Of the four types of conjunctions, there are short lists for three of them, which may be some comfort. Only subordinating conjunctions have a somewhat longer list of lexemes.

Coordinating Conjunctions

The **coordinating** conjunctions are known by the acronym '**fanboys**,' meaning 'for, and, nor, but, or, yet, and so.' These are all useful in joining clauses, but only four of them seem capable of joining individual words, as in these examples: 'strict yet kind,' 'give and go,' 'strong but silent,' 'life or death.' What English teachers love to explain is the punctuation of fanboys: between clauses, even if there are only two, they require a comma, but between smaller grammatical units, they only require a comma if there is a list of three or more items (not for only two).

A myth from elementary school that students need to shed at this point is that sentences are ungrammatical is they begin with simple coordinating conjunctions. It may be poor style to begin a sentence with a coordinating conjunction, but there is evidence coming that it is perfectly grammatical. In order to see for ourselves, let's take as an example of educated English from a book which sold about thirty million volumes during the thirty years since it was first published in 1979: the New International Version ('NIV') of the Bible. It was written by a committee of scholars and has been accepted by millions of readers who are native speakers of English. Here are three sentences in sequence from chapter 13 of the book of Acts (NIV), starting with verse 35:

> 48) "So it is stated elsewhere: 'You will not let your Holy One see decay.' For when David had served God's purpose in his own

generation, he fell asleep; he was buried with his fathers and his body decayed. But the one whom God raised from the dead did not see decay."

In the above text, three consecutive sentences begin with a coordinating conjunction: 'so,' 'for,' and 'but.' These three sentences beginning with coordinating conjunctions are clearly grammatical. This is meant to show that the elementary school rule is not about grammar, but about writing style. Is that evidence enough? I hope so. Judging for acceptability in matters of style is important, but it is not the same as judging for acceptability in grammar. So prescriptive grammarians may always raise questions of style as to the appropriateness of coordinating conjunctions as the first word in a sentence. But it is clear that such sentences are grammatically acceptable to native speakers of the language.

Correlative Conjunctions

There are traditionally five **correlative conjunctions** in English: 'both... and...,' 'either .... or...,' 'whether ... or...,' 'neither ... nor...,' and 'not only..., but also....' To that we should probably add 'the...the...' in sentences like 'The more the merrier.'

We should also note here that 'both,' 'either' and 'neither' may be used singly as either a determiner, a pronoun, or a quantifier, as discussed earlier. Of the five, only 'whether ... or' requires a phrase with a verb in it to follow each half of the conjunction. The other four in the traditional list can combine single nouns, adverbs, and adjectives as well as larger grammatical units. 'The...the...' can combine single adverbs and adjectives and larger grammatical units, but not nouns. It may be useful to develop some examples of these to help recall this information more clearly later.

49) Correlatives with various XPs ("phrases") (A=adjective, and so on)

   a) They are neither poor nor rich. (combining APs)

   b) They enjoy both classical music and rap. (NPs)

   c) They worked not only carefully but also quickly. (AdvPs)

   d) I don't know whether they'll decide to go home or they'll choose to stay for the weekend. (IPs)

Complementizers

The word '**complementizer**' describes the word 'that' in sentences where the verb requires a clause as its object or complement, such as 'I am hoping that you will come home.' The entire list of complementizers is 'that,' 'if,' and 'for.'

Further investigation shows that there are different complementizers for different types of complement clauses, as these sentences exemplify:

> 50) (a) I wondered if they would arrive on time
>
> (b) *I didn't know if to donate money to that campaign.
>
> (c) It was not too late for you to start a new life.
>
> (d) *It was not too late for you should start a new life
>
> (e) I am hoping that you will come home soon.
>
> (f) *I am hoping that you to come home soon.

Looking carefully at the above examples, we see in (a) and (b) that 'if' can only introduce indirect questions where the verb in the complement clause has a tense ('would arrive'), but not where it has no tense ('to donate'). The complementizer 'for' in sentences (c) and (d) can only introduce indirect statements (not questions) where the complement clause has no tense ('to start'). The technical term for the verb form 'to start' is '**infinitive**,' and we'll discuss that much later in this Guide under the heading 'non-finite clauses.' Infinitives have no tense. The complementizer 'that' in sentences (e) and (f) can only introduce indirect statements (not questions) where the complement clause has a tense ('will come').

Subordinating Conjunctions

Subordinating conjunctions form a rather long list. There are at least thirty-three, in fact. Here is an example with 'because':

> 51) They went home early because it started to rain.

As seen in this example, the addition of a subordinating conjunction turns a complete sentence ('It started to rain') into a clause that cannot stand on its own. Subordinate clauses are one type of dependent clause. This is one of the diagnostic characteristics of subordinate conjunctions and the subordinate clauses that they mark. In addition, subordinate clauses can also be identified by their mobility. Note how the 'because' clause can be moved to the front of the sentence: 'because it started to rain, they went home early.'

A list of the subordinating conjunctions would have to include the following ones, which are divided into semantic groups for ease in remembering: 1) those about time (after, before, when, while, since, until); 2) those about causes and effects (because, since, now that, as, so (that), in order that); 3) those about contrast (although, than, though, even though, whereas, while); and 4) those about conditions (if, unless, only if, whether or not, even if, in case (that)) (Bryson).

It's worth noting at this point that at least six words on the list can serve dual functions: 'after,' 'as,' 'before,' 'since,' 'than,' and 'until' can also serve as prepositions, as in 'after dinner/as a student/before class/since last year/than me/until spring'. The other listed subordinating conjunctions can only introduce full clauses

Five Types of Auxiliaries

Auxiliaries are sometimes called 'helping verbs' and sometimes called 'auxiliary verbs.' In English sentences where they appear, they always precede the main verb. The first sentence in the example set below gives several examples of auxiliaries in one of the diagnostic sentence for verbs. There are thirteen or fourteen auxiliaries in English, divided into four groups: 1) modal auxiliaries (in four and a half pairs: can, could, will, would, may, might, shall, should, and must), 2) aspectual auxiliaries ('have' – marking the perfective aspect and 'be' – marking the progressive aspect), 3) the passive auxiliary 'be' (for passive voice), 4) the dummy auxiliary 'do' (for emphasis, negation, and the interrogative form in the simple present and simple past tenses), and 5) the non-finite auxiliary 'to'.

The two 'be' auxiliaries can be distinguished clearly. The aspectual progressive auxiliary 'be' is always followed by a verb's **present participle**, ending in '-ing', like 'is working.' The passive auxiliary 'be' is always followed by a verb's **past participle**, like 'was kidnapped.' It's important to note that 'have,' 'be' and 'do' can also serve as main verbs, in addition to being auxiliaries. We see the auxiliary 'do' in sentences like 'What do they want?' and 'They don't know.' It's a little early in the course to explain the non-finite auxiliary 'to,' but here is a short explanation. First we need to say (simply) that 'finite' means that a verb has tense, and non-finite means that a verb has no tense. Here are a pair of sentences that demonstrate that difference.

52) A contrast between a finite and a non-finite clauses:

(a) Which is the place <u>for us to go first</u>?

(b) Which is the place <u>that we should go first</u>?

In comparing the underlined parts of the two sentences, we see that 'us' and 'we' are parallel and that 'go' in both sentences are in parallel positions. In between those two words, we have 'to' in the 'a' sentence and the modal auxiliary 'should' in the 'b' sentence. Here we see 'to' functioning as an auxiliary. It is not coincidence that the form 'to go' is called the 'infinitive' form of 'go,' since 'infinitive' means that it has no tense just as 'non-finite' does. That's a short explanation that we will come back to in several chapters.

Even though auxiliaries are sometimes called 'helping verbs' or auxiliary verbs,' there are good reasons not to include them in the same category as normal verbs. The diagnostic tests for verbs help show this. Here are the frame sentences repeated for convenience:

53) a) They should/may/can _____ . (or)

b) (The) <u>noun</u> _____ <u>good/healthy.</u>; such as 'The music sounds good,'
   or 'The patient looks healthy.'

Auxiliaries clearly cannot fit into either frame sentence for:

54) (a) *They should would. (or)

   (b) *'The music can good,' or *'The patient would healthy.'

It is also difficult to imagine a future tense use of any of the modals: *'will must,'
*'will should.' Of course, we cannot extend these unusable Aux+Aux strings to
include will+do or will + be or will+ have because these pairings seem to us not
as Aux+Aux strings but rather Aux+Main verb strings. Our minds switch
immediately to these items as full verbs, rather than as auxiliaries, so that is a
path that leads only to confusion. Other differences between the full verb usage
do, be, and have will appear when we discuss transformations, such as question
formation, and diagramming.

   Sometimes substitutes for modals are used in less formal registers. For 'will'
we use 'be+going to' (or very informal with 'gonna'); for 'must' we have 'have
to' ('hafta') or 'have got to' ('gotta'); and for 'should' we say 'be+supposed to'
('sposta'). These are sometimes called 'quasi-modals.'

Practice with Auxiliaries and Conjunctions

a) Identify the auxiliaries in the following sentences, where they appear.

   1. The children were doing their homework when the lightning struck.

   2. No one had any time to think about what they should do.

   3. None of them was used to needing to think so quickly.

   4. They would have left the house if a radio announcement had not
   stopped them.

   5. When they did look outside, they decided that staying inside was a
   much better idea.

   6. But, as they were discussing their options, the sun came out again, and
   their world returned to normal.

b) Identify the types of prepositions, conjunctions, and auxiliaries in the
following sentence:

As far as the young prince was concerned, it was time for them to honor a man to whom they all owed a great debt and who not only could have been, but almost was, killed, and had thereby increased the tribe's reasons for pride.

The Negative Particle 'Not' and Other Suspected Non-adverbs

Traditionally, 'not' has been labeled an adverb. A little review will show that 'not' does not function the way normal adverbs do. It doesn't pass the frame sentence diagnostics: *'They told the story (very) not.' *'They handled the situation (very) not.' Morphology doesn't work: *'not-er,' *'not-est.' And it shows no ability to change position: '*(Not) they did (not) tell the story *(not).' For this reason, 'not' has been separated out and is called the negative particle. It doesn't seem to fit any other category well. Even a word like 'never,' which also fails the first two diagnostic tests, can show some variability in its sentence position (adding 'did' for reasons we'll get to later on): '(Never did) they (never did) tell the story *(never did).'

There are a couple of other adverbs that might be called into question at this point, such as 'then,' and 'there.' We'll continue to call them adverbs, even though forms like *'there-er' and *'then-est' are clearly unacceptable. The reason is that they do make sense in the frame sentences, albeit using 'right' as an optional qualifier works better than 'very': 'They told the story (right) then.' 'They handled the situation (right) there.' So, for now, these two can remain safely inside the adverb category. This same explanation applies to words like 'once' and 'twice,' as in 'They told the story once.' 'They handled the situation twice.'

Practice with Several Lexical Categories

Identify the types of verbs, verb particles, prepositions, and auxiliaries in the following sentences:

1. Samuel needed to tell someone; he hadn't felt really and truly inspired for several years.

2. He knew that he could easily become an expert in art and languages and exceptional music, but really he'd just been giving in to whatever made him happy.

3. He thought that he must be missing out on his artistic opportunities; he had to wear a hat now just to pen a few creative lines.

4. At least he never got into painting; he never would have been able to keep up with developments in painting.

5. Someone had asked him where he got off thinking things like this.

6. He turned things around by asking others where they thought they were going with their comments.

b) Identify the types of verbs, verb particles, prepositions, and auxiliaries in the following sentence:

> The young prince did decide to make up a new name for the monument and hoped that would put off the need to worry about other problems such as how to keep his brothers from taking his kingdom away and allowing historians to consider him a failure.

Red-flag Words

Having worked through the various lexical categories and sub-categories, we can now pause and ask which words are the most likely to cause problems as we get ready to analyze phrase and sentence structure. Which words should carry a mental red flag for extra care as we prepare to encounter the entire spectrum of grammatical structures? They are ones that might be one category or a completely different one, depending on the grammatical context. Among the words high on such a list would have to be 'for,' 'to,' and above all 'that.' But there are also others: after, before, since, than, one, do, have, be, read, and hard. They're all hard in a their own ways. Let's take them in reasonable groups where we can fit them into groups.

1) **'One'** - quantifier, pronoun, or noun? The characteristics of a pronoun discussed above are not very helpful here, since 'one' can stand alone as either a noun or a pronoun, but the meaning is strikingly different. When we say, 'I'd like five ones please' it's being used as a noun. It's when we say, 'One can never be too careful' that we're using it as a pronoun. When it follows a determiner, as in 'I'll take that one' or 'the one thing that I'd most like…' then it's a quantifier. When it refers to a quantity, even without a determiner or noun, it's also a quantifier, as in 'One's enough.'

2) **'To'** – preposition or infinitive marker? Again, the preposition needs an noun phrase as its object, such as 'give it to him.' As an infinitive marker (which we've mentioned as a type of auxiliary), 'to' is always followed by a verb without any inflectional endings, as in 'they want to stay.'

3) **'Too'** – adverb or qualifier? In 'They have too much debt,' it's a qualifier. But in 'That applies to me, too,' it looks most like an adverb.

4) **'For'** - complementizer or preposition? The same rule for prepositions in #1 above applies here, as in 'They bought it for me/dinner.' In addition, 'for' introduces entire clauses, much like the subordinating conjunctions above, except that the clauses look different: 'They bought it for me to eat tonight.' Here 'for' is followed not only by an object pronoun, but after that comes an infinitive ('to' + verb) and the rest of a complete **predicate** (whatever completes/complements or modifies the verb). Subordinate conjunctions cannot introduce this kind of clause.

As we will discuss under '**empty categories**,' all of the words listed in numbers one and two can be deleted, leaving only a reduced form of a clause. This then leads to grammatical hide and seek, which students can get very good at.

5) '**Five,**' **and other cardinal numbers** - quantifier or noun? Distinguishing quantifiers from nouns was discussed in number one above. So we can say, 'I'd like these five,' and we're using a number as a quantifier. Or we can say, 'the fifteen most difficult words to analyze grammatically...' and it's also being used as a quantifier. 'I got a five on the quiz' is an example of noun usage. This is similar to buying 'a fifth' of something (a noun).

6) '**after,**' '**as,**' '**before,**' '**since,**' '**than,**' **and** '**until**' - subordinating conjunction or preposition? For each of these, just remember that a preposition must have a noun phrase as its object. So, it's a preposition if followed by an object pronoun or another noun phrase: 'after/as/before/since/than/until me/dinner.' It's a conjunction if it's followed by an entire clause: 'after/as/before/since/until we ate dinner.' Notice that 'than' is the only conjunction that doesn't work for the clause '...we ate dinner.' 'Than' is somewhat different from the rest of the list, but putting it here helps us give it a good slot to remember it in. Only 'than' and 'as' show themselves to be conjunctions in another context: when followed by a subject pronoun, as in 'better than I (am),' or 'as good as he (is).'

7) '**This,**' '**that,**' '**these,**' '**those,**' '**his**' - determiner or pronoun? The same characteristics that help us distinguish 'that' as a pronoun from 'that' as a determiner also work for 'this,' 'these,' 'those,' and 'his.' Each of them will fit into either of the first two example sentences in number four above.

8) '**That**' - compelementizer or determiner or pronoun? Determiners introduce noun phrases which always have a noun as their head, such as 'that green and red hat.' But when 'that' stands alone as a noun phrase, it's functioning as a pronoun, for instance, 'I saw that.' Then, other times, 'that' introduces an entire clause, as in 'I know that you know.'

9) '**Hard,**' '**fast,**' '**late,**' '**high,**' **and** '**low**' - adjective or adverb? Here we need to see what the word is modifying. If it's a noun, the modifier is an adjective, as in 'a hard day's night.' If a verb is being modified, the modifier is an adverb, as in 'live fast and die hard.'

10) '**Be,**' '**do,**' '**have**' - auxiliary or verb? When one of these occurs as an auxiliary, it is always followed by a main verb, as in 'I do (sometimes) see/ I am (always) looking/ I have (often) wondered...' When it is the head of a VP, with only complements and modifiers after it (and perhaps an auxiliary before it), it is the main verb, as for instance, 'I did my chores/They are very talented/We have time.'

11) '**Read**' - intransitive, transitive or ditransitive verb? Here we can simply count the number of objects and end up with a classification: none=intransitive,

one=transitive, two=ditransitive. Examples, in order, as a) She's reading (for fun), b) We read our textbooks (very faithfully), and c) They're reading my children a story (out on the porch).

These may be the ten (plus one) plagues of a grammar student, so it's good to learn how to deal with them. Notice that 'that' appears in both numbers seven and eight. And 'one' belongs to both numbers one and five. But we see 'that' used much more frequently, so it's probably the most annoying (or important) entry in the above list.

Grammatical Roles

We return to the idea that other categories modify verbs, adjectives and adverbs besides adverbs. Here are two of those other categories.

    55) After the party, we went home.

Here the word 'home' describes where we went. And 'after the party' describes when we did that. Each one modifies or describes the verb 'went.' So they are being used adverbially, yet neither is an adverb. 'After the party' is a prepositional phrase which is used adverbially, even though there is no adverb in the phrase. We'll discuss phrases in the next chapter. The focus here is the difference between lexical categories and grammatical functions or roles. Let's look at the word 'home' in this context. What's the lexical category of 'home' then? If it's adverbial, perhaps it can be comparative or superlative. Can something be 'more home' or 'most home' or 'homer' or 'homest'? So we see that the word fails these morphological tests for adverbness. We're not talking about 'homier' or 'homiest,' since that comes from 'homey,' which is a different word.

If we notice that the qualifier 'very' modifies adverbs as well as adjectives, as in 'They walked very slowly,' this will turn out to help us, so let's pursue that for a minute. This is a syntactic test, since it considers how words can be combined in a sentence. Can we insert 'very' into the sentence "After the party, they went home" as a modifier of 'home'? No, we can't, so we need to mark that test sentence with an asterisk, indicating its unacceptability: *'After the party, we went very home.'

By looking at the frame sentence above for a noun, we notice that the word 'home' fits there very well: "They have no home (to speak of)." This is confirmed by morphological testing for plural and possessive: 'They have two homes,' and 'The home's attractiveness lay in it's location in the mountains.' So the word 'home' is a noun; that's it's lexical category. But in the sentence above it is used as an adverb. That's its grammatical role. This could be slightly unsettling, but it may be a comfort to know that not many nouns can be used this way. Call it an exception if you will.

One notable part of the Germanic heritage of English is that nouns can act adjectively, as we noted during the discussion of types of adjectives. A phrase like 'the steamboat insurance company' shows that both 'steamboat' and 'insurance', which are nouns, can act adjectivally in modifying the noun 'company.' Such constructions are not found in Romance languages, like French and Spanish.

The main point to remember here is that lexical categories and grammatical roles do not always overlap. So they need to be considered separately.

Summary List of Sub-types of Lexical Categories

Adjectives: attributive only, and predicative only, (non-) gradable

Adverbs: manner adverbs, sentence adverbs, interrogative adverbs, relative adverbs, and conjunctive adverbs.

Auxiliaries: modals, aspectuals, one passive auxiliary, and the dummy auxiliary

Conjunctions: simple coordinating conjunctions, correlative conjunctions, complementizers, and subordinating conjunctions

Determiners: articles, possessives, demonstratives, personal, interrogative, relative, and indefinite.

Intensifiers (or Qualifiers): those that double as adverbs, those that don't.

Nouns: common, proper, (non-) count, abstract, and concrete

Pronouns: demonstrative, personal (subject, object, or possessive), indefinite, reflexive, intensive (or emphatic), reciprocal, interrogative, and relative pronouns

Prepositions: simple and phrasal, and very few postpositions.

Quantifiers: numbers and indefinites.

Verbs: linking, intransitive, transitive, prepositional, ditransitive, transitive prepositional, and complex transitive

Verb particles: adjacent, non-adjacent, and movable particles

Table 3 Indefinites

Indefinite Pronouns

One	some	any	none		another
One	someone	anyone	no one	everyone	any other
self	somebody	anybody	nobody	everybody	no other
	something	anything	nothing	everything	others
more, most, enough, fewer, less, much, either, neither, each					

Indefinite Determiners

	some	any	no	every	another
					other
more, most, enough, less, much, either, neither, each, such					

Indefinite Quantifiers

all, many, few, several, both, half

Practice with All Categories and Subcategories

Identify the lexical category and sub-category of each word in each of the following sentences (adapted from Butcher and Lang).

1. As Menelaus was the brother of Agamemnon, who was recognized as the chief of the petty kingdoms of Greece, he could call on the whole force of these kingdoms.

2. No prince signed on with the league of Troy from a home more remote than that of Odysseus.

3. So after they had defeated Troy, he prepared himself for the longest and most perilous homeward voyage of all the Greeks.

4. The Odyssey takes up only the last six weeks of the voyage during which Odysseus had gone from one adventure to another.

Chapter 4: Phrasal Categories, Phrasal Roles, and Phrase Structure

Identifying a Phrase

In some introductory materials, phrases are called '**constituents**' and students are given methods of **constituent testing**. That is the same as identifying phrases. This approach to grammar is called a '**phrase structure**' approach. Phrases need to be identified in the context of a sentence in order to become useful as analytical tools. One sentence that seems to help students build up some confidence in identifying phases is this one:

1) Two rich business people are eating lunch happily at the restaurant near the beach.

While it's true that there are four standard methods of identifying phrases, the short answer diagnostic works well in most instances, except for pronouns. More about pronouns in a moment, but they all turn out to be noun phrases. If a string of words will stand by itself as a short answer to a (sometimes cleverly devised) question, that string of words is a phrase. It may take a little more thinking to say what kind of phrase it is, but we can be sure it is a phrase of some kind.

Using the above sentence, it's a useful exercise to underline all of the phrases. We might ask, 'What is the restaurant near?' Answer: the beach. Where is the restaurant? Answer: near the beach. So both 'the beach' and 'near the beach' are phrases. Finding a shorter phrase 'inside' a larger is one of the normal features of all natural (i.e., human) languages. The shorter is said to be '**embedded**' inside the larger one. Several more examples will add to the amount of theory that we have regarding phrases. Question: with what kind of attitude are the people eating? Answer: happily. Request: describe the kind of business people who eat at that restaurant. Response: rich. It's a response to a request, rather than a question, but it stands alone as a response, marking it as a phrase. And finally, what are the rich people probably doing at that restaurant while they eat? Answer: business. The word 'business' can also be a phrase. Here we have three one-word phrases. That's not a problem. There are something like twelve phrases inside the sentence, and the sentence itself is the biggest phrase, as we'll discover later when we discuss phrase structure.

Now a word about pronouns. Since pronouns replace noun phrases, and not simple nouns, as we mentioned in a very abbreviated discussion in the context of pronouns above, they are phrases. That reasoning is called the 'replacement test.' This is how we recognize pronouns as phrases even though "they" or "she" by itself will never stand alone as a short answer. It's not a problem that they are single words, since even single words can be phrases, as we just noticed with 'rich,' 'business' and 'happily.' This may seem odd, but the short answer test confirms some single words as being phrases. The fact that some nouns (plurals, proper nouns, abstract nouns) are single-word phrases is also the truth behind the elementary school mantra that 'pronouns replace nouns.' That's only true when the noun is itself a single-word phrase. Otherwise, it is not true as we saw earlier for singular count nouns, such as 'pen,' or 'book.'

In order to get used to showing phrases and the embedding of phrases, underlining is a useful kind of notation. When we underline phrases for the above sentence, we notice several layers of embedding. First 'two,' 'rich,' 'business,' and 'people' and 'happily' can be shown to be single-word phrases. Then two of them combine to form the phrase 'business people.' We might note that 'rich' and 'business' do not combine to form a phrase at all. After that, the 'rich' further combines to form the phrase 'rich business people.' Finally, these three combine with the quantifier 'two.' That is how the subject of the sentence is formed. This multi-layered process also takes place in the predicate of the sentence.

Underlining of Phrases

Two rich business people are eating lunch happily at the restaurant near the beach

The phrase that most students miss in the above array is the noun phrase 'the restaurant near the beach' because students make 'at the restaurant' into an independent PP early in their Thening process. It's a non-tragic error that we'll be able to clarify more easily when we work on diagramming. For now, the best way to approach the problem is to build every possible phrase from the right end of the sentence. That would have helped in first recognizing the larger noun phrase 'the restaurant near the beach.' If we need some sort of logical reason or reminder to work from the right to the left, let's think back to our elementary arithmetic lessons – addition, subtraction and multiplication all proceed from the right side to the left side of the problem – first the ones column, then the tens column, and so on. The same sort of reasoning applies to identifying phrases –

start at the right side with the least complex units and build gradually toward the left side.

There does seem to be one exception, though. The scanning of the verb phrase seems is that exception: we need to scan from left to right starting from the verb on the left to include all the objects and modifiers once they have been identified. We see this above in how the verb phrase builds from 'eating lunch' to 'eating lunch happily,' and then to 'eating lunch happily in the restaurant near the beach.' Many students wonder why 'eating' is not itself a phrase. The short answer is that it is a transitive verb in this sentence, so it is not complete without its object. Calling 'eating' a phrase would indicate that the verb here is intransitive.

As mentioned, please notice that 'rich business' is not a phrase. Many other adjacent word pairs do not form phrases in this sentence, such as 'is eating' or 'happly at'. So we note that, while we hope to find all the phrases in the sentence, we also hope to learn to recognize the combinations which are not phrases.

Phrasal Categories and Roles

Once we have identified a phrase, we'd like to be able to name it. The name of a phrase is derived from the most important word in the phrase, which is called the **'head' of the phrase**. So what's the head of each of the two phrases we just identified: 'the beach' and 'near the beach'? For this we need to be able to identify the lexical category of each word in the phrase. 'The beach' is composed of a determiner followed by a noun. Judged naively, which will do for now, it is a noun phrase (usually written **NP**). 'At the beach' is composed of a preposition followed by a noun phrase. Here the head is not part of the embedded phrase, but rather the new element in it, the preposition, making the whole phrase a prepositional phrase (usually written **PP**). In order to fill in some of the other phrase names, we can look back at the word 'rich' and recognize that it is an adjective. So, as a phrase, it is an adjective phrase (**AP**). And we notice that 'business' is also a phrase.

When we look at a sentence very much like the one we just worked on, we can now label all of the phrases that we have identified. If a word is not part of a phrase (an '**XP**'), it's convenient to label its part of speech without the 'P' for phrase. These words are not underlined. It may be useful to try to label the phrases in the practice sentence by yourself before looking at the solution below. So don't look at the next page until you have spent some time labeling the phrases that are underlined: <u>A lot</u> of <u>rich business people usually</u> eat <u>lunch</u> at <u>the restaurant</u> near <u>the beach</u>.

Labeling phrases

```
Two rich business people are eating lunch happily at the restaurant near the beach
QP   AP    NP       NP    Aux V     NP    AdvP  P  D    N          P    D    N
                    _____NP          _____VP                   _____NP    _____NP
          _____NP    _____VP              _____PP
_____QP/NP                              _____NP
                                                        _____PP
                                                  _____VP
_____IP
```

The phrasal name for a sentence is 'IP', and we'll talk about that later in this chapter.

Practice with Phrasal Typology

Identify and name the phrases in the following sentences:

1. Samuel had not felt very inspired for several years.
2. He knew a lot about the different kinds of artistic expression.
3. However, he'd often just given in to his laziness.
4. He thought about his many opportunities as an artist.
5. Fortunately, he never got into art history.
6. Someone had asked him about his deep pessimism.
7. He turned things around and asked others the reasons for their personal criticism of him at this time.

Grammatical Roles of Phrases

When we ask what other grammatical roles the various phrases play in the sentence, we need some vocabulary that might be familiar from middle school or junior high grammar lessons, for those who had such lessons. For a start, NP's can be **subject**s and **object**s. 'The beach' is an object of the preposition 'near,' in the above example sentence, "A lot of rich business people usually eat lunch at the restaurant near the beach," so the NP is a **prepositional object**. The phrase 'near the beach' describes the restaurant (and not the verb 'eat'), so it modifies the NP 'the restaurant.' Since it modifies an NP, it's working **adjectivally**, even though it's a PP and not an adjective. And here we see that we not only need to know what lexical category/ies a word belongs to, and what kind of phrase it belongs to, we also need separately to see what the word is doing in the phrase and what the phrase (often written **XP** when we're not speaking about a particular kind of phrase) is doing in the sentence.

One of the two other phrases we identified above will add a new insight to this discussion, namely that there is sometimes a contrast between lexical or phrasal category and its grammatical role. The word 'rich' is not a good example, since it's both an adjective and an adjective phrase, and it's modifying a noun. So it has an adjectival role in the sentence. No surprise there. But what part of speech is 'business'? It seems to be stacked with 'rich,' so is it an adjective, too? The frame sentence for adjectives gives us the following: *'The business man was very business.' This shows that 'business' doesn't work in the predicative position. And it can't be modified by 'very.'

We'll hold on to the idea or theory that it could be a non-gradable adjective, but let's move on and test it for another lexical category. Might it fit better as a noun? Let's see if it has a plural – businesses. In fact, adjectives don't and can't have plurals, so that's the end of the non-gradable adjective theory. How about the frame sentence for nouns: 'They don't have any business.' That's not bad. So we'll call it a noun. But it still seems stacked with 'rich,' and it's certainly telling us something about the kind of people they are. So its grammatical role is adjectival, even though its lexical category is 'noun'. It doesn't even matter whether we think about 'business' as the first half of a compound noun, or simply an independent noun modifying 'people.' In either event, its role is still adjectival. And 'business people' is an NP whose head noun is 'people.'

In summary, a PP and an NP can each have an adjectival grammatical role. There are other examples of such divergences between grammatical role and lexical or phrasal category, but we will no longer be surprised when that happens. For the grammatical role, we will look at the function of the word in the XP (=phrase) or the role of the XP in the sentence. For the name of the XP, we will look for the most important word in a phrase (its head), the one that the other words are modifying.

Now we should ask what the spectrum of grammatical roles for an NP is. Is there anything in a sentence that an NP cannot do? If we go through the description of verb types, we will see that NPs can function as the subject of the verb, its complement, its direct object, its indirect object, or the complement of its direct object. This is not everything that a noun can possibly do in a sentence, but it is a complete list of all the ways a noun can be a complement.

Phrasal Structure

One question about phrases that we will now ask is, what about the parts of a phrase that are not the head – what are their grammatical roles? How many possible roles are there inside a phrase? We'll start with the PP that we identified earlier 'near the beach.' 'Near' is the head of the phrase, and we'll move on from there.

Prepositional Phrase (PP) Structure

The first question is whether the NP 'the beach' is a required part of the PP or not. If so, it is a complement; if not, it is a **modifier**. In discussing verb particles, we said that some of them double as prepositions and others double as adverbs. But are there cases of prepositions that are neither a preposition nor a verb particle nor an adverb? No, there aren't, even when that seems to be the case. If we start with the hypothesis that the NP is a complement and test for that, we'll be making a good start. We can get a feel for the preposition's need for an NP object by leaving it out. So in our model sentence, this means leaving out the NP object (or complement) of the prepositions 'near' and 'at':

2)   (a)*A lot of rich business people usually eat lunch at the restaurant near.

      (b) *A lot of rich business people usually eat lunch at.

In both examples, the sentence-final preposition requires an NP object as its complement. This turns out to be a general property of prepositions. Or at least that they must have some object. So we'll restate the general property this way: a preposition requires an object as its complement in order to make a PP. There are no single-word PP's, in contrast to the single-word NP's and AP's that we encountered above.

Nonetheless, English is so rich and flexible that two other phrasal categories besides an NP can also serve as a proper object for a preposition. In a few instances, such as 'out from under the car' we have two prepositions in a row – 'from' and 'under'. In this case, we consider the smaller PP to be the object of the larger PP, so 'under the car' is the object (or complement) of 'from'. In a more common instance, such as 'We wondered about how they were doing,' the object of the preposition 'about' is an entire clause: 'how they were doing.' Both a PP and a clause are thus also possible objects of a preposition in a PP. All three (NP, PP, and clause) can serve as the complement of a preposition.

Now, what would a modifier for a PP look like? Here are some examples, and we should notice that the modifiers precede the head of the phrase (the preposition):

3)   (a) strictly between us

      (b) six feet under the ground

      (c) straight up the ladder

That's it for the possible grammatical roles in a PP: a head, a complement and a modifier. This is also the entire spectrum of possibilities in a verb phrase (VP), and an adjective phrase (AP). An adverb phrase (AdvP) has only two possible roles: the head and any modifiers; adverbs never have a complement.

Verb Phrase (VP) Structure

We've discussed verbs that have no complement (intransitive verbs), verbs that have a single complement (transitive verbs and prepositional verbs), verbs that have two complements (ditransitive verbs and transitive prepositional/adverbial verbs), verbs whose subject receives a semantic complement (linking verbs), and verbs whose direct object receives a semantic complement (complex transitive verbs). Perhaps a walk-through will help us analyze whether we're looking at a verb with a complement or a modifier. Here's a short sentence.

4)   They looked really tired.

How did they look? 'really tired.' So 'really tired' is a phrase. We need to ask what the lexical categories of the two words are. Here 'tired' is an adjective, and 'really' (meaning 'very') is a qualifier. And 'tired' is the main part or head of the phrase, making the entire structure an AP. This series of considerations is an out-loud analysis, modeling what students need to be doing in their heads every time they analyze a phrase, so please make sure that each step of this is not only clear, but that it's possible to apply this series of steps to any of a zillion other phrases in the English language.

Having identified the lexical categories and the phrasal category, we can continue on by looking at how one goes about **testing for modifers**. This is a standard way to test grammatical roles within a phrase. The AP 'really tired' would be perfectly grammatical without the word 'really.' That's the easiest way to test for modifiers – take them out and see what's left. If the remaining word or phrase is grammatical and complete (although missing some perhaps interesting information), what was removed is a modifier. If the remaining word or phrase is not grammatically complete, what was removed is a complement. Here 'They looked tired' is perfectly grammatical and 'really' just gives us some extra information, so it's a modifier.

Now we can return to the discussion about the role of the AP 'really tired' in the sentence. Is it a modifier or a complement? We go through the same set of diagnostic tests. Remove it and what's left? 'They looked.' If we consider this grammatical, we must also notice that the verb 'look' has shifted meaning in order to stay grammatical. That's a sign that we removed a complement. 'They looked' is no longer an answer to 'How did they look?' as we had with 'They looked tired.' Instead, 'they looked' is the answer to a very different question, something like, 'when they discovered that John was missing, did they call for him or look for him?' Even then, 'they looked' does not sound very convincing as an acceptable answer in my dialect, but this is my best attempt to salvage what's left of the sentence after removing the AP 'really tired.' This seems to be clear evidence that the AP is a complement of the verb 'look' when it means something like 'seem.' In this meaning, 'look' is a linking verb, so we shouldn't be surprised that the AP is a complement. That's one of the characteristics of a linking verb. If we had started this inquiry by determining that that meaning of 'look' is a linking verb, we would have missed the chance to test the AP as either a complement or a modifier.

In summary, we could have taken either of two approaches to the following question: 'Is 'really tired' a complement or a modifier?' We could have first asked 'What kind of verb is 'look' and decided that it is a linking verb and therefore requires an NP or AP complement, which would make 'really tired' a complement. Or we could remove the AP from the sentence, as we did, and see if what's left is grammatically complete and correct. It turned out that the meaning of 'look' in 'They looked' is not the same as the meaning of 'look' in 'They look really tired,' which means that the AP is a complement necessary to that particular meaning of 'look.' Either way works, and students need to have a good grasp of each one.

In this context, we can look at the issue of modifiers for VPs. Since they modify verbs, these modifiers are called **adverbial modifiers**. Adverbs, prepositional phrases, and clauses can fulfill this role, so let's look at an example of each.

5)   I usually read the paper at seven o'clock before I go to class.

In analyzing phrases, we start by identifying all of them. In this case we have 'I' (pronoun NP), 'usually' (adverb AdvP), 'the paper' (NP), 'at seven o'clock' (PP), and 'before I go to class' (clause). There is an NP inside the PP and several phrases inside the clause, but we'll ignore them for now. Why? Because they don't aid our analysis. Students need to be able to identify each and every phrase or **constituent**, including its name, its structure and its role in larger phrases and in a clause, but for this discussion, it's fine to take a little shorter route for the sake of efficiency.

So, with laser precision, we delete everything except the subject and the verb: 'I read.' This is correct, but the meaning of the verb is 'I am literate,' which is not the original meaning. So a complement is missing, namely the NP 'the paper.' This affirms our earlier discussion saying that the direct object NP is considered necessary (a complement) even for bivalent verbs which can be either transitive or intransitive. What about the rest of the phrases and the clause? What we have left now is this: 'I read the paper.' This is a complete and acceptable sentence, even though it's missing some interesting information, such as when I read the paper. This short-cut has led us to the conclusion that 'usually,' 'at seven o'clock,' and 'before I go to class' are all modifiers. The clause is adverbial because it modifies a verb. We can also begin with the semantic information that each phrase answers the question 'when,' which (along with where, how, and why) is a typical meaning for an adverbial. Moving from semantics to syntax, it's useful to mention that adverbial clauses usually begin with subordinating conjunctions like 'before' or 'while,' which means that being able to recognize and identify subordinating conjunctions can be a great help in analyzing VP structure.

A short interlude about phrasal naming is in order here. The adverbial modifier 'before I go to class' needs its own phrasal name. We can already tell that it has a complete sentence ('independent clause') inside it, since 'I go to class' is a complete sentence and can stand by itself. But 'before I go to class' cannot stand by itself, so it is called a dependent clause. Its phrasal name is complementizer phrase ('CP') since the word 'before' introduces it in the same way the complementizer 'that' introduces other dependent clauses like 'We know that she will be on time.' We notice especially that what we see in our example is also generally true: a dependent clause is larger than an independent clause, since it has an entire sentence ('IP') inside it.

Returning to the variety of adverbial modifiers, we ask this question: what else in the syntax allows us to confirm that certain modifiers modify the verb and nothing else? We can do more than just intuit this; we can also analyze and show that they modify the verb. How? We can show this by isolating each modifier with the verb: 'usually read,' 'read at seven o'clock,' and 'read before I go to school.' These are reasonable interpretations and contrast markedly with an analysis that attempts to show that any of the modifiers could modify either the subject or the direct object in the left-over sentence: *'I usually,' *'I at seven o'clock,' *'I before I go to school,' *'usually the paper,' 'the paper at seven o'clock,' or *'the paper before I go to school.' All are unacceptable, further confirming our hypothesis that each of the three modifiers modifies the verb.

Using the underlining notation will summarize the structural roles in the VP:

6)   Structural roles in a VP

<u>I</u> <u>usually</u> <u>read</u> <u>the paper</u> <u>at seven o'clock</u> <u>before I go to class</u>
NP m:AdvP h:V   c:NP   m: PP   m: clause

Concluding, we can say that VPs can include one head verb (which might be a verb phrase itself), up to two complements (for ditransitive or transitive prepositional/adverbial verbs), and any number of modifiers. When we say 'one head,' we need to note that using coordinating conjunctions to produce a coordinate structure such as 'read and enjoy the paper' is quite all right, and still produces 'a head.' That head is the first element in the coordinate structure, which we'll discuss under 'coordinate structures.'

Adjective Phrase (AP) Structure

In the prior discussion, we looked at an example sentence and asked, 'How did they look?' and answered, 'really tired.' So 'really tired' is a phrase. We asked what the lexical categories of the two words are, and noted that 'tired' is an adjective, and 'really' (meaning 'very') is a qualifier. Since 'tired' is the head of the phrase, the entire structure an AP. That much we saw in the prior discussion. Qualifiers may serve as modifiers in an AP. What else can serve as a modifier in an AP? What about the following APs?

7)   (a) ten inches wide

     (b) ice cold

     (c) white hot

     (d) helpful in the kitchen

     (e) intellectually rich

In examples a-c above, the head of the phrase is the final word, which is an adjective. In the first two examples, the modifier saying 'how wide' or 'how cold' is a noun. So nouns can serve as modifiers in an AP. The third example shows that sometimes an adjective, such as 'white' can modify the head of an AP. And the fourth one shows a PP modifying an adjective. The final example is an adverb modifying an AP.

It remains to ask whether adjectives can have complements. The answer is yes, and here are a couple of examples:

8)   (a) fond of/averse to constructive criticism

(b) subject to/tired of sudden fluctuations

While it's clear that 'fond,' 'averse,' and 'subject' must have PP complements, since they cannot be used grammatically without a complement (as native speakers can confirm), what about 'tired'? Can't it be used without a complement, as in 'The hike made us really tired'? True, but notice that the meaning of 'tired of' is not the same. Being 'tired' from a hike refers to physical tiredness, but being 'tired of (change/spaghetti/losing)' is a psychological state. This shows that the psychological meaning requires a complement, even though the physical meaning does not. This contrasts with the use of the PP in a phrase such as 'tired to the bone,' where the PP following the adjective is clearly a modifier.

Using the underlining notation will show the differences between the two APs that we have been discussing.

9)   An AP with a complement or a modifier

       (a) <u>tired of spaghetti</u>   (b) <u>tired to the bone</u>
         AP   c: PP   AP   m: PP
                     _____AP   _____AP

In each case the adjective is followed by a PP, but in one case the PP is a complement ('c') and in the other case, it is a modifier ('m'). In summary, APs can include one head, one complement, and many modifiers. Examples of a coordinate structure for a complement would be 'tired of spaghetti and meatballs.'

Practice with Adjective and Verb Phrases

a) Identify the adjective phrases in the following sentences and label their heads, complements, and modifiers.

1. It was quite a balmy summer evening when our servant-hearted hero emerged slowly from some sort of oppressive darkness.

2. As he focused his intense his intense, white light on the strangely curvy path in front of him, he cautiously moved his blood-shot eyes from left to right.

3. In several small ways, this experience was similar to a second birth.

4. Now stopping, now falling, never turning to the left or right, he continued upward along the unpredictable rock path.

5. No one saw him during this heroic return from a hole a mile deep.

6. Andrew was delighted that his parents had bought him a brand new car.

7. Steven's burned his fingers when he touched the piping hot stove top.

8. After the worst day of her life, Emily realized that she did not like roller coasters.

9. When he was fairly young, John quickly rose as a huge star in the music business.

b) Identify the verb phrases in the above sentences and label their heads, complements, and modifiers.

Adverb Phrase (AdvP) Structure

Adverb phrases have the fewest structural possibilities – they only have a head and perhaps a modifier, but never a complement (as far as I know). Examples with modifiers that are qualifiers are quite easy to find: 'very silently,' and ' quite beautifully,' for instance. But the standard examples of adverbs modifying adverbs seem often to use qualifiers with '-ly' suffixes. Is 'surprisingly well' an example of an adverb modifying an adverb? Let's check to see if 'surprisingly' fits either of the frame sentences for adverbs, and contrast it at the same time with the word 'satisfactorily':

10)   (a) They told the story (very) surprisingly (or)
           (b) They handled the matter (very) surprisingly.
           (c) They handled the matter (surprisingly) well.
           (d) The handled the matter satisfactorily.
           (e) They handled the matter satisfactorily well.
           (f) They told the story (very) slowly.
           (g) They told the story slowly well.

It seems from the above examples, that some words with '-ly' suffixes are basically qualifiers and don't work verb well as adverbs (a-c, f), while other words with '-ly' suffixes are basically adverbs and don't work very well as qualifiers (d-e, g). This is an area where the student's own dialect will be an important factor in deciding these differences. Using only the above examples, we might conclude that qualifiers cannot function as adverbs and vice-versa, but even a single exception would sink that theory, so we'll refrain from generalizing from such a small number of examples. We can conclude, however, that adverb phrases have either a lone head word (as in (d) above), or both a head word and a modifying qualifier (as in (f) above).

Practice with Adverb Phrases

Identify the adverb phrases in the following sentences and label their heads and modifiers.

1. Sometimes I wish that I could just go outside and jump around.

2. It's a feeling I often get late at night when I'm typing my most chal
lenging papers.

3. Tomorrow morning, I'm sure that things will move along incredibly
well.

4. I'll wake up, walk briskly downstairs and really enjoy that first cup of
tea.

5. Perhaps I'll even patiently wait for the toast to pop out.

6. It's raining harder outside now, which will help me concentrate
completely intensely.

7. When he was fairly young, John quickly rose as a huge star in the
music business.

8. He could sing beautifully, and he wrote well thought-out songs.

9. Radio stations soon began to air his music.

10. People around the country also began to get a taste for that genre,
and interestingly enough the rest is history.

Noun Phrase (NP) Structure

Noun phrases include four possible structural roles (a head, a complement,
modifiers, and a **specifier**), making them potentially more complex than the four
phrase types that we have discussed so far: PP, VP, AP, and AdvP. An example
will allow us to recognize all four parts:

11) the intentional destruction of the city

First, we recognize the head of the NP noun ('h') 'destruction' followed by its
complement ('c') 'of the city.' We should check briefly to see if 'of the city'
might be a modifier. If we drop it from the phrase, we get 'the intentional
destruction,' which seems incomplete by itself, so we'll affirm 'of the city' as a
complement. 'Intentional' we recognize as an adjective, and confirm that it can fit
it easily enough in its frame sentence: 'The intentional insult seemed very
intentional.' In order to check to see if it's a modifier, we also drop it from the
phrase and get 'the destruction of the city,' which is grammatically complete even
though it's missing some interesting information. So 'intentional' is a modifier
('m') inside the NP. Now we need another name for the structural role of the
word 'the.' The word that theorists came up with is '**specifier**' ('s'). Sorry it's not
more descriptive, but we can see that the determiner specifies whether the NP is

definite or indefinite. We notice that 'the' could be replaced with a possessive noun like 'Nero's.'

So possessive nouns in NPs also have the role of specifiers. We notice that 'Nero's' is itself a phrase. Sometimes specifiers are phrases, such as 'Nero's', and sometimes they are not, such as the determiner 'the.' If 'the' can be the specifier of an NP, then we expect – correctly – that all determiners can also be specifiers of NPs. And if a possessive noun phrase like 'Nero's' can be a specifier, then we expect – again correctly – that all possessive NPs can also be specifiers. This includes longer possessive NPs; so we can agree that the phrase 'the next door neighbor's' is the specifier in the larger NP 'the next door neighbor's new car.'

PPs may also be modifiers within an NP, as in 'the destruction of the city by night last week', where 'by night' is a modifier. 'Last week' is an NP also acting as a modifier in the larger NP.

A more complicated kind of modifier for an NP is a relative clause, which always follows the NP it is modifying (its **'head noun'**, which is really a 'head NP'). In the previous sentence, the clause beginning with 'which' is a relative clause. Being able to recognize and identify the lexical categories of relative pronouns, relative adverbs, and relative determiners can be very helpful in analyzing NPs of this sort. It deserves repeating here that many of these markers of relative clauses can also be deleted, which means we need to be alert to see if they can be inserted where they have been deleted. Let's look back at the kinds of examples given in chapter 2 and notice that most relative adverbs and some relative pronouns may be deleted:

12) Relative adverbs 'when' and 'why' are deletable, but not 'where'

(a) There's the hospital <u>where</u> I was born.

(b) This is the week (<u>when</u>) the big decision will be made.

(c) There is no logical reason (<u>why</u>) I should stay at home this evening.

13) Relative determiner 'whose' is not deletable

That's the man <u>whose</u> house we visited yesterday.

14) Object relative pronouns 'whom,' 'that' and 'which' are deletable

(a) Those are the people (<u>who(m)</u>) we saw yesterday.

(b) That's the dog (<u>that/which</u>) we saw yesterday.

If we underline the phrase structure of the final example above, we notice a couple of blanks, but the large NP containing the relative clauses is the main point here:

15)

That is the dog which we saw yesterday.
NP   s:D h:N m: ?P
____NP _____CP

Above, 'dog' is called the '**head noun**' (even though it would be more accurate to speak of 'the dog' as the 'head NP') of the relative clause 'which we saw yesterday.' This is not surprising since it is the head of the NP containing the relative clause. We'll identify the phrasal name of a relative clause later when we discuss subordinate clauses and noun clauses. It's a CP, and that will take a little more detail to explain well. So we'll put that off for a while. Notice that 'which' and 'that' would both be acceptable with only a difference in level of formality.

There is another grammatical structure that is similar to a relative clause in some ways, although it is not a clause, but rather an NP. NPs are sometimes followed by another NP which refers to the same thing (the **referent**) and uses different words while adding some new information. It's sort of like a reflection from another angle, giving a new insight. A couple of examples will help us focus better:

16) (a) My dog, the gray one there, usually eats twice a day.

(b) Mr. Jones, our neighbor, often helps watch our house.

(c) Our neighbor Mr. Jones often helps watch our house.

The commas in the first two sentences indicate that the second NP in each example could be deleted as a modifier. In each case, the second NP refers to the same entity (a dog in the first example and a man in the second) as the first. The technical name of such an 'NP-reflection' (not a technical term) is '**appositive.**' My apologies for the obscure opaqueness of the term 'appositive.' If an appositive is a modifier, it is set between commas, as above, and it is called a **non-restrictive appositive**. If it is a complement, however, there should be no commas, and the appositive cannot be removed without losing necessary information.

If we changed the order of the two noun phrases in the second sentence above, 'Our neighbor Mr. Jones often helps watch our house,' we would have an example of an appositive which is a complement. This is called a **restrictive appositive**, at least if the speaker in the sentence has more than one neighbor. Why? Since the speaker has more than one neighbor, the term 'our neighbor' requires the NP 'Mr. Jones' to identify which of the neighbors is being referred to. So 'Mr. Jones' is a complement to 'our neighbor' in the third sentence above. Restrictive appositives are frequently proper nouns definitely identifying a previous, descriptive NP.

Summing up, we can note that any given NP can have a specifier (only one, however), one head, one complement, and any number of modifiers. Some modifiers, such as relative clauses, can be quite long.   Specifiers can also sometimes be pretty long, as in 'The girl next door's aunt moved in yesterday, where the specifier is a possessive NP 'the girl next door's.'

Practice with Noun Phrases

First, a) identify the noun phrases in the following sentences, and then b) identify any relative clauses in the following sentences.

1. George, who had rescued many from a burning inferno, looked out on the clear bay.

2. He was upset about his current state of health that prevented him from moving from his chair on the porch.

3. "Explain to us the methods which enabled you to survive the 1999 earthquake."

4. The man whom George was facing moved in closer to hear more clearly.

5. "Let me ask again whose lives you were hoping to save in your first descent."

6. George's son, the one who came each day to help him, prepared to ask the guest to finish his conversation shortly.

7. He thought back to an earlier time when his father would have enjoyed this conversation.

8. He wondered about the reason why he now let any of these conversations take place at all.

9. The article that ran online praised George for his many accomplishments.

10. That was the day George, now a shell of himself, turned 85.

Determiner Phrases

In more highly theoretical approaches to grammar or syntax than this one, a great deal has been written about determiner phrases. In an effort to main a consistent approach to grammar here, it is useful to mention the unusual status of possessive nouns as determiners. The above section on NP structure provided a glimpse of this phenomenon in its final sentence: "Specifiers can sometimes be pretty long, as in 'The girl next door's aunt moved in yesterday, where the specifier (of the sentence) is a possessive NP 'the girl next door's'. " Such specifiers should be recognized as determiner phrases (DPs).

17) Possessive NPs as determiner phrases

a) The girl next door's aunt moved in yesterday

b) Judy's (just that much is a DP)

It should not be surprising to note that the phrase 'the girl next door' is an NP. What makes it a DP is the possessive " 's" at the end of the phrase. So this possessive marker must be the head of the DP. This same principle holds true for very short possessive nouns, such as "Judy's," where we can see that the proper noun 'Judy' is also an NP by itself. When it becomes possessive, it can be a determiner, as in 'Judy's aunt Helen.' So our first generalization can be that a DP has an NP inside it. And our second is that its head must be the possessive marker because that's what qualifies it to become a DP.

What is the structural role of the NP inside the DP? The only choices are complement, modifier or specifier. If the NP is an obligatory part of the DP, then we're down to a choice between a complement and a specifier. Let's look at other phrases in English and ask what the order of their specifiers and complements is. In English, we have seen that the head can come first, followed by its complement(s) as in PPs, such as 'at home,' where the order is head-complement, and basic (unmodified) VPs, such as 'discussing finances,' where the order is also head-complement.

In other phrases, the specifier comes before the head, leaving the head in the final position, as in basic NPs, such as 'this time'. If an NP has a complement, that is phrase-final, such as 'our hope for the future,' with its specifier-head-complement order. In still others, the specifier is first and the head is in a medial position, as in basic IPs, such as 'we can succeed' and CPs, such as 'since you asked,' with their specifier-head-complement order. This gives us a fairly clear picture that specifier-head-complement is the normal order of syntactic phrases in English. In the examples above, we see two examples showing that the DP has an obligatory NP before the apostrophe-s, that is, before the head D. So our tentative conclusion, based on the specifier-head-complement order in English is that the NP before the apostrophe is the specifier of the DP.

Does the head D have a complement? It certainly should, since every determiner must be followed at some point by a noun or an NP. If the obligatory NP following an apostrophe-s is considered the complement of D, then the subject of the sentence is a big DP in the specifier-head-complement order. It is this logic which would allow us to consider the subject of every sentence a DP rather than an NP.

Instead of following that approach to its logical (and theoretically somewhat satisfying) conclusion, however, we can more easily and intuitively continue to call the subject of a sentence an NP, rather than a DP. The determiner (and DP) is then classified as the specifier of the NP subject, rather than calling the determiner the head of a DP subject. This is more intuitive and consistent with the approach taken so far in this approach to grammar. Bereft of its possible complement (the subject NP), a DP now only has its specifier NP and its head and no other structure. The role of the DP in the sentence is confined to that of the specifier of a larger NP. This is consistent with the term 'determiner' in that determiners are always and only specifiers of NPs.

Just as some determiners (the demonstratives, for example: this, that, these and those) are homophonic with demonstrative pronouns, we can also think of examples where a DP can function pronominally, as in 'That's my Mom's!' In both instances, we can imagine a noun phrase sitting invisibly behind the pronominal NP or DP, 'my mom's (car).'

Quantifier Phrases

By themselves, all quantifiers are also phrases (QPs). This can be seen in example a) below, where each quantifier can stand alone as the short answer to a question.

18) QP structures

a) How much/many would you like? Four/ (very) Many/Several/Half

b) I'll take these five; I'll take this many.

c) I'll take these five apples.

d) I'd like (*these/*the) two/many of the apples

e) I'd like these two on the counter

f) the magnificent seven

g) the magnificent seven heroes.

h) the seven beautiful heroines.

i) *the seven beautiful

j) the seven

In example sentence (a) above, the answers 'four,' 'many,' 'several,' or 'half' would all be grammatically acceptable answers. The use of 'very' before 'many' suggests that 'many' is functioning like an adjective with a qualifier. This can also occur with '(very) few.' However, 'very' cannot be used with the numbers or any of the other indefinite quantifiers in this way, so this seems to be an exception that needs a separate explanation that does not consider it to be an adjective. A short answer may be that 'many' and 'few' may not be full QPs every time they are used. Sometimes they may need a specifier or complement to become a phrase, much like singular count nouns are not full phrases without a determiner. In combination with other lexical categories, quantifiers can follow determiners and still be the head of the phrase, as in b) above: 'I'll take these five.' In this usage, the QP seems very much like an NP. In fact, we can imagine an implicit NP that we've left out, which we could record like this, 'I'll take these five (NP).'

In noting the parallel structure of a QP with an NP, we can ask whether the structure of a QP can have all the roles found in an NP. Does it not only have a possible determiner as its specifier ('these two'), but also possible modifers between the specifier and head ('the seven green dragons'), and possible complements ('the end of two trips') and PP modifiers ('the sixth house on the left') following the head noun, just as an NP can have?

A typical example of the complement of an NP is an of-PP, such as 'the end of the trip.' A QP can have a similar structure, as in 'the five of them.' This works well with numbers, as in this example, but not with indefinite quantifiers or without a demonstrative pronoun in the PP: *''I'd like the two/the many of the apples.' If we remove the first determiner, though, the sentence improves immediately: 'I'd like two/many of the apples.' The selection of possible complements seems somewhat restricted for QPs. If there is no determiner in front of the quantifier, though, complements seem quite acceptable: 'some of this (discomfort),' or '(not) many of these (soccer players)'. So in this way, the structure of QP and NP complements are similar, but not identical. NPs and number-QPs can have both a specifier and a complement, but indefinite QPs can only have a complement if they have no specifier.

Both types of phrases can also have modifiers, but there seem to be some differences. The number-QP with a determiner can also have adjectives modifying the head Q, as in 'the magnificent seven.' This structure also mirrors that of an NP as in 'the magnificent horses.' But again, it seems that there is an implicit NP: 'the magnificent seven (NP).' The determiner+QP sequence can also become a constituent inside an NP, as in 'the magnificent seven heroes.' Here the order is D-A-Q-NP. It's noteworthy here to recognize that the preferred order for the NP with an embedded QP that contains an adjective usually has the adjective following the QP, as in 'the seven beautiful heroines.' This order is D-Q-A-NP.

The two sequences also seem to have different interpretations. In D-A-Q-NP, the Q-NP is a QP ('seven heroes' as a single idea). There the adjective modifies the QP. But the D-Q-A-NP order seems to have A-NP as an NP modified by the Q (where 'seven heroines' are not seen as a single idea). Here the QP contains the A-NP. This is another way in which the NP and the QP are not parallel: the placement of the Q relative to the adjectives changes the apparent structure and meaning of the composite phrase (the larger QP or NP).

It's also notable that a number-QP with a determiner can be a constituent inside an NP, as in 'I'll take these five apples,' which an NP cannot do, *'I'll take (these apples) cores' or *'I'll take (this apple) core.' It's true in both of the NPs just mentioned that the string is grammatical, but the determiner+ N(P) combination is not a constituent inside the larger NP. The combination in each case is a compound noun 'apple core(s)' without the determiner. So a QP with a determiner that is inside an NP is evidence that the QP is not functioning like an NP even though the two structures are sometimes mirror images of each other. The grammaticality of the sentences 'I'll take (these apples') cores' or 'I'll take (this apple's) core' gives us a clue that the QP inside an NP may be functioning similarly to a DP (determiner phrase).

Since the QP is similar to an NP in several ways, it's common in many grammars to call QPs pronouns when they are used without a following noun, such as 'these five' or 'the fifth.' Indeed, these examples are like pronouns in the sense that they refer to another noun (an antecedent) somewhere earlier in the context. Unlike pronouns, however, number-quantifiers can follow determiners, as in the examples just mentioned. Pronouns cannot normally follow a determiner: *A her/ *my it/ *these mine/*her who. Where a determiner-pronoun combination is acceptable, the meaning is changed, as in 'an it.' So both a QP and a pronoun (which is an NP) are similar to NPs, but their structures are not the same.

One final reminder should be repeated from the chapter on lexical categories that, in other usages, numbers should be considered nouns, as in 'I got a ninety on the test.' Here, 'ninety' is clearly a noun, and could even have a plural form if there were three nineties on the test.

Sentence (IP) Structure

Now we are ready to fill in some of the blanks that we noticed earlier in this chapter. Strangely enough, sentences have the same kind of basic structure as noun phrases in the sense that they each can include a specifier, a head, a complement, and many modifiers. Many textbooks compare an NP to a sentence in its structure. So the NP 'Nero's intentional destruction of the city' is structurally parallel to the IP 'Nero intentionally destroyed the city.'

The approach to IP structure taken here does not follow that of some traditional grammar books, so we will end up looking at sentences from both the traditional and a more modern point of view. It's useful to see the reasons for this divergence between the two approaches, so we will look at some of the features in the structure of a sentence which can be analyzed two different ways. The first aspect is the number of basic structural roles in a sentence. To begin, we review the idea that some adverbs can move quite freely within the sentence:

19) Adverb mobility/flexibility within a sentence

a) Slowly, they are sorting through the debris.

b) ? They slowly are sorting through the debris.

c) They are slowly sorting through the debris.

d) They are sorting through the debris slowly.

This movement is characteristic of manner adverbs and other adverbial structures (such as PPs used adverbially), although not all types of adverbs or adverbials will be acceptable in all four positions, as we recall. The usefulness of this observation is that the only slots open to adverbs are at the major divisions within the sentence – its seams as it were; an adverb cannot puncture the structure of another XP and occupy a space within it. What we see, then, as the major breaks inside the above sentence are the slots before and after the word 'are.'

For those whose native-speaker judgment is not convinced that sentences (b) and (c) above really show boundaries within the sentence, here is another pair which demonstrates the same two clause-internal positions for adverbs:

20) Adverb mobility/flexibility within a sentence (2)

(a) We probably should leave early.

(b) We should probably leave early.

Here the two clause-internal positions are 1) before and 2) after the word 'should.' How are 'are' in the first set of sentences and 'should' in the following pair of sentences similar? They are similar in that both are auxiliaries: 'are' is a progressive aspectual auxiliary and 'should' is a modal auxiliary. We already have a pretty clear idea that 'are' and 'should' are not part of the subject. What we need most to see here is that the auxiliary is not part of the main verb phrase, either. So the sentence is now seen as having three main parts: subject, auxiliary, and verb phrase. This differs from the more traditional view that the sentence has two parts: the subject and the predicate.

Having established a reason for looking at the sentence as having three basic parts, we are well on our way to an explanation of the term 'IP' as the phrasal name for a sentence. 'IP' stands for '**inflected phrase**.' We note that the word 'inflection' has to do with verb tense, as is shown in the 'inflectional suffixes' that present-tense he/she/it verbs have ('-s' as in lives, catches, and writes) and that past-tense verbs have ('-ed' as in wedded, missed, and burned). But which of the three parts of the sentence carries the inflection? In the 'slowly' set of sentences, the auxiliary 'are' is clearly present tense. Its past tense forms are 'was' and 'were.' This is in contrast to the main verb 'sorting' which has no tense, only aspect (progressive). It's clear that we could not add '-s' or '-ed' to 'sorting.'

In the 'probably' pair of sentences, 'should' is not so clearly carrying tense, but its main verb 'leave' lacks any tense just as clearly as the main verb 'sorting' does in the previous set. It's even clearer, in fact, since it would be possible, but unacceptable, to add tense to the verb 'leave' and say *'should leaves' or *'should left' because only the auxiliary can carry tense. If the auxiliary carries tense, it is one of the most important parts of the sentence. This idea is captured in calling the sentence an inflected phrase, since that points out that the head of the inflected phrase ('IP') is the auxiliary, which carries the inflection.

Now that we know why a sentence (also called a main clause in other contexts) is called an 'IP,' we can return to the idea why the sentence is often described as having only two parts: the subject and predicate. This is because sometimes the auxiliary combines with the structures that follow it to form larger phrases before all of them combine with the subject to form a complete sentence. The syntactic tool that will show us this combining process is called '**shared string coordination**.' The basic idea is seen in the following sentence, which is adapted from Andrew Radford's *Syntactic theory and the structure of English: a minimalist approach* (106-107), as are the basics of the topic of shared string coordination.

21) Example of shared string coordination

Question: What did your roommate suggest?

> Answer: to try to appeal (but to try not to beg) for extra time to finish my paper.

The sentence is a shortened form for 'to try to appeal for extra time to finish my paper but to try not to beg for extra time to finish my paper.' But the '**shared string**' of words 'for extra time to finish my paper' is not repeated. In order for that string of words to be deleted, it must be a **constituent**, that is, some kind of a phrase. With that information, we can look at a series of shared string structures that tell us quite a bit about the structure of an IP, especially concerning the relation of the auxiliary to the VP.

> 22) a) He might have been (or he might not have been) reviewing the class notes.
>
> b) She might have (or she might not have) been reviewing the class notes.
>
> c) He might (or he might not) have been reviewing the class notes.
>
> d) ? She (but not he) might have been reviewing the class notes.

In the first three 'shared strings,' we see examples of a phrase that is one word longer than the one before it. For some of these phrases we do not even have names yet. The first sentence shows that 'reviewing their notes' is a phrase. This is a VP, which unsurprisingly, consists of a transitive verb and its complement (the direct object). Next comes 'been reviewing their notes,' which we can call a **progressive phrase**, since its head is the verb 'be' (in its perfect participle form 'been') which requires the progressive '-ing' ending on the main verb. The third shared string of words is 'have been reviewing their notes,' which we can call a **perfective phrase**, since its head, the verb 'have,' requires the past participle '-n' on the following verb indicating a perfect aspect. Finally, we have the shared string of words 'might have been reviewing their notes,' which is the main focus for this section of the Guide. In this case 'might' is the auxiliary, and it seems to be just as grammatically acceptable as the three before it.

If we ask what the sentence might be if the 'shared string' were repeated, however, we see that it isn't really a shared string at all: *She might have been reviewing the class notes, but not he might have been reviewing the class notes. Is this just because the word 'not' needs to occupy a different position in the sentence? Is there some confusion because both 'she' and 'he' are both in the sentence and weren't in the first three? The short answer is that we cannot create a shared string structure for the string 'might have been reviewing the class notes.' The clearest, most relevant explanation is that 'might' here is carrying the tense for the sentence (something 'have' and 'been' are not doing, incidentally), which makes it the head of an IP. Every IP in English needs a subject, or specifier, so the string starting with 'might' does not qualify as a constituent (phrase) without its subject NP. So, up to now, it looks like sentences have three basic parts, rather than the traditional subject-predicate split.

Almost immediately we run into a kind of sentence that makes us wonder whether the auxiliary is really the most important part of a sentence. 'What about'

– some alert student asks – 'a sentence like this one, which apparently only has two parts: "Edward grows tomatoes as large as grapefruit"? The subject is 'Edward,' and the predicate is 'grows tomatoes as large as grapefruit,' and we have no sign of an auxiliary anywhere. Now what?

We need to develop a little background about auxiliaries to answer that question. The answer lies in one of the functions of the auxiliary. What happens when we ask 'yes/no' questions about declarative statements such as the 'slowly' and 'probably' sentences above? How are such questions formed?

23) Yes-no question formation with auxiliaries

(a) They are sorting through the debris. ->

Are they sorting through the debris?

(b) We should leave early. -> Should we leave early?

In each case, the yes/no question is formed by the movement of the auxiliary to sentence-initial position (called 'fronting'). Suppose there is no obvious auxiliary, as in the sentence, 'Edward grows tomatoes as large as grapefruit.' How do we produce as yes/no question from this sentence? Every speaker of English can do it, but we need to ask about the way the mind moves the information around. The answer will perhaps surprise some readers: the auxiliary, which we cannot see, but which is carrying the information about the verb tense (take this on faith for a moment), is helped become visual by the insertion of the verb 'do,' which can carry the information on tense, person, and number contained in the auxiliary.

This 'dummy do' (called that since it only carries the information on tense, person, and number and has no meaning of its own) is fronted to create the yes/no question. So, in this approach to grammar, we can decide that the tense information ('inflection') that the auxiliary carries was not quite as invisible as we thought. It is being carried in the 's' on the main verb 'grow.' The information that it's carrying is this - 'present tense, third person singular of the verb.' So how did it get there? The standard answer to that is that it was originally in the auxiliary's standard position between the subject and the main verb, and it had to move to the main verb to become grammatical and visible. This process is just as easy to imagine as the auxiliary fronting in creating the yes/no question.

To help us visualize this, a couple of pictures or diagrams are probably worth a thousand words. The information saying 'present tense, third person, singular' for verbs is carried in the suffix '-s,' which is shown in the auxiliary position in (a) below. The arrow in the sentence below shows the movement of the '-s' suffix to the end of the main verb. This is called 'tense hopping' because the information carried by the auxiliary (in the suffix) is moved down onto the main verb. This movement only happens in the simple present tense – as in our example here – and the simple past tense, with the suffix '-ed.' The verb 'grow' doesn't become *'growed' in the past tense for historical reasons that we don't need to go into here.

24) Tense hopping example

Edward -s grow tomatoes as large as grapefruit.
  |___↑

Tense hopping is a common kind of auxiliary movement in the formation of declarative statements.

The other kind of auxiliary movement that we just discussed is **auxiliary fronting** in the formation of yes/no questions. Auxiliary fronting occurs for both visible (and audible, of course) and barely visible (suffix '-s' or '-ed') auxiliaries. When the auxiliary is not a full word (as in '–s' or '–ed'), English supplies the **dummy auxiliary** 'do' in an insertion process called '**do support**.' Then there is no tense hopping necessary. An example of do support is shown in sentence (a) below. In a declarative sentence, the insertion of 'do' would be most appropriate for an emphatic statement, such as a retort to someone's doubtful opinion that Edward couldn't possibly grow such big tomatoes. Below that, in (b) is a diagram of the fronting movement of the dummy auxiliary 'do' when the statement is transformed into a yes-no question, as indicated by the question mark at the end of the sentence.

25) 'Do-support' and auxiliary fronting

a) **Edward -s grow tomatoes as large as grapefruit.**
      ↑
      do

b)   **Edward does grow tomatoes as large as grapefruit?**
  ↑_____|

c) Does Edward grow tomatoes as large as grapefruit?

This answers the earlier puzzle about sentences where there is no visible auxiliary, such as the sentence 'Edward grows tomatoes as large as grapefruit.' What we have just done is show that all declarative sentences, whether they have a visible auxiliary or no visible auxiliary, have three essential parts – a subject, an auxiliary, and a verb phrase.

The two processes that show how an auxiliary is a separate part of the sentence, **auxiliary fronting** and **do support**, are both rather recent developments in terms of the 1500-year-long history of the English language. Only four hundred years ago, Shakespeare was perfectly comfortable with the more standard (Germanic) fronting of the main verb, as in the following examples.

26) Shakespearean fronting of main verbs

a) "Belong you to the Lady Olivia, friends?" (Duke Orsino in Twelfth Night, V, i, 9)

b) "Signior Hortensio, come you to part the fray?" (Petruchio in Taming of the Shrew, I, ii, 22)

c) "But died thy sister of her love, my boy?" (Duke Orsino in Twelfth Night, II, iv, 105)

Modern Germanic languages, such as German and Dutch, still front main verbs in yes/no questions. Translating Shakespeare's question "Died your sister from her love?" into modern German or Dutch produces exactly the same word order, word for word, as Shakespeare's, but it's perfectly standard German and Dutch: 'Starb deine Schwester wegen ihrer Liebe?' (German), and 'Stierf je zus vanwege haar liefde?' (Dutch). This is a historical change that has happened in English grammar during the past four centuries or less.

Going back to the sentence like the one that we worked on at the beginning of the chapter, let's try to label all of the structural roles within each of the phrases. The same kind of underlined array we used earlier will work for this, too. It's convenient to use 'h:' to represent the head of a phrase, 'm:' to represent a modifier, 'c:' to represent a complement, and 's' to represent the specifier. We can approach this in stages, like this:

27) A process for labeling structural roles in XPs

a) identify all the lexical categories – abbreviations are placed above each word (soon to include empty categories – wait)

b) identify words which are themselves phrases

c) identify compound lexical items

d) first-level phrases – the simplest ones – starting from the right edge

e) first-level combinations of phrases

f) second-level combinations of phrases

g) further combination of phrases

h) second-level VP

i) complete VP

j) complete IP

28) One rich businessman is eating lunch unhappily at the restaurant near the beach

Q	A	N	N	aux	V	N	Adv	P	D	N	P	D	N
One	rich	business	man	is	eating	lunch	unhappily	at	the	restaurant	near	the	beach.

b)   AP   NP   N   NP   AdvP

c)   N

d)   h:V   c: NP   s:D h:N   s:D h:N

e) h:Q m:AP c:N   h:P c:NP

f)   h:NP   m:PP

g)   h:P   c:NP

h)   h:VP   m: AdvP

i)   h: VP   m: PP

j) s: QP   h: Aux c: VP

The subject QP is the specifier of the sentence (IP), the auxiliary is its head, the VP is the complement of the auxiliary, and the AP, AdvP, and PPs are modifiers inside the NP and VP.

Practice with Phrasal Structure in Simple Sentences

a) Identify and name the phrases and their heads, complements, modifi ers, and specifiers in the following sentences.

> 1) The two boys, and their mom, were fed up with ropey play dough between their toes.

> 2) Then they found out about a new kind of modeling clay without fiber.

> 3) Their mom was grateful for this new idea for their afternoon playtime.

> 4) She had really disliked the mess on the floor every afternoon of the week.

> 5) She sometimes took out some of her pent-up frustration on her long-suffering husband.

> 6) After the first day with no afternoon mess, they all went out to dinner as a celebration.

b) Identify and name the phrases and their heads, complements, modifiers, and specifiers in the following sentence (adapted from Butcher and Lang) (note, just leave out the word 'however' in the phrasal structure):

Odysseus' personal narrative to the Phaeacians of his adventures in the previous ten years, however, takes up two nights of the six weeks in the narrative of the Odessey.

Traces of Movement and Empty Categories

Tense hopping may seem somewhat subtle the first time we encounter it, but the example of the simple present and simple past tense suffixes '-s' and '-ed' give us perhaps the clearest idea of tense, number, and person information moving from the auxiliary position onto the main verb. This movement of the suffix onto the main verb is completely automatic in English. Additionally, every native speaker of English who wants to ask a yes/no question automatically fronts the auxiliary, as well, even to the extent of adding a dummy auxiliary 'do' so that it can be fronted. At this point, we only need to add one important concept to our analytical toolbox. In each instance of movement, we need to trace the original position of the moved word or constituent and connect it to the final position. In analyzing the structure of sentences where movement has occurred, we use the convention of an empty category (marked 'e') to represent the place where the movement started.

What Difference Does It Make?

We then immediately face the question of whether the mind keeps track of these empty categories, which are sometimes created by created by movement, as we know, and other times simply by deletion. The short answer is 'Yes, the mind does keep track of these empty spaces (technically also called '**traces**') in the structure of the sentence.' Is there any evidence for that? And what can we tell others when they look at us as if we were crazy to believe in something that we can't see or hear? If we look at contractions that fuse with (technically '**cliticize to**') the previous word, we can see that our minds do keep a record of the original position of the moved word or phrase. In the following example, we see in 'a' that the auxiliary 'have' can cliticize to the modal auxiliary 'should.' But in 'b' we see that when 'should' is fronted, 'have' cannot cliticize to the word 'they' directly in front of it. Why should that be? It's because 'they' is not really directly in front of '-ve.' This solution is shown in 'b' below, where the empty category from the fronting of 'should' is occupying the slot between 'they' and '-ve.' Since the contraction '-ve' is not directly adjacent to 'they,' it cannot cliticize to it.

29) a) We should have left earlier -> We should've left earlier

b) What should we have done? -> * What should we've done?

Please note that some shortened form of 'have' may sound comfortable for sentence 'b,' but it is not the cliticized form that rhymes with 'rave,' such as in the sentence 'They've gone home.' If we listen to ourselves carefully we will hear the difference. This gives us some evidence (to share with family and friends, perhaps) that these traces of movement are very real parts of the structure of sentences and real parts of our mental grammar. That's why we make note of them.

Ambiguity and Phrasal Structure

Ambiguity is part of English grammar from the smallest units of language to the largest. Let's take a short tour and then move on to phrasal structures again and look at their sources of ambiguity. At the smallest level, American English has some sound patterns that irritate British English speakers for many reasons, one of which is the resulting ambiguity. Compare the SAE (standard American English) pronunciation of 'metal' and 'medal.' What's the difference? None. Is the central consonant pronounced with a [d] sound or a [t] sound? Neither, in fact, but with a so-called 'flap' (represented by the symbol [ɾ] in the International Phonetic Alphabet). In SAE, we don't hear any difference between 'metal' and 'medal' until the stress moves away from the first syllable in such words as 'medallion' and 'metallic.' The flap creates ambiguity at a phonological level.

At the level of word structure, another form of ambiguity appears. If someone asked for a definition of the word 'unbindable,' there are two possible answers: a) possible to unbind or b) impossible to bind. This is ambiguity in whether the word's structure is 'unbind+able,' which is the first meaning, or 'un+bindable,' which is the second meaning. This is amibiguity at a morphological level. It is called **structural ambiguity**, since it is a reflection of the word's two possible structures.

At the level of phrase structure, we can look at a compound noun such as 'copper pipe racks.' This is ambiguous between 1) pipe racks that are made of copper (copper + pipe racks) and 2) racks for storing copper pipe (copper pipe + rack). Using the underlining notation introduced earlier, we can see the difference in the phrase structure.

30) Structural ambiguity

```
        N     N     N          N     N     N
a) copper  pipe  racks  b) copper  pipe  racks
     NP     NP    NP         NP     NP    NP
   m:NP   m:NP  h:NP        m:NP  h:NP  h:NP
   m:NP          h:NP              m:NP  h:NP
```

In the above example, the top lines are the same But the lower lines, which show the formation of the first and second levels of phrases, are different in two important ways: which two words combine to form an intermediate NP and what the role of that NP in the three-word compound noun is. This is also called **structural ambiguity**, since it's a reflection of the word's two possible structures.

At the level of clausal structure, ambiguity looks very similar to the ambiguity of phrasal structure because clauses are simply larger phrases, as we can see by the convention of calling a sentence an inflected phrase (IP). Structural ambiguity at a clausal level often involves several clauses, an additional complexity that we will discuss somewhat later mostly under the rubric 'dangling participles.' Just to give us something to look forward to, however, here is an example of ambiguity at a clausal level:

31) a) Question: When did she say that she would be leaving?

Answer a: yesterday (meaning: she said that yesterday)

Answer b: tomorrow (meaning: she'll be leaving tomorrow).

b) On the right side of the road, we saw that a number of cars had stopped to look at the marvelous scenery.

Looking at the first sentence, we recall having already discussed **auxiliary fronting** in connection with the formation of yes/no questions. An explanation of the above ambiguity will fit into the discussion below about forming questions with wh-words (who, what, when, where, why, and how, and also which and whose), which are also fronted. The second sentence could mean that we saw something from the side of the road, or that cars had stopped at the side of the road, or that the marvelous scenery was on the right side of the road. In this instance, we attribute this to **PP-fronting**. This short tour of ambiguity can be great fun in English classes, since the students usually have had some experiences with it, but lack a more comprehensive overview.

Practice with Structural Ambiguity

Identify structural ambiguity in the following sentences and tell what the two possible meanings are (Anonymous. "Funniest…").

1.   Police Alert on Stolen Drugs, Newcastle Chronicle 22 September 2006

2.   Lord to Decide Future Next Month, Calgary Sun 19 November 2006

3.   Rare Flower Found On Site A Plant, Says Developer, Guardian 10 July 2006

4.   Lloyds Sell Goldfish to Morgan Stanley For £1bn, Independent 21 December 2005

5.   Report Shows Need For Paper Cuts, North Wales Weekly News 30 December 05

Coordinate Structures

Phrasal structures that have coordinating conjunctions have the same identity as the lexical items or phrasal structures which they are made up of. Two nouns can combine to form a (coordinate structure) noun, and two noun phrases produce a bigger NP. This is also true for verbs and prepositions. Here again, we notice that we need to distinguish between lexical items that are phrases by themselves and those that are not. There are different ways to make this distinction, but the context of an entire clause is generally the most convenient way to test these coordinate structures. Several examples should make this a little clearer:

32) Types of Coordinate Structures

      N   N

a) The <u>wheel and axle</u> was invented about ten thousand years ago.

b) The guests were glad to help <u>wash and dry</u> the dishes.

c) It was great fun to run <u>up and down</u> the sand dunes.

d) <u>Cars and trucks</u> have been around for more than a century.

e) My friends <u>washed the dishes but didn't dry them.</u>

               PP   PP

f) The children ran <u>up the ladder and down the slide.</u>

The first three sentences above contain examples of individual nouns, verbs and prepositions which are not themselves phrases. We should notice also that their coordinate structures with 'and' are also not phrases. We can test this (and prove it) by asking "What was invented about ten thousand years ago?" and confirming that *"wheel and axel" is an unacceptable answer; only "the wheel and axle" will stand alone as a phrase. Noticing that the verb in the first sentence is singular is consistent with this conclusion, since the string 'wheel and axel' is considered a singular (count) noun. As we saw in the section on phrase structure, singular count nouns are not themselves phrases.

In the second and third example sentences, we can see that the verbs 'wash and dry' have a single object and that they are both transitive verbs. If we ask "What did the guests do?" the answer *"Wash and dry" is unacceptable. This is also logical semantically as well, since we do not know what they were washing and drying – clothing comes to mind as a possibility. In contrast, "wash and dry the dishes" will stand alone, and is a complete phrase. The third example sentence contains two prepositions with a single object, and they function much like the two verbs with a single object functioned in the second sentence. An acceptable answer to "Where did they run?" can be "up and down the dunes" But *"up and down" by itself has a different meaning. A different meaning tells us that we're missing a complement. 'Up and down' begs the question of 'up and down what?' if we want to maintain the original meaning.

In the final three examples, we see plural nouns which each function as a complete phrases. They combine to become coordinate NPs, coordinate VPs, and coordinate PPs where each of the components is itself an NP, a VP or a PP. It is worth noting here that the two elements that are combined are not only the same in being a phrase or not (let's call this '**constituency**,' that's the technical term), but also in belonging to the same lexical or phrasal category : both nouns, or both NPs, or both verbs, and so on. For larger (IP, CP) phrases, we can see that two sentences can combine to form a bigger (compound) sentence if they are connected by a comma. But if they are broken into two sentences separated by a period, we have a different question. The coordinating conjunction in this case points to a context outside the sentence.

Correlative Coordination

The correlative conjunctions either-or, neither-nor, both-and, whether-or, not only-but also, and the-the follow the same rule as discussed for coordinating conjunctions: the elements that they combine need to be the same in both category and constituency. A small number of examples helps us see this consistency.

33) Examples of correlative structures

a) They were neither rich nor poor. (two APs)

b) They are the same in both type and constituency. (two NPs)

c) They needed to either go home right away or find shelter quickly. (two VPs)

Correlative constructions have one very attractive use for teaching situations, whether in a classroom, in a tutoring session, or in making a point about using conjunctions to connect parallel grammatical structures (phrases): they define the boundaries of the two structures/phrases very neatly. This is shown by the contrast in the following two sentences between using the coordinating conjunction 'or' or the correlative conjunction 'either...or' in the same context:

34) Clear phrasal boundaries with Correlatives

a) Many smokers try to stop by switching to a brand they dislike or a low tar cigarette.

b) * Many smokers try to stop by switching either to a brand they dislike or a low tar cigarette.

c) Many smokers try to stop by switching to either a brand they dislike or a low tar cigarette.

d) Many smokers try to stop by switching either to a brand they dislike or to a low tar cigarette.

In example sentence (a) above, it is implicit that the writer means 'switch to NP1 or NP2,' which is correct. But readers may read the sentence by processing it with the expectation that the flow will be 'switch to X or to Y,' and feel odd when they do not see a second 'to.' They are essentially reading as in sentence (b), which is incorrect. Sentence (b) makes the point clearly that the two phrases are not parallel by defining the beginning boundary of each of the two phrases: the first phrase begins with 'either' (+PP) and the second with 'or' (+NP). Readers might decide to go back and re-read the sentence to process the alternative choices again. We should notice how much clearer the alternatives are stated in sentences (c) – (d). The reading with two NPs is given in (c). The reading with two prepositions (and two PPs) is given in (d). Thus, it is possible to show that two coordinate phrases are either parallel or not parallel with correlative conjunctions more clearly than with coordinating conjunctions.

Mixed-category Coordinate Structures

One of the characteristics of coordinating conjunctions is that they combine two words or phrases that belong to the same category: two nouns, or two verbs, but not a noun and a verb, for instance. Generally, it sounds awful when we mix categories in coordinate structures, as seen in these examples:

35) Unacceptable mixed coordinate structures

a) *They like to go for walks or biking. (PP-or-VP)

b) *They wanted a dog and to go home. (NP-and-IP)

Such mixing is unacceptable in both spoken and written English. In other instances, especially with correlative conjunctions, we can fool ourselves into believing that some inequality inside the coordinate structure is allowable, when it isn't really. Here are a couple of examples:

36) Unacceptable mixed correlative structures

a) *We should either go to the shore or to the mountains.

b) *They wanted neither to become too rich nor too poor.

One handy characteristic of correlative conjunctions makes our analysis pretty straight-forward: each or the two words in this type of conjunction marks the beginning of one phrase, so we can easily compare the two phrases (or several phrases, if there is a list of items) to see if they are of the same type. In the first example above, 'either' precedes the word 'go,' which identifies its phrase as a VP. Following the correlative 'or,' in contrast, we see the word 'to,' which in this case is a preposition heading up a PP. So, for purposes of prescriptive grammar, this combination is totally unacceptable. The second is like the first; after 'neither,' we see that the phrase begins with 'to+verb,' which in this case is an auxiliary+verb (take that on faith if necessary), which heads up a reduced clause (an IP), yet the phrase following 'nor' is the AP 'too poor.' This is also unacceptable in a prescriptive sense, although we can accept such mixing in spoken English.

Finally, we need to recognize that some mixed categories are acceptable for both spoken and written English because of **lexical gaps**. In other words, when there is no word of a given category in English, we may discover mixed pairs that have – by consistent use – become acceptable. One of the most frequent examples that we use without thinking is this one:

37) Is it more useful to work through these issues orally or in writing?

Here we notice that we are dealing with two lexical gaps: there is no verb form to produce a phrase like *'in oralling' which would match 'in writing', and there is no adverb like *'writtenly' to match 'orally.' In instances of this kind, popular use defeats the ingrained preference for grammatical parallelism.

One way to explain the structure of such a phrase is to notice that we can use a coordinating conjunction as the head of a phrase that passed the short-answer test for **constituency**, as shown in this set of example sentences:

38) Q: What's Johnnie want for Christmas – a bike?

A: and a train set.

A: *and to visit Disneyland

Q: What was an early mechanical invention – the wheel?

A: and axle

As we might expect, the coordinating conjunction still requires a complement phrase that is the same lexical or phrasal category as the phrase or word that it is connecting, as is seen by the unacceptability of the 'and to Disneyland' response. What kind of phrase do we have with "and a train set"? It passes the 'stand-alone' test for constituency, but is it a 'conjunction phrase' (ConjP) or perhaps a 'coordinating conjunction phrase' (CCP)? The approach we are taking suggests that it should be called one of the two terms rather than not have any name at all. The conjunction is seen as the head of the phrase.

This does not conflict with the general principle that coordinate structures have the same name as the individual categories from which they are formed. Two NPs in a coordinated structure still form an NP. Now we are adding the idea that there is an intermediate phrase between the two NPs. Since subordinate conjunctions always form dependent clauses, it may be more convenient to call this sort of phrase a CCP to distinguish it from conjunction phrases (dependent clauses) headed by subordinating conjunctions. Grammatically, the CCP can function as an independent clause in the case of sentence-level coordination, although not for smaller coordinated phrases. This point about sentence-level coordination was discussed in the previous chapter with an example from the New International Version of the book of Acts. The intermediate CCP between two parallel phrases tells us which of the two NPs (for example) in a coordinate structure is the head of the larger one – it is the first of the two, because the second NP is inside a larger CCP.

This standpoint leads us into a discussion of two other questions: what should we think about sentences which begin with a coordinating conjunction? And what can we say about mixed-category coordinate structures? Compound sentences, like this one, raise no questions at all: "Sam likes cherry pie, and his brother likes apple pie." But such a sentence can also be punctuated as two sentences: "Sam likes cherry pie. But his brother likes apple pie." Notice that the second sentence would also be a sentence without the word 'but:' "his brother likes apple pie." When the coordinating conjunction is included, however, the sentence refers to a context outside itself. Therefore, we can use the idea of a CCP in this instance to show that English does sometimes embed information in one sentence that refers to information is another sentence. We know that this is true of pronouns, in the sense that they sometimes refer to another NP outside of the sentence for their meaning. So a sentence which is a CCP also refers to a context before it that adds meaning to the sentence. Does that also hold for the exception that we just mentioned? Let's try it and see.

39) Q: Will we be doing the final exam in writing?

A: and orally.

Here we can talk about the 'and orally' response as a conjunction phrase. Normally, the conjunction would only accept an identical PP category like 'in writing' to connect with, but because of the lexical gap, it will accept an AdvP 'orally.' Given the discussion above 'orally' is an AdvP, and 'and orally' is a CCP. The CCP keeps the AdvP from being a candidate for the head of the coordinate structure because only the first element can become the head. The whole phrase is then named after the first element, which would make 'orally and in writing' an AdvP, and 'in writing and orally' a PP. There are undoubtedly more sophisticated solutions to this problem, but this will do for our purposes now.

Practice with Correlative CCP

Evaluate the following sentences and correct them if necessary.

1. Neither eggs or broccoli has touched Nick's lips in the last few weeks.

2. He thinks he is slowly wasting away either from mental exertion with grammar or all the repetitive music he's been listening to.

3. Really, it's not that big of a deal since he ate both his own lunch and somebody else's several hours ago.

4. He thinks his roommates might be pretty hungry after losing either most of their fruit supply or perhaps several of their lunches during the past several days.

5. Either he should manage his finances better or learn to look more carefully at the names written on the sacks of food in the refrigerator.

6. Well, it doesn't really matter now; he thinks they're well fed enough and quite satisfied either eating a sandwich or possibly some toast with jam.

7. Kyle not only eats non-dairy foods but also starts away from meat products.

8. I think they talked about either their plans for the weekend or exercising.

9 Not only is the family rich, but they love to spend time together.

Summary

We now have enough information (but probably not yet enough practice) to break any sentence in the English language into phrases of various sizes, label each phrase, and determine its structure in terms of a head (single or compound) with its complement(s), modifier(s), and perhaps a specifier (for NPs or IPs). In order to do that, we call first on our earlier skill in identifying the lexical category of each word in the sentence. In order to label a phrase, we use the category of the most important word in that phrase (its head), which is the one that the other words are modifying or complementing. For the grammatical role, we will look at the function of the word in the phrase or the role of the phrase in the sentence. We will talk about grammatical roles more when we discuss Reed-Kellogg diagramming. We notice now already that there are instances when the grammatical role and lexical or phrasal category are not the same. In fact, a PP is always either adjectival or adverbial. There is no such thing as 'prepositional' grammatical role in English.

Practice with Phrase Structure in Complex Sentences

For each of the following sentences identify all of the phrases contained in the sentence and label each phrase's head, and if there are such elements, the phrase's complement(s), modifier(s), and its specifier.

1. Although a bit rough on shoes, couches, and cats, she is the best dog in my family.

2. Every time I leave her in my friends' back yard while we talk, she will sit by the door and wait for me.

3. Once, when she found a squeaky toy, she didn't let go of the thing for weeks.

4. She will chase after any kind of ball; without any hesitation, she will tear after it until she brings it back to me so I can throw it again.

5. My favorite memory of her is when I was reading on the floor and she came up to me and laid her head on my shoulder.

6. If she ever dies, I promise myself that I'll throw a funeral for her with a wake and everything.

7. After my friend talked with that athlete, she reminded him that his great running and jumping did not mean that he could fly.

8. A dance team that moves together wins together.

9. The restaurant owners who treated their customers and employees poorly ran themselves right out of business.

10. A few people were confused when they read the headline "Miners Refuse to Work After Death".

Clausal Structure

Earlier, we discussed the structure of a main clause and identified the subject NP as the specifier, the auxiliary as the head of the clause, the VP as the complement of the auxiliary, and we noted the possibility of a number of modifiers inside the NP and VP. In cases of multiple auxiliaries, such as 'may have been playing,' we noted that only the first auxiliary is the head of the IP, and each following auxiliary is the head of a smaller phrase inside the IP. These phrases need to be named, so this Guide uses the most predictable names, which are based on the functions of the auxiliaries serving as their heads. In their left-to-right order, they include the modal auxiliary as the head of the Inflected Phrase (IP), the perfect aspectual auxiliary 'have' as the head of the Perfect Phrase (PerfP), the progressive aspectual auxiliary 'be' as the head of the Progressive Phrase (ProgP), and the main verb, as usual, as the head of the Verb Phrase (VP). In dialects that allow multiple modals, such as in the sentence 'We might should be leaving soon,' the second modal would be the head of a Modal Phrase (ModP). Using the underlining convention of chapter 4, the standard progression looks like this:

40) When the phone rang, they might have been watching TV.

> When the phone rang, they might have been watching TV.
> _____VP
> _____ProgP
> _____PerfP
> _____IP

Dependent clauses, as exemplified in the above example by the clause 'When the phone rang,' expand the IP into a **complementizer phrase** (CP), which is the main topic of the next section.

The Structure of IP, CP, and Multi-clausal Sentences

Compound sentences are the least complicated kind of multi-clausal sentence. They consist of two or more simple sentences (= 'independent clauses' = "IPs") bound together by a coordinating conjunction (one of the 'fanboys') or by semicolons or colons. The number of IPs that can be so connected is theoretically unlimited, so style and mental processing limits are the main restrictions on how long such sentences become.

Besides compounding, multi-clausal sentences are generated by combining one of more dependent clauses with an appropriate number of independent clauses. Such a sentence is called complex if it contains a dependent clause. Here again, there are no theoretical limitations to the length of such sentences, only practical ones.

This next point may be too abstract to discuss until we get to phrase structure diagramming. But let's go through the analysis once here and return to it again later for a second look. Dependent clauses can be adjectival, adverbial or nominal. The dependent clauses are themselves called CPs (**complementizer phrases**), but the entire sentence containing the dependent clause is itself an IP. The entire sentence only becomes a CP if an auxiliary or a wh-word is fronted, as happens in direct questions, indirect questions, or exclamations.

What should we say about the sentence, "In April, many students look forward to their summer vacations" where 'in April' has been fronted to the left of the main clause IP? Is it located outside of the IP, in either the head of CP, like a complementizer or fronted auxiliary, or is it in the specifier position in the CP, like a fronted Wh-word? If a fronted PP like 'in April' is part of a larger CP, our question can then be rephrased like this, "Can a fronted PP become either the head or the specifier of a CP?" It probably couldn't be a head, since it's not carrying any inflectional information or acting as a complementizer. In order to ask whether it can be the specifier of CP, we can check to see if it is competition with fronted Wh-words for the position. A sentence such as the following will help us:

41) Noticing empty categories

Q: In April, what do many students look forward to?

with 'e's: 'In April, what do many students e look forward to e ?'

Here we see that there is a position to the left of the specifier of CP ('what,' in the above sentence) where the fronted PP can move to. If we say that the IP and the CP should have similar structures, it would be logical to say that the IP should also have a position for PPs and (probably) other **adjuncts** (modifiers) to move to. This gives both the IP and the CP a fourth possible grammatical role or slot that it can accommodate: a modifier to the left of the specifier position. This is intuitively attractive, since it would be odd for a modifer (such as the PP 'in April') to occupy either a head position that normally only accomodates a complementizer (or an auxiliary) or a specifier position, when the fronted PP is clearly a modifier, rather than specifier.

Now we have a straight-forward way of talking about the structure of a sentence such as "Slowly$_1$, John e opened the door e$_1$." The manner adverb was originally in sentence-final position, which we mark with an 'e.' In this position, it modified the verb 'opened.' By marking the original position with an 'e,' we preserve that piece of information. From this position, it was fronted to the (just-discussed) modifier position to the left of the specifier-of-IP position. By co-indexing the adverb with the empty category, we state that it's still modifying the main verb. If this discussion seems a little abstract at this point, we'll bring it back to earth in a more concrete way in the discussion about phrase structure diagramming where the movement of adverbs will be diagrammed and the landing space defined clearly.

Adjectival CPs always modify an NP, and usually follow that NP directly if they have not been moved; adverbial CPs modify a verb and are characterized by their ability to move similar to the way that adverbs can; nominal clauses can occupy any of the eight positions occupied by an NP (subject, direct object, indirect object, subject complement of a linking verb, object complement of a complex transitive verb, object of a preposition, complement of an adjective, and appositive). Up until now, no example of a nominal clause functioning as the object complement of a complex transitive verb has been identified, so perhaps only seven of the eight possible NP slots is available to nominal CPs.

We will see these relationships graphically when we diagram such sentences in phrase structure trees, which is in chapter eight.

Practice Recognizing CP Modifiers

Some dependent clauses (including reduced ones) in the following sentences have moved, others have not. For CPs that have not moved, there is only one question: what are they modifying (an AP, NP, VP, IP, or CP)? For CPs that have moved, please answer the following questions 1) where did they move from, 2) what are they modifying (if anything), and 3) are they part of the IP structure or part of the CP structure in the sentence after they move?

> 1. When the children first awoke in their vacation lodge, the flowers were slowly opening in the summer sun.
>
> 2. The sunlight was streaming through their window as well, which woke them from their slumber.
>
> 3. What had been two lumps under the bedcovers was transformed into two people who were ready to meet the day.
>
> 4. It was to be a glorious day, so the pair was quick to throw back the covers and head for the kitchen, where Mom was already busy.
>
> 5. Mother's eggs and toast and sausage were almost ready, so, while they waited, they watched the illuminated dust float throughout the room.
>
> 6. Until you have seen illuminated dust in the morning sunlight, you can hardly say you have lived.

Chapter Overview Practice

For any given sentence, mark all of the phrases, their heads, and any complements, modifiers, or specifiers.

1. Jamie and all her best friends took a fantastic road trip during their last spring break.

2. They traveled across the country in an old, beat-up car.

3. Their rugged journey took a heavy toll on that 14-year-old vehicle.

4. It broke down countless times along the way back home.

5. Emily's best friend reads fiction novels about vampires, werewolves and all sorts of fantastic creatures.

6. She, however, only reads dystopian stories.

7. This type of story is a relatively new genre of literature

8. It features characters who are fighting against an oppressive government system.

9. Paul would rather spend his free time watching T.V. series online.

10. Under the right circumstances, he might watch an entire series in a matter of a few days.

Chapter 5: Types of Clauses: Main and Dependent (Adjectival, Adverbial, and Nominal)

Main and Dependent Clauses

Clauses come in two basic types: **main (or 'independent') clauses** and **dependent (or 'subordinate') clauses**. The main difference is that only main clauses can stand by themselves as a sentence, while dependent clauses are not complete sentences by themselves. In this approach to grammar, we'll assume that all clauses have an auxiliary (whether we see it or not) and a verb. Stated in another way, when we're looking for the clauses in a sentence, we'll identify them by their verbs. Phrases without verbs, such as NPs, APs, AdvPs, and PPs do not, therefore qualify as clauses.

VPs do not qualify as clauses when they do not have auxiliaries, but since the auxiliary is sometimes barely visible or not visible, we will look for and test for a clause wherever we see a verb. Dependent clauses may not be complete sentences in themselves, but they generally have a complete sentence inside them. Often, but not always, the dependent clause is a main clause preceded by another word which has been added to the front of the sentence, usually a subordinate conjunction or a complementizer. This means that dependent clauses usually have more structure than independent clauses. Here is a contrasting pair of clauses.

1) (a) We went home,

    (b) before it got too late.

The first clause is an independent clause, and the second is a dependent clause because of the subordinate conjunction 'before.' Without the conjunction 'before,' it would be an independent clause, namely 'It got too late.' Subordinate conjunctions and complementizers often serve as markers signaling the beginning of a dependent clause. There are three kinds of dependent clauses, and their names simply describe their grammatical roles in the sentence: **adverbial or adverb clauses** (which modify a verb), **adjectival or adjective clauses** (which modify an NP), and **nominal or noun clauses** (which have the same grammatical roles as NPs do). Since dependent clauses are larger than independent ones, it is not surprising that they have somewhat more structure than independent ones. After all, an IP structure has no room for the markers that signal the beginning of a dependent clause. And a dependent clause always has an IP inside it. Because one of the markers that is easiest to recognize is the complementizer 'that,' dependent clauses beginning with 'that' (and by extension, all dependent clauses) are called 'complementizer clauses,' which is abbreviated 'CP.' The head of a complementizer clause is the complementizer, if there is one.

Adjectival Clauses

We can think back a notice that our discussion about adjectival clauses has already begun. In chapter 2, we discussed relative adverbs, relative determiners, and relative pronouns as lexical sub-categories. In chapter 3, we discussed relative clauses under 'NP Structure' because a relative clause is always embedded in a larger NP headed by its head noun. There we covered some of the most important concepts about adjective clauses, since most adjective clauses are relative clauses. **Relative clauses** always modify a head noun or head NP. Since they modify a noun or NP, they are called adjectival. They often, but not always, are signaled by a relative pronoun, determiner or adverb (collectively called **relative markers**).

It is opportune at this point to mention that there is a difference between a relative clause which is the complement of the noun it is modifying and a relative clause which is a modifier to the noun it is modifying. An example will help us focus on the difference:

2)   (a) Members of the hiking team, who compete nationally, often carry packs weighing sixty pounds.

(b) Members of the hiking team who compete nationally often carry packs weighing sixty pounds

Asking the question, 'Who carries sixty-pound packs?' shows us the difference between the two sentences. If we look at the first sentence, the answer is 'members of the hiking team,' meaning all of them. If we look at the second sentence, the answer is, 'not all of the members of the hiking team, but only those who compete nationally.' The difference is that the first relative clause is a modifier and only adds extra information. The commas tell us that the relative clause can be lifted out of the sentence and still leave its main message intact: members of the hiking team often carry packs weighing sixty pounds.

The second sentence, however, has no commas marking the relative clause (if it's punctuated correctly, as it is in this case). The relative clause is a complement to the head noun. It is necessary to determine the meaning of the head noun: which members of the hiking team do we mean? So the first relative clause modifying the hiking team would be marked 'm,' just like the relative clause 'which we saw yesterday' is in the previous example sentence. The second relative clause modifying the hiking team would be marked 'c.' The difference is important to the meaning of the sentence and the presence or absence of commas should signal that difference. Traditional grammar presentations call relative clauses which are complements '**restrictive relative clauses**.' The relative clauses which are modifiers are called '**non-restrictive relative clauses**.'

For students who are not charmed by these names, please take heart; many others do not find the names very descriptive or helpful either. It may help to remember that restrictive = complement, and non-restrictive = non-complement (or modifier). If the relative pronoun is 'who,' it can be used for both restrictive and non-restrictive relative clauses. But this is not true for the pair 'that' and 'which,' which are often considered interchangeable. Suppose we try to insert 'that' into the previous sentence: *'But this is not true for the pair 'that' and 'which,' that are often considered interchangeable.' Of the two only 'which' can signal a non-restrictive relative clause. The practice sentences should help us understand this difference in a practical way.

As we discussed, relative clauses can be either complements of the head NP or modifiers of the head NP. If they're complements, they're called **restrictive relative clauses**. If they're modifiers, they're **non-restrictive relative clauses**. One of the trickiest aspects to analyzing sentences with relative clauses is that the relative marker (either a **relative pronoun** or **relative adverb** in this case) may have been deleted. Relative determiners are never deleted. Such deletions belong to a discussion on '**reduced adjectival clauses**,' which we'll get back to later.

To continue our discussion, we need to notice that sometimes a clause that is not a relative clause can also function adjectivally. Here is one example:

3) The day after they finished their final exams was devoted to moving everything out of the dorms.

The clause 'after they finished their final exams' is introduced by a **subordinating conjunction** and not by a relative marker. So it is not a relative clause. But it is modifying the head NP 'the day,' so it is adjectival. Any word for a period of time, from 'nanosecond' to 'day,' 'week,' 'year,' 'period,' 'time,' 'century,' 'millennium,' or 'age' can be the head noun for this sort of adjectival clause where 'after,' 'before,' 'until' or 'since,' marks the beginning of an adjectival clause which is not a relative clause. So non-relative adjectival clauses are about time.

Adverbial Clauses

Adverbial clauses almost always start with a subordinating conjunction, and these conjunctions get deleted under very different circumstances from relative clause markers. In fact, subordinating conjunctions are usually not deleted, which makes most adverbial clauses easy to spot. When we see a subordinating conjunction, we should assume we're looking at an adverbial clause (except for the adjectival clauses about time that we just discussed). Where there is a deletion, we end up with a reduced adverbial clause, which is a discussion for another time. Confirming their clausal category as adverbial is also eased by their main syntactic characteristic: like adverbs, they can usually move. This is not true of other dependent clauses. So, if a clause can be moved, it's bound to be adverbial. Here are a couple of examples.

4)   (a) We went home before it got too late.

(b) Before it got too late, we went home.

(c) They succeed because they're so industrious.

(d) Because they're so industrious, they succeed.

Practice Identifying Clauses

Identify the dependent clauses in the following sentences and label them adjectival, adverbial, or neither.

1. Ashley decided to move before she was supplanted by the next tenants.

2. Although she was usually very tolerant, the neighbors had gotten to her.

3. She did not relish packing up all her equipment, which was heavy.

4. As soon as she finished her breakfast, she decided it was time for her to pack up.

5. Then she thought that a coffee would probably give her the energy she needed.

6. Hours later, she wearily lifted the last of the boxes she'd packed up, and she limped out the door with it.

Nominal Clauses

Nominal clauses are also called noun clauses, since 'nominal' means 'like a noun.' A nominal clause is a clause that has the same grammatical role as a noun in any given sentence: it can function as the subject of a sentence, the object of a verb or preposition, or the complement or appositive of another **XP** (phrase). Reviewing a little, we remember that an **appositive** is the second NP of two (usually adjacent) NPs. It adds more information and restates or reflects from another angle what the first NP is referring to. Clauses can also reflect an NP in the same way. **Appositive clauses** also immediately follow an NP and restate what the NP is while adding a little more information. There is an example in the set of example sentences below to help visualize this more clearly.

The most characteristic marker for nominal clauses is the complementizer 'that,' but wh-words (and 'whether') as well as the complemetizers 'if' and 'for' are also important markers for nominal clauses. Here are examples demonstrating the various grammatical roles of nominal clauses, showing a variety of markers for nominal clauses. 'Nominal clause' is abbreviated 'CP(N),' in this set of example sentences, where CP means 'complementizer clause':

5) Types of nominal clauses

(a) Whether they can book another flight today is a question.
('whether' marking a subject CP(N))

(b) They discussed how they could get home on time.
('how' marking a direct object CP(N))

(c) They wondered about where to get good information.
('where' marking a prepositional object CP(N))

(d) The message that El Al had open seats cheered them up.
('that' marking an appositive CP(N))

(e) They gave whomever they were next to a big hug.
('whomever' marking an indirect object CP(N))

(f) The reason for joy was that they could leave very soon.
('that' marking a subject complement CP(N))

(g) A bystander was amazed that things worked out.
('that' marking an adjective complement CP(N))

(h) For them to be at home for Granma's funeral was a
comfort. ('for' marking a subject CP(N))

(i) All the relatives knew they would be glad to get home.
(deleted 'that' sort of hiding a direct object CP(N))

(j) That they would arrive on time was now a certainty.
('that' marking a subject CP(N))

(k) *They would arrive on time was now a certainty.
(unacceptable deletion of 'that' from subject CP(N))

The example of an adjective complement clause (g) deserves a little attention. Traditionally, all adjective complement clauses are considered nominal (e.g., Klammer, Schultz and Dellat –Volpe 333, 336-337). If we test the example above, we can agree with that perspective. We can ask 'amazed at what? and the 'that'-clause answers the 'what' question. Answers to 'what' and 'who' questions are generally nominal in the same way that answers to 'how,' 'why,' 'where,' and 'when' questions are generally adverbial. But couldn't we also ask 'amazed why?' and find our answer in the 'that'- clause, as well? In order to stem any tide of confusion, let's agree, until we have some better answer, that we'll consider any adjective complement clause that can answer a 'what' question to be a nominal clause. It's fine to line up with the traditional approach as long as the data will support it, so that's a fair choice.

The cautious student then thinks, but is not willing to ask out loud, "Might there be adjectives whose 'that'-clauses do not answer a 'what' question?" That is a question worth asking. What do we think of a sentence like "I'm happy that you're coming home soon" ? Can we ask 'happy what?' and get an answer from the 'that'-clause?

There are two ways to think about that. 'What' can mean 'fill in the blank,' or it can mean, 'name the referent for that idea.' If we think of 'what?' in a context of 'He's a student as Missi-what High School?' the 'what' simply asks someone to fill in the blank. So the answer could be 'Missisauga,' and we don't know whether the blank that got filled in is nominal, adjectival, adverbial, or, as in this case, no identifiable grammatical category at all. In that sense, 'happy what' asks for a 'that' clause, and any 'that' clause will do. Should we then conclude, using that approach, that all adjective complement clauses are indeed nominal, since they all answer the fill-in-the-blank meaning of 'what'? Not really. If the fill-in-the-blank meaning of 'what' will accept anything at all, then we can't use it to call clauses nominal or adjectival or anything else, because it doesn't distinguish anything.

So we're back to the other meaning of 'what,' which asks for a certain referent. In my dialect, 'happy what?' has no meaning at all, but 'happy why?' does mean something, and the 'that'-clause answer the 'why' question much better than the 'what' question. So this Guide again leaves the question open and suggests that a data-driven approach may diverge in some places from the traditional one. When we discuss Reed-Kellogg diagramming in chapter nine, we will simplify our lives by following the traditional approach. In this section, we'll say that adjectives followed by complement clauses can be tested with wh-questions to determine if they are nominal or adverbial. If 'what' works, then we'll consider it nominal. If not, as in 'happy-why?', we should, for the sake of being consistent, call it adverbial.

In the third from last example sentence (i) above, we see that 'that' can sometimes be deleted from direct object nominal clauses. This can cause a moment of doubt for the student trying to decide whether the clause 'they would arrive on time' is a main/independent clause or a dependent one. The problem is that 'they would arrive on time' can stand by itself, so it passes the test for independence. Nonetheless, it is still considered a dependent clause because the deleted 'that' is still considered part of the clause. In the next section, we will talk more about deleted clause markers and other deleted words.

The complementizer 'that,' however, cannot be deleted from subject nominal clauses, as seen in the final example sentence. *'They would arrive on time was now a certainty,' is ungrammatical and cannot mean 'That they would arrive on time was now a certainty.' So the main problem in identifying deleted signal markers for nominal clauses is to be aware of the possibility of a clause serving as a direct object in VPs like 'know that,' 'hope that,' 'wish that,' 'said that,' 'asserted that,' and similar verbs of cognition and communication. With all such verbs, the complementizer 'that' can be deleted.

Example (h) with the complementizer 'for' has a verb without any tense, called an '**infinitive**.' The clause is therefore called **non-finite**, and we'll talk about that in one of the next sections. The rest of the sentences all have **finite** verbs or finite auxiliaries. Finite here means that they have a verbal tense, either present or past.

In many instances, the relative pronouns 'which' and 'that' are interchangeable, with only a difference in style. But there is one use of 'which' that is unique. It can introduce a relative clause that modifies not an NP but an entire independent clause. Here is an example of an independent clause functioning as the head of a relative clause:

6)   We haven't gotten last semester's grades yet, which is really surprising.

Here, the relative clause 'which is really surprising' is not modifying a head NP, but rather the entire main clause 'we haven't gotten our grades back yet.' If we say that all dependent clauses are either nominal, adjectival, or adverbial, what is this one? It cannot move, so it's not adverbial. It's not modifying a noun, so it's not adjectival. So it's called nominal, even though it doesn't seem to take the place of an NP in the sentence it's in. It's clear that it's modifying a sentence, which makes it like a sentential adverb. So the most logical name would be adverbial, but that's not its traditional label. This is the second nominal clause that does not have a corresponding NP slot in a sentence since adjectives do not have NP complements, but they can have nominal clauses as complements.

In summary, then, adjectival clauses always follow an NP and describe it; adverbial clauses usually have clear markers (subordinating conjunctions) and can usually move to the front or end of the sentence; nominal clauses often have complementizers which mark them clearly, and they can substitute for NPs in any of the many grammatical roles that an NP can fill (subject, various object roles, several complement roles, and the appositive role).

Practice with Nominal Clauses

Identify the dependent clauses in the following sentences and label the grammatical role of the nominal clauses.

1. Because of the storm, it had become dangerous for us to travel, so we just stayed in our cabin with the small tour group.

2. Since we were going to be there for a while, we decided that it would be fun to play some games.

3. While some of the group thought of games we liked, others called the emergency information center to ask how long we would be stuck.

4. The prediction that we would be able to travel when the skies cleared up was an encouragement to us.

5. For us to entertain ourselves for that long looked like a severe test of whether we could get along well with each other.

6. Nonetheless, those who had thought up fun games were confident that they would not run out of ideas until the coast was clear.

Practice Identifying Clausal Types

Identify all the subordinate clauses – adverbial, adjectival, nominal whether finite or non-finite. Identifying verbs should help locate the clauses.

> 1. After Troy fell, Odysseus touched at Ismarus, the city of a Thracian people, whom he attacked and plundered, but by whom he was at last repulsed.

> 2. The north wind then carried his ships to Malea, the extreme southern point of Greece. which, if he had rounded safely, would probably have allowed him to reach Ithaca in a few days, where he would have found Penelope unvexed by wooers and Telemachus a boy of ten years old.

> 3. But this was not to be.

> 4. The 'ruinous winds' drove Odysseus and his ships for ten days, and on the tenth they touched the land of the Lotus-Eaters, whose flowery food causes those who ingest it to forget their past.

> 5. Lotus-land was possibly in Western Libya, but it is more probable that ten days' voyage from the southern point of Greece brought Odysseus into an unexplored region of fairy-land.

> 6. Egypt, of which Homer had some knowledge, was but five days' sail from Crete, which means that Lotus-land, at ten days' sail from Malea, was well past the limits of the discovered world.

> 7. Memorial Day, which is a cherished American Holiday, is a time when families and friends get together around a nice meal and remember how service men and women sacrificed for them.

> 8. Whoever is lucky with the weather can feast on a meal in the backyard while they enjoy some sun and quality conversation that they might not have had otherwise.

> 9. While the food is a big draw, it is important to remember, however small the remembrance may seem, those that fought for the freedoms which many Americans enjoy.

> 10. Memorial Day remains a significant yearly milestone in the calendar of those who are grateful to live in America.

Reduced Clauses and Empty Categories

We have noticed in several sections above that relative markers and complementizers may be deleted in English. These deleted words are also considered **empty categories**. The ability to delete certain words from a sentence is one of the grammatical characteristics which gives English such power and flexibility of expression. It also means that we, in developing an adult understanding of grammar, need to become more sensitive to parts of sentence structure that we cannot see or hear. This was mentioned in connection with auxiliaries earlier, so perhaps it would be helpful to try again to convince ourselves that our minds really do keep track of empty categories. Perhaps the easiest example is a command. In these sentences 'e' represents the deleted words or empty categories:

7)   Empty categories in imperatives

    (a) e Go wash your face.

    (b) e Go wash his face.

    (c) e Go wash your faces.

In the first sentence, the empty category is the subject of the sentence 'you.' But we wonder if the object 'your face' somehow gave us a clue that the subject is 'you.' That is not so, and we can show that by changing 'your face' to 'his fact' in the second sentence. The 'e' in the second sentence still means 'you.' So how do we know what the empty category is? We have a mental structure for every possible sentence in English and they all have subjects. So when we don't see one, we know that it must have been deleted, and our mind supplies one. The third sentence shows us that we can sometimes use clues in the sentence to decide whether the subject is singular or plural 'you.' In the first sentence, the subject is singular; in the second sentence, the subject could be singular or plural; and in the third sentence, the subject must be plural.

Another kind of structure in English where we see evidence that our minds keep track of the complete structure of a sentence even when part of it is not visible (or audible) is called '**gapping.**' For background, let's recall the unsurprising fact that joining two phrases of the same kind with 'and' produces a bigger phrase of the same kind, such as 'men' (NP) + 'and' + 'women' (NP) = 'men and women' (NP), or 'hit the ball'(VP) +'and' + 'run around the bases' (VP) = 'hit the ball and run around the bases' (VP). We can confirm the NPs for ourselves by noting that the pronoun 'they' can refer to 'men' or to 'women' or to 'men and women,' since they are all NPs.

For the VPs, we can say 'They told him to hit the ball and run around the bases, and he did so.' Here the word 'so' refers to 'hit the ball and run around the bases,' since 'so' can substitute for a VP. We can take a moment here to remember that the word 'pronoun' is a misnomer, since it only replaces NP's and not simple nouns. 'Pronouns' are really 'pro-NPs' if we wanted the name to be accurate. In this sense, the word 'so' should be called a pro-VP, since it can replace a VP. With that as background, we can look at the following sentence, which seems at first glance to break the rules. This is a sentence with a '**gap**' in it, as mentioned at the beginning of a previous paragraph.

8)   I wonder why your sister likes cherry pie and your brother e peach cobbler.

Here the conjunction 'and' connects 'your sister likes cherry pie' with 'your brother peach cobbler.' The first XP (phrase) is clearly a sentence with a subject, auxiliary (which tense hopped), verb and NP complement. The second XP is simply two NPs 'your brother' and 'peach cobbler.' What happened? Our minds have automatically filled in the two empty categories in the second XP, so that it should be written, 'your brother e peach cobbler,' where the 'e' is for the missing verb 'likes,' which contains the main verb and the auxiliary's tense, number and person information.

Contrasting two very similar sentences adds to our impression that the mind accounts for empty categories. The following two sentences seem quite similar, but only the first one is acceptable. Why should that be?

9)   (a) 'I've finished rewriting the paper, so we could now submit it to the editors'

(b) *'I've finished rewriting the paper, which we could now submit it to the editors.'

Why is the second one unacceptable? Because 'it' is occupying the position of an 'e,' and the mind will not let both the 'e' and the word 'it' occupy the same space. This is a small effort to show that the mind actually keeps track of entire sentence structures, even when some of the words have been deleted or moved. We see other, sometimes comic, examples of this in the sections on **reduced adverbial clauses** and **sentence transformation**s.

Reduced Adjectival (Relative) Clauses (Finite and Non-finite)

A little while ago, we noticed that one of the tricky aspects to analyzing sentences with relative clauses is that the relative marker (the relative pronoun or relative adverb) may have been deleted. If we look again at some sentences containing fairly typical examples of relative clauses and other adjectival clauses, we can see (by looking at the words inside the parentheses, which are 'optional') which of the relative markers can be deleted. When the relative marker is deleted, the result is a **reduced relative clause**.

10) Creating reduced relative clauses by deleting relative adverbs

(a) There's the hospital <u>where</u> I was born. (may not be deleted)

(b) This is the week (<u>when</u>) the big decision will be made.

(c) There is no logical reason (<u>why</u>) I should stay at home this evening.

11) No reduced relative clauses from relative determiner deletion

That's the man <u>whose</u> house we visited yesterday.

12) Reduced relative clauses from deleted relative pronouns

   (a) Those are the people <u>(who(m))</u> we saw yesterday.

   (b) That's the dog <u>(that/which)</u> we saw yesterday.

   (c) That's the man <u>who</u> helped us buy gas yesterday. (no deletion)

13) No reduced adjective clauses by deleting non-relative marker

   The day <u>after</u> they finished their final exams was devoted to moving everything out of the dorms.

14) No reduced relative clause by deleting the 'which' of clausal head

   We haven't gotten last semester's grades yet, <u>which</u> is really surprising.

Relative determiners (like 'whose' in 11) above are never deleted. Neither are relative pronouns which are the subject of the verb in the relative clause (like 'who' in 12)(c)). Nor is a subordinating conjunction ever deleted such as 'after' when it introduces an adjectival clause (as in 13). Nor is 'which' when its head is an entire clause (as in 14). The relative adverb 'where' follows a different rule, since it can only be deleted if we add 'in' to the relative clause: 'the hospital I was born in.' This makes 'where' the equivalent of 'in which,' and seems to show that only the 'which' part can be deleted, leaving the 'in' part behind. This is like deleting one semantic feature from the relative adverb 'where.' Besides those listed above, all the rest of the relative clause markers can be deleted, leaving an empty category, or several empty categories. These are reduced relative clauses. Here are some more example sentences with the empty categories written in:

15) (a) The man we met yesterday... -> The man e we met yesterday... ('e'= who/whom/that)

   (b) The man washing his car over there... -> The man e e washing his car ... ('e e'= who is/was)

   (c) The man blushing over there... -> The man e e blushing over there... ('e e'= who is/was)

   (d) The blushing man over there...-> no relative clause is left.

In the first example, only the relative clause marker is deleted. The resulting reduced relative clause is still **finite** because it still has its auxiliary. The second and third examples show us that a maximum deletion from a relative clause is the relative marker and the auxiliary. If the auxiliary is deleted, so is the information about tense, and the resulting reduced relative clause becomes **non-finite**. The final example shows us that we can reduce the relative clause to the point that the clause disintegrates by moving it in front of the head noun. In (d), the word 'blushing' is a **VP used adjectivally** as a modifier to the noun 'man.'

Another term for such a VP is **gerundive.** We will return to gerundives when we discuss phrase structure diagramming. We should notice that we cannot call such a VP an AP because it doesn't fit the frame sentence and cannot accept a qualifier, as in this sentence: *'The blushing man is very blushing.' One detail that will help us pigeon-hole the rearrangement of a relative clause as in (d) is to note that this is only possible with intransitive verbs. If we try the same movement with a transitive verb and its direct object, it is unacceptable: * 'The washing his car man over there...' A transitive VP cannot be used adjectivally in this way in English, although this type of relative clause is quite normal in languages such as Chinese.

Another way that we can manipulate a reduced relative clause until it disintegrates is by fronting it.

16) (a) The man e e washing his car over there has just asked his girlfriend to marry him.

(b) e e e washing his car over there, the man has just asked his girlfriend to marry him.

The second sentence, with the fronted reduced relative clause (not a technical term, so just read a little farther for the real term) seems to mean something entirely different. Rather than two empty categories, it seems to have three, namely, 'While he was washing his car over there, ...' Thus, fronting the reduced adjectival clause has turned it into a **reduced adverbial clause.** This is not really very surprising, since only adverbial clauses can move. So it's not surprising that movement destroys an adjective clause this way. We will discuss this further in the section on reduced adverbial clauses.

Practice Identifying Reduced Relative Clauses

Identify the adjectival clauses in the following sentences as either reduced or not.

1) Flying between storm clouds is one of the most memorable experiences some travelers ever have.

2) The air rising inside the clouds creates strong up-drafts that can jolt the plane and lift a passenger out of his or her seat.

3) Some pilots choose a route the passengers cannot fathom and fly deftly around each succeeding cloud.

4) For the stewards and stewardesses travelling such routes often, this can be a time when they can give passengers a little more personal attention.

5) Since it's impossible to distribute any of the food or duty free items normally offered, they take turns reassuring the passengers they can

identify as uncomfortable.

6) The amount of danger the crew and passengers are exposed to depends on the pilot's skill in dealing with the situations that arise.

Reduced Adverbial Clauses (Non-finite)

Just as we can delete the relative markers introducing a variety of relative clauses, we can also delete the subordinating conjunctions that introduce adverbial clauses. In the case of adverbial clauses, however, it seems that we cannot delete only the subordinating conjunction or only the NP subject. In no case are we able to keep the auxiliary in a reduced adverbial clause, so they all end up being **non-finite**. In the following example sentences, we notice that a series of two or three empty categories is possible and normal.

17) (a) While mowing his lawn, John discovered a tiny leprechaun.-> While e e mowing his lawn, John … . ('e e'= he was)

(b) Mowing his lawn, John discovered a tiny leprechaun. -> e e e mowing his lawn, John … . ('eee'= while he was)

(c) John discovered a tiny leprechaun while mowing his lawn.-> John …while e e mowing his lawn. ('e e'= he was)

(d) ! John discovered a tiny leprechaun mowing his lawn. -> John discovered… e e e mowing his lawn. ('e e e' = while he/it was) OR->John discovered… e e mowing his lawn. ('e e' = which was)

(e) Bowled over by his discovery, John took the leprechaun to his psychiatrist. -> e e e bowled over by his discovery, … (e e e=Since/Because he was)

The first two sentences show that we can remove either the subject and the auxiliary of the adverbial clause while leaving the subordinating conjunction in place, or we can delete both of these and the subordinating conjunction as well. For clarity, let's call the reduced relative with three empty categories a '**participial clause**,' since it begins with the verb's **present participle** 'mowing.' In some (traditional) grammar explanations, it is called a **participial phrase**, which is all right, since all clauses are some sort of phrase. The specific term used in some texts when referring to the reduced clause with only two empty categories is an '**elliptical clause**,' since '**ellipsis**' is another word for deletion or omission.

The fourth sentence is also a participial clause, since it begins with the verb's **past participle** 'bowled over.' If we need to distinguish the second and fourth sentences from each other, we'll call the first one a '**present participial clause**' and the fourth one a '**past participial clause**.' Here again, we should also be familiar with the words used in traditional texts: '**present participle phrase**' and '**past participle phrase**.'

The contrast between the first and third sentences shows that the reduced adverbial clause can be placed at the end of the sentence without changing its meaning. This is true as long as the reduced clause still has its subordinating conjunction. But the flexibility of movement can be deceptive, as we see in the fourth sentence. Our mind would rather fill in the blanks of the moved participial clause in that position as a relative clause.

When we look at the contrast between the second and fourth sentences, we see that a participial clause cannot be placed immediately after an NP without becoming ambiguous. In fact, we should probably say that the mind recomputes the meaning completely, rather than saying that there are two possible meanings. The effect of the movement of the reduced clause to a position after an NP is so radical that we are likely to interpret the participial clause as meaning 'John discovered a wounded leprechaun (which was) mowing his lawn' rather than 'John discovered a wounded leprechaun (while he was) mowing his lawn.' This tells us something important about empty categories. Verbs in English need subjects, and when we delete the subject and leave the empty category with no context, the mind will search for and construct a context and fill in the blank subject by identifying the empty subject NP with (technically called being **co-indexed with**) the closest noun or NP in the neighboring clause. Here's a way of showing the indexing of the empty subject NP to the nearest visible/audible NP:

18) (a) e e$_i$ e Mowing his lawn, John$_i$ discovered a tiny leprechaun.

(b) John discovered a tiny leprechaun$_i$ e$_i$ e mowing his lawn.

The difference between the interpretation of the empty subjects in the two reduced clauses results from the almost automatic choice of the nearest NP in an adjacent clause as the co-referent. In order to remember more easily what the subscript 'i' means, we can say that it stands for '**identical**' or 'identified with' for the two words that it links together. The meaning of the two NPs is the same when they are co-indexed, and the subscript 'i' indicates this.

There is another form of reduced adverbial clause which does not begin with a subordinating conjunction or a participle, but rather with an adjective. Here is an example and an explanation of its three empty categories:

19) Reduced adverbial phrase with deleted verb 'be'

(a) e e$_i$ e Rich to the point of embarrassment, Carnegie$_i$ decided to build public libraries.

(b) Since he was rich to the point of ...

In this case, the empty categories include 'be' as a linking verb rather than an auxiliary. Earlier, we said that an easy way to define a clause is a structure with an auxiliary and a main verb. Since the main verb and auxiliary here have been deleted, it would be consistent with our previous definition of a clause to call these structures 'phrases,' instead of clauses. This is not a point to get stressed out about since some scholars refer to structures like 'rich to the point of embarrassment' as **adjective phrases** and others refer to them as **adjectival**

clauses. We should notice that the dependent clause or phrase 'rich to the point of embarrassment' has been fronted, so it is functioning adverbially in our example sentence above. Therefore, it should properly be considered a species of **adverbial phrase or clause**. We'll return to this structure when we discuss sentence diagramming.

Practice with Reduced Adverbial Clauses

a) Identify and categorize the reduced adverbial clauses in the following sentences.

> 1. While lying out on the beach, I decided that I should apply some sunscreen.
>
> 2. Still enthusiastically learning to surf, my cousin from the city discovered this outdoor truth a little late and got a bit of a burn.
>
> 3. We both paused later in the afternoon, warming up from the sun, to get a big drink of water.
>
> 4. Warned about sharks in the water, we were very cautious for the rest of the afternoon
>
> 5. Safely back home, the first thing we thought of was cold lemon ade.
>
> 6. Still enthusiastic about catching some waves, my cousin is planning tocome again next weekend.

Distinguish the the reduced adverbial clauses from the reduced adjectival clauses in the following sentences.

> 1. Although a bit rough on shoes, couches, and cats, she was the best dog I had ever known.
>
> 2. Every time I left her in my friends' back yard while talking, she would sit by the door waiting for me.
>
> 3. Once she found a squeaky toy another friend's dog owned and she didn't let go of the thing for weeks.
>
> 4. She grew up playing games of fetch and would go after anything you threw to her.
>
> 5. My favorite memory of her is when I was reading on the floor, she came up and laid her head on my shoulder.
>   *ee I was*
> 6. While^enjoying her companionship, I promised myself that, when the time came, I'd throw a funeral for her with a wake and everything.
>
>   *reduced adverbial clause*

Dangling Participles

Having seen how the mind processes empty subjects, we can move to an area where some comical errors occur. Participles don't actually 'dangle,' but they do get co-indexed in odd ways. The term 'dangling' is older than co-indexation theory, so we'll use the traditional term even though it is quite metaphorical. Here are a couple of examples that sometimes make people smile (or grimace):

20) Dangling participles (reduced clauses)

   (a) e e$_i$ e *Covered with chocolate sauce and strawberries, Americans$_i$ love ice cream sundaes.

   (b) e e$_i$ e *Broiled to a golden brown, I$_i$ really enjoying salmon steak with garnish.

   (c) e e$_i$ e Lost deep in the Amazon forests, the investigative reporter$_i$ found an unknown tribe.

   (d) e e$_i$ e *Flowing with gold dust, many adventurers$_i$ were attracted to the streams at Sutter's Mill.

In each case, the empty subject is co-indexed with the subject of the main clause, resulting in readings that in (a) the Americans are covered with chocolate sauce and strawberries, in (b) the speaker 'I' is broiled to a golden brown, in (c) the investigative reporter was lost deep in the Amazon forests, and in (d) many adventurers were flowing with gold dust. For teachers and tutors of English, such sentences, and much more humorous ones, are great fun to make up and tell their students about. Often though, teachers do not have to make them up at all. Surprisingly enough, this sort of error is quite common in the writing of high school and college students and even college graduates. There are a number of web-sites which also collect such gaffs:

> http://www.fun-with-words.com/ambiguous_headlines.html
> http://monster-island.org/tinashumor/humor/headline.html
> http://www.departments.bucknell.edu/Linguistics/synhead.html
> http://www.squidoo.com/funniest-headlines. htm

Practice with Dangling Participles

Identify and correct the dangling participles in the following sentences.

1) Walking by the lake, the stars twinkled in its reflection.

2) Running as fast as he could, his classmates cheered Jeremy on with all their enthusiasm.

3) Exhilarated by the fjords, the boat trip was one of Jan's most moving experiences.

4) Still holding their candy, the store manager chased after the young shop-lifters.

5) After being stirred vigorously, the bartender put ice in the drink.

6) Springing easily from limb to limb, the biologist observed the lemurs.

Reduced Nominal Clauses

As we noticed in discussing nominal clauses, the **complementizer** 'that' can be deleted from clauses functioning as direct objects, especially for verbs of cognition and communication, such as 'thought (that),' and 'said (that).' Here's an example with the complementizer marked as an empty category.

21) They said e they would come on time.

The complementizer must be introducing a direct object clause for this to be acceptable. As we can recall from the discussion of nominal clauses, some of them are **non-finite**. At this point, let's take a further step by noting that non-finite nominal clauses, too, can be reduced. Example sentence 98) (h) 'For them to be at home for Granma's funeral was a comfort' can be reduced, but its meaning will change meaning in an interesting way because of the deletions:

22) e e To be at home for Granma's funeral was a comfort.

When we delete the complementizer 'for' and the pronoun 'them,' the mind cannot find another appropriate NP to co-index the empty subject to, so what happens? The meaning of the subject NP becomes general and changes to 'anyone.' Giving another example where the main verb is something besides the linking verb 'be' will allow us to see two types of this reduced nominal subject clause.

23) Reduced and unreduced nominal clauses

    (a) For us to go there at this time of night would be foolish.

    (b) e e To go there at this time of night would be foolish.

    (c) For us to be going there at this time of night would be foolish.

    (d) e e e e Going there at this time of night would be foolish.

In both the second and fourth example sentences above, we notice that the deletion of the subject pronoun allows the meaning of the empty subject to shift and to become 'anyone.' The final sentence has four empty categories, which is a little extreme. For that reason, this structure has been treated in various ways by different scholars, as we will see when we diagram nominal clauses and reduced nominal clauses. Traditionally, a verb form ending in '–ing' is called a **gerund** when it is used nominally (and a **gerundive** when used adjectivally).

Clauses of Comparison and Degree

Often we use entire clauses to compare ideas or events. This is so even though parts of the clause may have been deleted. In the following example 'than' is used as a conjunction. We see that the dependent clause has been reduced. Its auxiliary and main verb can optionally be deleted, and the subject complement (AP or NP) must be deleted at the end of sentence if the empty verb and adjective are the same as the visible verb and adjective (not counting the '-er' suffix on the visible adjective).

24) My Dad is stronger than your Dad (is) (*strong).

In the example above, 'than' introduces a CP as the complement of an adjective. It's interesting in this context to note that some texts list 'than' among the conjunctions, but not among the prepositions. In the above examples, we clearly see 'than' functioning as a conjunction. We have discussed 'than' above as being used sometimes as a preposition and sometimes as a conjunction. To carry that point a little further, let's notice that 'than' functions as a preposition in a sentence like this one, 'The way you solved the problem was much more elegant than how we tried to do it.' Here the fronted wh-word 'how' is occupying the specifier of CP position, and there's nowhere left in the CP structure for a second specifier. This means that 'than' cannot be functioning as a conjunction. So we'll say in this case that the CP after 'than' is the object of the preposition 'than.'

An example of 'than' with an IP object, where we might consider it a conjunction is this sort of sentence (with two **gerunds**): 'Your leaving us would be harder than our staying here without any income.'

Before we finish the discussion of comparisons with 'than,' we should note that the empty adjective does not have to be deleted if the two verbs or adjectives are not the same, as in the following example.

25) My dad is more enthusiastic about politics than your dad is concerned about environmental protection.

If we leave out the word 'concerned,' we notice that the mind fills in the empty category with the same meaning as the previous adjective. This means that there is a mental link between the empty category and a visible category, which we can show by a subscript 'i' meaning 'identical' on the visible word and the empty category, like this:

26) My dad is more enthusiastic$_i$ about politics than your dad is e$_i$ about environmental protection.

Other grammatical constructions that form a group that is often discussed with clauses of comparison are clauses of degree, such as 'so... that ...,' 'too ... for...,' and '... enough ... to.' Here are a number of example sentences showing these structures:

27) (a) The experimental plane is as well-designed as (what₁) we had

expected e₁ (=something) from such a large company.

(b) The experimental plane goes faster than e₁ e (the speed₁ that) a

plane has ever traveled e₁ (that speed) before.

(c) That's the fastest planel e₁ (that₁) anyone has ever built e₁ (=a plane).

(d) We were so exhausted that we could not walk another mile.

(e) The temperature had risen too high e e (for anyone) to hike outdoors.

(f) Our roommates thought that we were wise enough e e (for us) not to take such a risk.

The above set of sentences give us typical examples of (a) a clause of equality, (b) a clause of comparison, (c) a clause that is a complement to superlative adjective, (d) a finite clause of degree, and (e) and (f) two non-finite clauses of degree (more in the next section on 'to+ verb' forms, which are called **infinitives**). In the first one, we see a noun clause introduced by a deleted wh-word 'what.' In the following two sentences, we notice that we ordinarily delete the NPs which would allow us to analyze the dependent clauses as head nouns followed by relative clauses. In the first sentence in the chapter and in the (b), (d), (e), and (f) sentences in the above set, we see complement clauses that are complements to the AP that they follow ('stronger,' 'faster,' ' so exhausted,' 'wise enough,' and 'too high')

Superlatives are sometimes used to generate empty categories as is seen in a sentence like this 'My dad is the best e,' where we need more context to know what noun is represented by the empty category. It is clear that 'best' is still functioning as an adjective here, and not as a pronoun since it is preceded by a determiner.

The example in 24) above also shows why it is hard to justify talking about a string such as 'than your Dad' as a prepositional phrase with an NP object and ignoring the deleted auxiliary, verb and complement or modifier. In terms of grammatical analysis, we need to recognize the more complete grammatical structure even when we would never say or write all of it.

In other instances, an entire clause is visible, such as in (d) above, where there is no empty category. In our diagramming of sentences in chapters eight and nine, we will return to our discussion of these empty categories.

Practice with Empty Categories

a) Identify the empty categories in the following sentences and label them or find a lexical replacement. Please also mark the empty categories left by tense hopping.

> 1. Opened sixteen weeks and three days ago, the situation at Tilly's Candle Shop now looked critical.

> 2. Tilly' told her husband that this great adventure was too risky for them to keep investing their savings in.

> 2. She had tried to attract the large pensive man's attention when she first met him at the junior college they both attended.

> 3. She had immediately said 'yes' when he knelt down on his denim-clad knee and offered her the largest diamond she'd ever seen.

> 4. Unfortunately, while working at the factory, he had a devastating fall.

> 5. They would have moved closer to their parents if he hadn't been hurt so badly that he couldn't return to work.

> 6. He never healed well enough to do his old job, so it was extremely fortunate Tilly had just finished her credential process as a teacher.

> 7. With her teacher's salary, she could pay all their bills, which was a great comfort.

> 8. When they started the candle shop, they had hoped to attract enough customers to begin saving for their retirement.

b) Just for fun: which of the following is ambiguous in terms of its empty categories? Why is only one ambiguous?

> 1) They loved adventure more than job security.

> 2) Joan loved the Beatles more than her husband.

Chapter 6: Non-finite Clauses

We have been using the vocabulary of non-finite clauses rather informally. Discussing it more formally, or rather, more comprehensively, should – hopefully – fill in some of the gaps left by that informality. Let's go over why non-finite structures like 'to go' are called 'non-finite clauses' in this Guide and not 'infinitive phrases,' as they are in many text books. Non-finite clauses all have verbs and complete VPs, including all the complements of the verb, so that satisfies our working definition of a clause with an empty specifier and auxiliary. They are often reduced clauses, as we noticed in the section on reduced noun clauses where removing 'for + NP subject' from the sentence 'For us to go there at this time of night would be foolish' resulted in the mind recomputing the subject as 'anyone.'

Let's look again at what 'finite' and 'non-finite' mean in an effort to be able to recall those terms. We traced the meaning of the abbreviation 'IP' to the term '**inflected phrase**,' meaning that a sentence (or main clause) has an auxiliary that carries certain information about the verb's tense, number and person. The most direct example is the suffix '-s' in an example such as, 'She cares about other people.' The suffix was introduced as the result of 'tense hopping' from the auxiliary position to the main verb. The '-s' carries the information that the verb is in the simple present tense, is third person (he, she, it, or they), and is singular (not we, you-all, or they).

So the '-s' is appropriate for a verb with a 'he,' 'she,' and 'it' as the subject. Nothing new so far. '**Finite**' means that it's possible to count the number of something, while 'infinite' means that it is beyond being counted. When an auxiliary or verb carries information about '**number**' it is either singular or plural, and that is what is meant by finite. When there is no information from the auxiliary about number (or tense, or person), it is beyond counting, so that verb is '**infinite**' and is called '**an infinitive**,' and the clause is called '**non-finite**.'

As we saw in the previous chapter, a complete non-finite clause, such as 'For us to go there (at this time of night...)' begins with the complementizer 'for' followed by an object pronoun, followed by 'to,' followed by the uninflected form of the main verb (also called the **base form**) and the rest of the VP. It is not a coincidence that this structure mirrors the order of constituents of a finite dependent clause, such as 'If we would go there (at this time of night, ...)" Here we see a subordinating conjunction followed by a subject pronoun, followed by the modal auxiliary 'would' followed by the bare infinitive form of the main verb 'go,' followed by the rest of the VP.

Both the complementizer 'for' and the subordinating conjunction serve the same purpose: they introduce and mark the clause as a dependent clause (or 'CP'= **complementizer phrase**). In a more technical sense that we will return to when we discuss phrase structure diagramming, both 'since' and 'for' are the specifiers of their CP. We will discuss the empty head positions of these CPs in that same discussion on diagramming. Both the pronoun NPs are the specifiers of their IPs. Both 'should' and 'to' function as the auxiliary for their dependent clause. Both verbs are in the uninflected or **bare infinitive form**.

It may be odd to think about 'to' functioning as an auxiliary for a non-finite clause. We know auxiliaries as the carriers of information about tense, person, and number. And we know that infinitives do not have tense, person, or number. So, the auxiliary 'to' does not have any of that information to carry. What's the point of an auxiliary particle like 'to' that doesn't do anything? One of the conclusions in the introduction to the section on 'Sentence (IP) structure' above was that 'the sentence is now seen as having three main parts: subject, auxiliary, and verb phrase.' The existence of the particle 'to' as an auxiliary even when there is none of the normal auxiliary information to carry seems to confirm this three-part division of English sentence structure. It's there because that's part of the basic structure of a clause in English, even if it seems to be doing nothing. But perhaps that's not all. Please read on.

Modal auxiliaries and the auxiliary 'to' function in the same way in another grammatical structure where the main verb can be deleted. The process is called '**ellipsis**' of the entire VP (the complement of the auxiliary), and can be seen in the empty categories in these parallel finite and non-finite clauses:

1)   (a) I'd rather not go to lab today, but I know I should e.

       (b) I know I should go to lab today, but I just don't want to e.

In each of the above sentences, we see 'should' or 'to' indicating the ellipsis of the VP. This is evidence that supports the idea that the word 'to' really is the auxiliary for non-finite clauses. Since auxiliaries by their nature carry tense and number, it's something of an oxymoron to talk about non-finite 'to' as an auxiliary when it, by definition, carries neither tense nor number. Perhaps we should call it a quasi-auxiliary. But it is conventionally called the non-finite auxiliary, so we won't challenge conventional wisdom here. It is the head of the non-finite IP, just as the modal (or other) auxiliary is the head of the finite IP. They can also have the same complements, and can allow ellipsis of their complement VP's in parallel ways.

We have already talked a little about **reduced infinitive clauses** in the section on reduced nominal clauses. We noticed that the deletion of the complementizer 'for' and the subject pronoun could lead to a different interpretation of the clause, as in this example from earlier:

2)   Reduced and unreduced infinitival clauses

(a) For us to go there at this time of night would be foolish.

(b) e e To go there at this time of night would be foolish.

In the first sentence the subject is 'we,' which is expressed in the object pronoun 'us,' but in the second sentence the subject is 'anyone.' This happens when there is no context for the empty subject. But when there is a context, we return to the principle that we saw in the section on reduced adverbial clauses above. If the NP subject of the non-finite clause is left out, the mind will search for a context and fill in the blank subject by identifying the empty subject NP (technically called being **co-indexed** with it) with the closest noun or NP in the same or neighboring clause. In many cases, however, if the subject of the main clause and the subject of the non-finite clause are the same, the subject NP of the non-finite clause must be empty. The following sentences exemplify this:

3)   Obligatory empty categories in infinitival clauses

(a) Our desire is for you to become a doctor.

(b) Our desire is for him/her to become a doctor.

(c) Our desire is for them to become doctors.

(d)*Our desire is for us to become doctors.

(e) Our desire is e e to become doctors.

The contrast between the final two sentences is where our focus mainly falls. By way of warm-up, however, we notice that the first three sentences allow any subject besides 'we' as the subject for the complement clause referring to the NP 'our desire.' In the fourth example sentence, though, we notice that the 'we' of 'our desire' may not appear as a subject pronoun in the non-finite clause; the subject position of the non-finite clause must be empty in order to express the idea that the two clauses have the same subject.

There is an informal way of getting around the constraint against having 'our' and 'us' in the above sentences, namely the sentence "Our desire is for ourselves to become doctors." What should we think about this exception to the rule? Why should a reflexive pronoun work where a personal object pronoun cannot? Each type is used as an object pronoun. Each type is used in these sentences in the role of the subject NP in a non-finite (nominal) clause. Yet one is clearly constrained and the other is not. The reflexive pronoun is clearly acting exceptionally here, and the fact that it can only be used informally in this type of sentence may be the source of the exception. Other informal usages of the reflexive pronouns (such as 'theirselves', and 'hisself') also behave differently from formal usage.

This (generally) obligatory deletion of the co-indexed subject is also true for verbs like 'want,' 'hope,' 'long,' and 'desire,' as shown in the examples below:

4)   (a) I want you/him/us/them/*me to succeed.

(b) I long for you/him/us/them/*me to succeed.

We notice in the first sentence that the complementizer 'for' must be deleted, but that in the second sentence the complementizer must be expressed. This seems to be an idiosyncrasy of the verb; some verbs require an expressed complementizer 'for,' others require its deletion, and still others, such as 'like,' seem to be flexible, as seen in the sentence, 'I'd like (for) you to be there' where both options are acceptable.

Bare Infinitives (Or Infinitives without 'To')

Recognizing **bare infinitives** is intrinsically more difficult than recognizing infinitives with the complementizer 'to.' This makes sense because we're missing an important marker. Standard examples of bare infinitives include complements to the verbs 'watch' and 'hear,' and some examples with the grammatical structure 'all we did was.....,' or 'they made him...' An example of the listed verbs would be like this: "They watched him climb the tree." The verb 'climb' here has no tense, and is therefore non-finite.

The first two verbs belong to a class of verbs that we should be aware of and try to list more completely: 'notice,' 'feel,' 'see,' 'look at,' 'observe,' 'listen to,' and other **verbs of perception**. 'Smell,' and 'taste,' also belong to this list, but it is hard to imagine a context where it would be meaningful (and semantically appropriate) to say something like, 'They smelled the flowers leave the room.' And 'taste' apparently cannot be used in this context at all, since we don't do much observing of outside events with our sense of taste.

With many of the verbs of perception, the present participle form with '-ing' is possible as well as the bare infinitive, and the meaning of the two can sometimes be quite different:

5)   Comparing bare infinitive and present participle clauses

(a) I watched him e climb the mountain (i.e., he succeeded).

(b) I watched him e e e climbing the mountain (i.e., we don't know if he succeeded).

In terms of structure, bare infinitives, as in 5 (a), should be considered to have a deleted 'to' as a single empty category. The v+ing present participle form, in contrast, has the three empty categories of a full CP: complementizer, NP subject, and auxiliary in front of the verb. Concerning 5(a), we have some historical evidence to support the existence of this single empty category, since the auxiliary 'to' used to be expressed in the time of Shakespeare.

6)   Shakespearean examples of an undeleted auxiliary 'to'

(a) ...pure surprise and fear/Made me to quit the house. (First Gentleman in Pericles, Prince of Tyre, III, ii, 24)

(b) I had rather hear you to solicit that/ Than music from the spheres.. (Olivia in Twelfth Night, III, i, 72)

(c) I go, sir; but I would not have you to think that my desire of having is the sin of covetousness: (Clown in Twelfth Night, V, i, 27)

The second sentence demonstrates a verb of perception with the auxiliary 'to' expressed where our present-day English would use a bare infinitive. In the other two sentences, we see examples of two other grammatical structures where the bare infinitive is used today, but which were full infinitives four hundred years ago. From this we conclude that we should assume the existence of an empty category 'to' in bare infinitives unless there is a strong reason not to. If the infinitives have an auxiliary, are they analyzable as covert clauses? The aux is the head of IP, so the question becomes whether they also have an implicit subject (=specifier). And the answer to that is yes. We can always co-index the relevant visible NP to the empty specifier/subject of an infinitive. And where there is no visible NP to co-index with, the infinitive will be interpreted as 'anyone' or 'everyone.' We saw an example of the lack of a visible NP subject at the beginning of the chapter in the sentence 'e e To go there at this time of night would be foolish.' There is no NP for the empty subject of 'e to go' to co-index with, so the sentence means 'for anyone to go there..'

When we talk about a non-finite clause as a CP with an IP inside of it, we run into another conundrum – isn't an IP another term for a sentence? How can the CP 'for us to go there' have an IP inside it? Is 'us to go there' a sentence? No it isn't. Since it's non-finite, it can never be a sentence. Nonetheless, it is an IP, since it has the characteristic syntax of an IP: an NP subject followed by an aux (non-finite) followed by a VP predicate. So non-finite clauses can have an embedded IP even though the IP is not a sentence.

Other examples of grammatical structures that support bare infinitives are listed here:

7)   Other examples of bare infinitive (underlined)

(a) My big brother made me eat the rhubarb

(b) The driver has the mechanic check the car carefully.

Reduced Infinitival Adverbial Clauses (Or 'Adverbial Infinitives')

As we have learned to expect with adverbials, one of the best diagnostic tests is whether the adverbial can move in the sentence. This is also true of adverbial non-finite clauses.

8) (a) One must be very motivated e_1 e_2 to adapt successfully to a new environment. (e_1 = for, e_2 = oneself)

(b) To adapt successfully to a new environment, one must be very motivated.

In the example sentences, we see the non-finite clause move from its normal position in (a) to its clause-initial position in (b), where it is separated from the main clause by a comma in order to indicate this movement. We also notice two deletions that have created empty categories: the complementizer 'for' and the subject NP meaning 'oneself.' As discussed above, since the empty NP here has the same co-referent as the subject of the main clause, it must be deleted in the non-finite clause. Some texts encourage students to use a longer form of the complementizer 'in order (for+ NP),' which is fine if it helps. But this may make it harder to notice that the NP subject has been deleted.

Absolute Phrases or Clauses (Or 'Nominal Absolutes')

Since **absolute phrases/clauses** are sometimes called '**verbless clauses**' (Clark 223), it is hard to imagine how they are clauses at all. Sometimes a text will note that the name 'nominal' in the term '**nominal absolutes**' is a misnomer, since they function adverbially. In each of the examples cited below, it is possible to construct a full clause by adding a subordinating (or coordinating) conjunction and a form of the verb 'be,' either as an auxiliary form of 'be,' or a form of the main verb 'be.' This reminds us of the section on reduced adverbial clauses where the main verb 'be' was also deleted from so-called adjective clauses, such as 'Rich to the point of embarrassment, Carnegie....'' It also reminds us that 'be' as a main verb is exceptional in English in a number of ways.

Let's look at some of some examples from a standard textbook augmented with information about the empty categories (Klammer, Schultz, & Volpe 409):

9) (a) e_1 The year's work e_2 completed, Santa lay down for ...

(e_1 = since/as/because, e_2= was (aux))

(b) e_1 His voice e_2 quavering, Charlie called ...

(e_1 = while, e_2 = was (aux))

(c) e_1 Help e_2 e_2 nearby, the team climbed confidently...

(e_1 = because/since , e_2 = was (aux), e_2 = verb (be))

(d) Jemika studied, e_1 her chin e_2 e_2 in her hand.

(e_1 = while, e_1 = was, e_2 = verb)

(e) The children waited, e_1 their faces e_2 e_3 forlorn.

(e_1 = and/but, e_1 = were (in aux position), e_2 = verb)

The first two have past or present participles of a verb, which allows them to fit into a recognizable pattern for a clause. The final three do not have this characteristic, which leads one to ask how to recognize them as clauses. This shows a clear weakness in the analysis which calls them all clauses equally. Absolute clauses/phrases fit into the exceptional behavior of the main verb 'be,' and we can learn to recognize them with that understanding. We can hold on to the idea that the removal of a conjunction and an auxiliary while leaving the NP subject is a phenomenon that we want to be alert for. If the verb form is still present, our task is very much easier. If the main verb is 'be,' its disappearance is part of what makes it unique among English verbs. The second idea to be aware of is that where three elements are deleted (conjunction, auxiliary and verb), leaving just the NP subject and part of the predicate, it may be possible to analyze such structures in other ways such as (d) 'Jemika studied (with) her chin in her hand.'

More Practice Identifying Empty Categories

Identify the empty categories in the sentences below and suggest possible lexical replacements.

> 1. Not used to life on campus, Jeff considering moving back home and commuting again.
>
> 2. More interested in competitive sports than during his high school years, he thought living on campus would allow him to try out as a walk on.
>
> 3. Unable to resolve the issue clearly, he went to the counseling center.
>
> 4. Unsurprised by Jeff's questions, the counselor helped him see the pros and cons of the choices he had.
>
> 5. Grateful he had sought outside advice, Jeff settled more firmly into dorm life and its challenges.
>
> 6. Encouraged by the coaches' initial reactions to his workouts, Jeff began a more intensive exercise program.

Reduced Infinitival Adjectival Clauses (Or 'Adjectival Infinitives')

Infinitival adjectival clauses, as the name implies, modify nouns. As is the case with other (reduced) adjective clauses, these must almost always immediately follow the noun that they are modifying. We have seen that **unreduced finite adjective clauses** always have relative clause markers (as in 'the person whom we ...,') or time-related subordinate conjunctions in their specifier of CP position (as in 'the day when we...'). **Reduced finite adjective clauses** have no such marker visible in their CP. **Non-finite nominal clauses** are often marked with the complementizer 'for.' **Reduced infinitival adjectival clauses** do not have a visible complementizer. But we can often reconstruct a deleted complementizer 'for' and the subject NP in reduced infinitival adjectival clauses. If it's functioning adjectivally, it will follow the noun immediately, just as other adjective clauses do. An example should help us go a step further here:

10) The best way e_1 e_2 to help Jack with his assignments is for someone to execute a plan e_1 e_2 to set the alarm on his cell phone so that it will vibrate every hour while he's studying.

[e_1= 'for' ; e_2 = someone; possible to insert 'us/ her/ them']

The 'way' above is described by the first the reduced infinitival clause as 'to help...,' so that infinitive is adjectival. The 'plan' above is described by the next reduced infinitival clause 'to set ...,' so that is also adjectival.

Reduced Infinitival Nominal Clauses (Or 'Nominal Infinitives')

When reduced infinitival clauses are used nominally, we would expect them to fulfill the same NP roles as other nominal clauses. This is correct. They can function as the subject of a sentence, the object of a transitive verb or preposition, the complement of a linking verb or a direct object, or an appositive. Often, the deleted complementizer and subject NP of such a clause can be reconstructed. Here are some examples:

11) (a) They don't like e_1 e_2 to eat more than 2500 calories a day.
(e_1=for,e_2=self (invisible), can also insert visible "us/you/him/her/them, but not *themselves) (direct object)

(b) e_1 e_2 To eat much more than that creates health risks. (e_1 = for, e_2 = anyone) (subject of the IP)

(c) Our hope is e_1 e_2 to protect our physical health. (e_1 = for, e_2 = self (invisible); possible to replace with visible you/him/her/them/*us) (nominal complement of a linking verb)

(d) Research has found a healthy diet to result often in a longer life. (your turn; where are the empty categories?)

In the first sentence, the dependent clause answers the question 'don't like what?' and is therefore the direct object of the main verb 'like.' We also notice that the dependent clause can accept any object NP that does not co-index with the subject NP of the main clause. In the second example sentence, the reduced clause functions as the subject of the main clause and has no context for the meaning of the deleted subject NP. As we have learned to expect, it is then interpreted to mean 'anyone.' In the third sentence, the reduced non-finite clause functions as the complement of the linking verb 'be.' In the final example sentence, we would expect to find a complementizer 'for' after 'found' even though it does not sound helpful at all. So we need to think about that some more.

The fourth sentence is therefore troubling, since it is looks like a complex transitive verb which is supposed to contain the complement of the direct object, as one would expect from verbs such as 'consider' or 'find.' Why, then, is it so unnatural to try to reconstruct the infinitive with a deleted complementizer and subject NP? The sentence, ?'Research has found a healthy diet for them/him/her to result often in a longer life' sounds oddly distorted, which was not true of the other reconstructions of reduced non-finite clauses. Why this strangeness? The infinitive actually points to an entirely different reconstruction: 'Research has found e a healthy diet (for them) 'aux' result often in a longer life.,' where 'e' is the complementizer 'that,' 'for them' is a PP, and 'to' is a replacement for a finite auxiliary such as 'will.' The nonfinite clause seems to be derived from the sentence, 'Research has found that a healthy diet will result often in a longer life.' It seems that such verbs as 'find' allow the finite auxiliary (like 'will') in the dependent clause to be replaced by the infinitive auxiliary 'to.' The occurs without the deletion of the subject of the non-finite clause. What remains seems to be a non-finite IP, which we have not encountered before. We will again, soon, though, when we discuss gerunds. In conclusion, the infinitive in the final example sentence is a non-finite nominal clause, but the infinitive form of the verb does not indicate a deletion of its complementizer and subject NP, which makes it quite different from the other examples in that set.

More Practice Identifying Clauses and Empty Categories

Identify the empty categories in the following sentences and explain whether the clauses (both finite and non-finite) are adjectival, adverbial or nominal.

1. Brent's roommate asked him to go surfing with him and he thought it might be interesting to try.

2. Before Brent started to go to school, he had to live with an aunt and uncle in their home by the sea.

3. The older couple loved to surf and frequently encouraged Brent to go with them.

4. Brent hated to get sandy, and he couldn't stand to rub on sunscreen as often as they wanted him to.

5. Consequently, Brent would walk to the edge of the sand and stop, re

fusing to go any farther and ready to fight all comers.

6. Now that he's older, Brent has overcome his unwillingness to try out new adventures, and he's willing to think about renting a wet suit   and a surf board.

Dangling Infinitives and Other Dangling Modifiers

As always, it can be great fun for the teacher, and can provide a bit of comic relief for the students, to create and explain dangling modifiers. Here are a couple of rather staid examples:

12) (a) e e To maintain a high grade point, exam preparation should always be emphasized.

   (b) e e To prepare well for the Halloween party, a scary costume is very important.

In the first example sentence, 'exam preparation' is trying to maintain good grades. In the second one, 'a scary costume' is going to prepare well for Halloween. Another kind of dangling modifier which occurs regularly in student writing is the PP headed by 'as.' Properly co-indexed, it is used this way: 'e_i As a student, I_i enjoy many extracurricular activities.' 'As' means something close to 'being' in this context, and can be interpreted as having an empty subject NP which is co-indexed with the subject of the main clause: 'e_i being a student, I_i enjoy many ....' This is perhaps easier to see when the co-indexing is absurd:

13) *As a student, extra curricular activities are very important.

This concludes our look at how the mind fills in empty categories that result from the deletion and omission of elements of dependent clauses. Next we'll look at empty categories that result from the movement of phrases from one position to another.

Gerunds and Gerundives

Gerunds and gerundives have the same form as present participles: they are verb forms ending in '-ing.' Gerunds are nominal, and thus serve the grammatical role of noun phrases in a sentence, and gerundives are adjectival, serving the role of adjective phrases. We can see that there are different kinds of gerunds and different grammatical (syntactic) roles that gerunds can have in a sentence. Gerundives are much simpler, since there are not different sorts of gerundives or different syntactic roles in a sentence for them. Let's talk about the simpler gerundive forms first. Here are some examples.

14) Gerundives

   a) It was hard to locate the quickly disappearing jet.

    b) The blossoming trees smelled heavenly.

Gerundives have the characteristics of a VP, but not those of a CP. They do not seem to contain empty categories for a complementizer, NP subject, or auxiliary. We see this when we think about the possibility of expanding the sentence 'It was hard to locate the quickly disappearing jet' to '*It was hard to locate the (for) us to be quickly disappearing jet.' This inability to expand is also logical in a theoretical sense, since the word 'the' acts as the specifier of a noun, in this case 'jet'. This creates a conflict trying to find a slot for a second specifier such as 'for.'

    Another limitation on the expansion of a gerundive is that not every verb type can become a gerundive. In fact, only intransitive verbs can, because there are also no empty categories to the right of the 'V-ing' form. Transitive verbs cannot, as we see in a sentence like '*The planting trees plan was approved.' The 'V-ing' form cannot even be expanded to allow a PP modifiers after it, as in '*The blossoming in April trees smelled heavenly.' Nonetheless, even though the gerundive does not have any empty categories to its left or any room on its right for complementizers or modifiers, it can allow adverbial modifiers which precede it, such as 'quickly' in the first example sentence above. So gerundives are best analyzed as VPs which are functioning adjectivally. We are already fam iliar with NPs that function adjectivally from a much earlier chapter in this course where we encountered compound nouns, and now we see that VPs can also act adjectivally.

    15) The completely nominal gerund

        The annual cutting of Jack's mane attracted a crowd that grew from year to year.

One more 'V-ing' form that we can discuss without much complication is exemplified in the above example of a gerund: 'The annual cutting of Jack's mane produced a crowd that grew from year to year.' This gerund is simply a noun; therefore, it is 'completely nominal.' We can refer to it simply as a **'nominal gerund'**. In more theoretical treatises, it is called, the 'ing-of gerund' (Siegel 2). We notice first that the 'V-ing' form is modified by an adjective 'annual,' and that the adverbial form 'annually' would not be acceptable.

    Second, we notice that 'cut' is a transitive verb and that 'cutting hair' would be a verb-plus-direct-object combination. Here, however, the direct object NP 'mane' is not the object of the verb, but the object of the preposition 'of.' Generalizing from that observation is the conclusion that 'the annual cutting of' is not a verb form at all, but an NP with a specifier 'the,' followed by room for adjectival modifiers preceding the V-ing form. This form is followed by an 'of-PP' complement that eliminates the possibility of having a direct object. So the nominal ("ing-of") gerund is grammatically and syntactically a noun. This particular example even seems to allow plural morphology, 'the many annual cuttings ..., ' although that is probably not the case for all nominal gerunds.

    Now we are ready to discuss two types of more typical gerunds without an 'of-PP'. The collective term for both of these is 'mixed category' structures

(Siegel 2) or 'defective' category grammatical structures (Jung 1) because they have traits of both nouns and verbs.

16)   Mixed category (verbal and nominal) gerunds

a) Joe loves skiing and snowboarding in deep powder.

b) Joe loves (their/Fran's and his) skiing and snowboarding in deep powder.

c) Joe loves (them/Fran and him) skiing and snowboarding in deep powder.

d) Sailing into a hard wind is a reminder of how exciting life can be.

e) (Our) Sailing into a hard wind reminded us that we're really alive.

f) (Us) Sailing into a hard wind reminded everyone that we're really alive.

The first three example sentences of gerunds above show gerunds functioning as the subject of a sentence, and the second three show gerunds functioning as direct objects. In fact, they can also function as prepositional objects ('We worried about getting sick'). In all three roles, they function nominally. In addition, they have many traits that remind us that they are verbal as well. They can be modified by adverbs of manner, but not usually by adjectives: 'Sailing steadily (*steady) into a hard wind... ,' In addition, these adverbs can move around gerunds as they do around verbs: 'Steadily sailing into a hard wind...' But we have expressions like 'It's clear sailing from here on out' where an adjective can modify a gerund. That's because some 'V-ing' forms have become perfectly acceptable as nouns, just as 'carpeting' has. Here we are focusing on the V-ing forms that have not become nouns in their own right.

The example gerund sentences above show us two other characteristics of gerunds. First is that they, like verbs, all have a subject, even if it is not stated. The unstated subject in (a) "Joe loves skiing and snowboarding in deep powder " is 'Joe' because the empty category in front of the verb 'skiing' will co-index with the nearby subject NP 'Joe'. This is also true for sentence (e) if we delete the word 'Our.' Since the word 'us' appears later in the same clause, the empty subject of 'sailing' will co-index with the object NP 'us.'

But what if there's no other NP for the empty subject of the 'V-ing' form to co-index with? That's what we see in the second example sentence below; the empty category takes on the general meaning of 'anyone' or 'everyone.' So the mind supplies a subject for the gerund whether it is stated or not and whether co-indexing is possible or not. This is how those three sentences would be marked with co-indexation.

17)   **The subjects of mixed gerunds** (no other empty categories marked)

a) Joe_i loves e_i skiing and snowboarding in deep powder.

b) Joe$_i$ loves Fran's$_i$ skiing and snowboarding in deep powder.

c) Sam doing aerial twists was quite a sight.

d) **e** Sailing into a hard wind is a reminder of how exciting life can be. (e=anyone)

e) e$_i$ Sailing into a hard wind reminded us$_i$ that we$_i$'re really alive.

The final important piece of information that we see in these sample gerund sentences is that the subject of the 'V-ing' form can be stated in two different ways. First, it can be stated as a possessive form, either as a possessive determiner ('their,' 'his,' 'our') or as a possessive noun ('Fran's'). It is logical to call this form the "**possessive-case gerund**". In some theoretical works, it is called a 'poss-ing' gerund for the same reason (Siegel 1, Jung 2).

The second possibility is that the subject of the gerund can be stated in an object or accusative case, either as an object pronoun ('them,' 'him,' 'us') or noun in the accusative (object) case ('Sam'). This second way of stating a gerund's subject can be captured in the term '**object-case gerund**'. This is easier to remember than the more theoretical term 'acc-ing' gerund (Siegel 1, Jung 2). Perhaps it is just as easy to simply call them 'possessive gerunds' and 'object gerunds.'

One way that the differences between the possessive and accusative/object gerunds can be seen is as a difference in the level of formality. The possessive form is the prescriptive written form, while the accusative (object) form is the more usual informal or spoken form. The spoken form of the gerund clause genuinely looks like a clause with a subject and verb, whereas the written form looks like a noun phrase with verb phrase embedded inside it.

Both types of the possessive and accusative gerunds seem to have all of the characteristics of a verb phrase. The auxiliary is always an empty category. In the written form of the gerund including the parenthetical material, there is a specifier slot to the left of the empty auxiliary in the gerund. In that specifier slot, we see a possessive determiner (our, their...), or a possessive noun, such as 'Joe's,' as appropriate. In order to see if both the formal forms of the gerund should be considered a type of clause, we would need to consider the specifier as a subject of the gerund, in just the same role as specifiers in inflected clauses (IPs). Oddly enough, there does not seem to be an empty category for a deleted complementizer in the poss-ing gerund clauses.

18) Possessive gerunds with empty categories lexicalized

a) Mary loves e skiing in deep powder.

b) Mary loves their/Scott's skiing in deep powder.

c) *Mary loves for Scott's skiing in deep powder.

We can accept a sentence like 'Mary loves their/Scott's skiing in deep powder,' but a sentence like *'Mary loves for Scott's skiing in deep powder' seems completely distorted. The difference here seems to be that possessive gerunds do not have complementizers that can be lexicalized the way other non-finite clauses do. Instead of CPs, should they then be considered IPs?

This is something of a puzzle. We generally try to lexicalize non-finite clauses with the non-finite complementizer 'for,' and the finite clauses with the finite complementizer 'that.' With possessive gerunds, that separation leads to the conclusion that gerund clauses are IPs but not CPs. That would make them the only dependent clauses in English that are not CPs.

This conclusion does not have a parallel for the accusative gerunds. If we look at accusative gerunds, their empty categories can be lexicalized to expanded to a complete CP. But there is one cautionary note as we start looking at empty categories to lexicalize. A sentence like 'For me, skiing is like going to heaven' does not create a CP (complementizer+specifier+VP) from the gerund, because 'for me' in that example is really a PP that is used adverbially. This we can see by the ability of 'for me' to occupy either a sentence-medial or sentence-final position, as in 'Skiing, for me, is like going to heaven'.

If we start with 'Skiing is like going to heaven,' however, another possible string of empty categories presents itself. This possibility would have an extra empty category: 'e e e e Skiing is like going to heaven.' The lexicalization would be as follows: 'For (someone/anyone) to be skiing is like going to heaven.' The first area to check is meaning – does the lexicalization distort the meaning of the original 'V-ing' form? If we think it does change the meaning, then this approach should be thrown out. If it doesn't, we can proceed to see if other subjects can be used, such as 'him' or 'Fran' or 'us'

19) Accusative/object gerunds with all empty categories marked

(a) Joe loves e Fran and him e e skiing and snowboarding in deep powder.

(b) e Us e e sailing into a hard wind reminded everyone that we're really alive.

Here is another example: 'For us to be using the playground properly is important (for others). The 'for others' PP at the end of the sentence helps show that the 'for us' at the beginning of the sentence is not a PP, but a complementizer-specifier combination. That is, 'for' is the head of the CP and 'us' is the specifier of the embedded IP. So this approach of looking at an accusative gerund to see if it is a CP seems to have promise. Looking at the complementary possessive gerund, however, is less promising: '*For their/Fran's to be using the playground properly is important (for others).

Thus we have mixed results for the two types of mixed category structures. What we have discovered is that an acc-ing gerund would need two auxiliaries inserted lexically to create a CP. The first auxiliary 'to' is non-finite as required by the non-finite complementizer 'for,' and the second progressive auxilliary 'be' is required to introduce the verb form with the progressive suffix '-ing.' At that point, the 'V-ing' form of the verb is no longer functioning nominally by itself, but is embedded (as a VP) inside a CP that is itself being used nominally, in this case as the subject of the sentence. Where the complementizer and double auxiliary are empty categories, the 'V-ing' form looks like it is functioning nominally by itself.

The possessive gerund can be analyzed as an IP if the possessive form is viewed as the specifier of the IP. This is somewhat counter-intuitive, since possessive determiners and possessive nouns are specifiers for NPs in every other context. So we leave the possessive as a puzzle which allows two approaches – either an NP with all the characteristics of a VP or an IP with a very odd specifier. In fact, we should not even call it an NP, but rather a DP (determiner phrase) with an embedded VP.

In sum, the split between formal, written English and informal spoken English is inconvenient in this analysis, but such a split seems to be indicated by the data. The informal object-case form shows more clearly how the mind can process the gerund as a clause. The formal possessive-case gerund is truly a mysterious beast grammatically: a DP with an embedded VP. This does not infer any criticism of the formal way of writing gerunds. They are what they are. Rather, mastery of the formal possessive way of writing gerunds can be seen as another area where students can write in a formal style that shows off the effects of a good education.

Chapter 7: Movement, Transformations, and Empty Categories

So far, we have seen how **empty categories** result from **auxiliary fronting** and **tense hopping** within the sentence. Now, we are ready to look at more of the ways movement of words and phrases creates empty categories in clauses. Phrases and clauses are the grammatical units (constituents) which are moved most commonly in sentences, but the way contractions move onto the previous word gives us an example of the movement of single words that are not constituents. This chapter divides movement into two types: those which all native speakers do automatically, and those which are optional and usually used for reasons of style. The first are sometimes called **syntactic movement**s or **obligatory movements**. The two we have already looked at - auxiliary fronting and tense hopping - are examples of syntactic movement.

Eight Obligatory Transformations

This section will briefly discuss nine types of syntactic movement. Such movement results in so-called **transformations** of the sentence. Movement always leaves a trace in the original position of the moved constituent. These traces are also called empty categories, as we discussed in chapter four.

One of Noam Chomsky's memorable examples of our mind's ability to keep track of traces of movement is the '**wanna' construction** in conversational English. Some students may not have this construction in their mental grammar, in which case, they will have to listen to and believe the grammaticality judgments of their fellow students whose dialects do have a 'wanna' construction. We'll start with two standard wh-questions, each paired with the same sentence in the form of an **echo question** (where the heavy stress is italicized):

1) (a) Who do you want to see?

    (b) You want to see *who*?

    (c) Who do you want to see you?

(d) You want *who* to see you?

For those whose dialects have the 'wanna' construction, there is an interesting difference between the top and bottom pairs of sentences: 'wanna' works fine for the first sentence: 'Who do you wanna see?', but it is impossible for the third sentence, * 'Who do you wanna see you?' Why should that be? As we should suspect, it is because the mind has kept track of the movement of 'who' from its original place as shown in the echo sentences. Here is the placement of the empty categories from the movement of 'who.'

2)   (a) Who do you want to see e ?

       (b) Who do you want e to see you?

As we can see, the two words 'want' and 'to' are next to each other in the first sentence, so they can combine into 'wanna.' But in the second sentence, we see that there is an 'e' between the two words 'want' and 'to,' so they are not next to each other and cannot combine into 'wanna.' It's only because the mind has made note of the place where the word 'who' moved from that 'wanna' cannot be produced in the second sentence. As long as the trace (or empty category) is between the 'want' and the 'to,' they are not next to each other, and they cannot combine.

Tense Hopping

Even though English verb forms express past, present, and future time, there are, strictly speaking, only two **verb tenses** in English: past and present. Future time is most often indicated by using the modal 'will,' which doesn't count as a verb tense, since it's not part of the verb itself. When there is a visible (or audible) auxiliary in the auxiliary position, it carries either past or present tense, and that tense doesn't have to 'hop' anywhere. It just attaches to the visible auxiliary.

Tense is quite obvious for the two aspectual auxiliaries (be and have) and the one dummy auxiliary (do), since they are very clearly inflected (present: am, is, are, has, have, do, does; past: was, were, had, did). But what about the modal auxiliaries, do they also carry tense? Yes, they do, at least historically, because all but one of them belong to pairs representing a present and a past form: shall/should, may/might, will/would, can/could, and the loner 'must,' which is historically a past tense of the Old English verb 'moten.'

So the tense only has to 'hop' when there is no visible auxiliary, which means it only happens for the simple present and simple past tenses, and only when there is no emphatic meaning and no negation (these two are discussed in the next section). One typical example is from our discussion of Sentence (IP) structure above.

3)   Tense hopping by the third-person 's' of the simple present tense

Edward -s grow tomatoes as large as grapefruit.

4)   Do-support instead of tense hopping

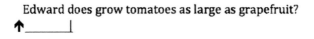

Edward -s grow tomatoes as large as grapefruit.
              ↑
              do

5)   Auxiliary fronting for a yes-no question

Edward does grow tomatoes as large as grapefruit?
↑_____|

When no do-support is needed, the suffix '-s' moves, as shown in 3) above, from the auxiliary position onto the main verb 'grow' and leaves an empty category/trace in the auxiliary position, as shown here:

6)   Edward e grows tomatoes as large as grapefruit.

It may be odd to realize, but in these two tenses, simple present and simple past, the head of the IP, that is, the head of the whole sentence, is an empty category. English sentence structure is odd enough that a number of different approaches all give useful perspectives.

Negative and Emphatic Sentences

The sentence immediately above would not show any sign of tense hopping if it were either emphatic or negative, as seen in the two following sentences:

7)   (a) Edward does grow tomatoes as large as grapefruit.

(b) Edward does not grow tomatoes as large as grapefruit.

(c) Edward did grow tomatoes as large as grapefruit.

(d) Edward did not grow tomatoes as large as grapefruit.

The 'dummy do' auxiliary is inserted in both the emphatic and negative forms of the simple present and the simple past tense, as shown above. So it turns out, for the only two tenses where we would normally expect to see **tense-hopping,** that it does not always happen because the 'dummy do' auxiliary allows the tense, number, and person information to be expressed in the auxiliary position with no movement. For these insertions of the 'dummy do', there are no empty categories to mark. We note here also that the negative particle is always positioned between the auxiliary and the main verb. In strings of multiple auxiliaries, it follows the first auxiliary, as in this sentence

8)   They should (not) have *(not) been *(not) doing that.

This insistence by 'not' to occupy the position directly after the main auxiliary is further evidence that the aux position is a unique position in the structure of English sentences. As we said earlier, the sentence has three main parts, not two.

Yes/no Questions

Auxiliary fronting is the hallmark of English yes/no questions, as demonstrated in a previous section. One important point here is that main verbs cannot be fronted, but only auxiliaries can, as seen in the contrast between the two examples here:

9)   (a) Did you e arrive yesterday?

       (b) *Arrived you e yesterday?

The fronted auxiliary is in a position outside of the IP where it started. This position is the head of CP, the head of the complementizer phrase. The fronted auxiliary is in a position outside of the IP where it started. This position is the head of CP, the head of the complementizer phrase. Here we notice that a question is an example of a CP that is not a dependent clause. Up until now, all the CPs that we have discussed have been dependent clauses. Now we see a CP which is a complete sentence by itself. This is somewhat remniscent of the discussion about non-finite clauses where we noticed that these particular IPs that were not independent sentences but, rather, dependent clauses because they have no tense. Here we have the converse situation: an independent CP.

　　As we noted above, the inability to raise main verbs in English is a relatively recent historical development which contrasts with other modern Germanic languages, where main verbs are still fronted in yes/no questions. There is only one exception left in English, which we'll look at in the next section. It is a lone remnant of that older Germanic syntactic fronting of the main verb.

'Be' Raising (Or Fronting)

In all varieties of American English, and many other varieties elsewhere, the verb 'be' is the only main verb that does not need any 'do' support for yes/no questions. When 'be' is the main verb, it can be fronted just the way auxiliaries can, as we see in the first two example sentences here:

10)   (a) They are students.

        (b) Are they students?

        (c) ! Do they be students?

        (d) Baa, baa, black sheep, have you any wool?

(e) ! Baa, baa, black sheep, do you have any wool?

The third example sentence above shows us how we should expect the English language to develop if it continues to change until 'be' joins the ranks of all the other main verbs in English. In the United Kingdom, there are still dialects where 'have' as a main verb can also be fronted. They are sometimes referred to as 'baa, baa black sheep' varieties of English (Radford). In those varieties, the use of do-support, as in the final sentence above, gives as clear a feeling of unacceptability as the use of do-support for the main verb 'be' in the third example above. In fact, there are some non-standard varieties of English where the third sentence is already acceptable. These varieties of English are acting as pioneers along the way to remove the final vestige of Germanic **main-verb fronting**.

But what's '**be-raising**' (or '**be-fronting**')? In a sense it's the opposite of tense hopping. Looking back at the first sentence in the previous set, we have two options where we can mark the empty category.

11)   Two ways to assign an empty category for main-verb 'be'

(a) They e are students.

(b) They are e students.

The first option represents a tense-hopping view of the inflected (finite) verb, which we have discussed above. The second view represents 'be-raising' or 'be fronting.' The reason that the second view is preferable is that is gives us a more unified explanation for the formation of yes/no questions. If we assume that the main verb 'be' is raised/fronted from the main verb position to the auxiliary position to pick up the tense, number, person information from the auxiliary, then it is in a normal (auxiliary) position to be further fronted for a yes/no question. If it is in the tense-hopping position indicated in the first sentence, then we would have to ask why other main verbs cannot also be fronted in yes/no question formation, as in the **baa, baa, black sheep varieties** and as in modern Germanic languages. So by saying that the main verb 'be' is in a different position from every other main verb in English, we have a more logical and satisfying way to explain why 'be' is so exceptional. We can also anticipate how this exception status of 'be' may change in the next decades or centuries.

Wh-questions (Or Information Questions)

Even though we have encountered the various wh-words in three different lexical categories as interrogative pronouns, interrogative determiners, and interrogative adverbs, all three of these lexical categories function very similarly in forming wh-questions. Two movements are involved in the formation of wh-questions: **auxiliary fronting** and then **wh-fronting**. The wh-word is fronted to the specifier position in front of the fronted auxiliary, which is in the head position. In order to see where the wh-word begins its movement, perhaps we should look for a moment at **echo questions**. We saw a couple of examples of echo questions in the

'What difference does it make?' section at the beginning of this chapter. My favorite scenario to introduce this type of question is to imagine that it is an evening in the living room of a house where an overwhelmed parent is reacting with considerable disbelief to the expressed hopes of a high school-age son or daughter:

12) **Echo questions**

    (a) You want to go see *who*?

    (b) You're going to drive a *what*?

    (c) You're planning to go *where*?

    (d) *Who* will be hosting the after-party?

    (e) You'll be swimming in *whose pool*?

    (f) You'll probably be home *when*?

Although these are called **echo questions,** they are not really questions at all in that they are also requests (or demands) for a repetition or reiteration of information that has already been expressed, but which is difficult to process immediately. In all of the examples above, the wh-word and the associated wh-phrase are in the position they must occupy before being fronted for a standard information question. We note that not only has the Wh-word not been fronted, but the auxiliary has not been fronted in echo questions either. Only the fourth example seems to have normal question order. This is exceptional and will need our attention after we look at the more usual examples.

    We can take any of the other examples above and turn it into a standard wh-question. Let's look at another example, this time with arrows to show movement. Although the movement of the auxiliary is not marked in the sentence below, we should recognize that the past tense was picked up by the auxiliary 'do' in the position just before the verb 'hit' and fronted to the position marked by the auxiliary 'did'.

13) Possible wh-word movements in wh-questions

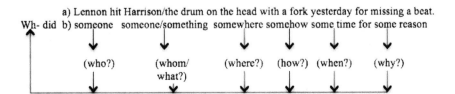

Now, if the fronted auxiliary is in the position of the head of the CP, which we think to be the case, what is the position of the wh-word called? Thinking back to the structure of an IP, there is only one non-modifier position to the left of the head of IP: its specifier position. So we see that the CP is the third of three types of phrases that need to have specifier positions to explain their structure: NPs, IPs, and CPs.

It may already be clear from the italics in the set of echo questions, but just to make sure, let's notice that the two-word 'whose'-NP is fronted as a unit. This is what we can always expect from the three wh-determiners. Either the NP or the PP including the NP is acceptable for fronting. Whether the preposition 'in' is considered part of the unit to be fronted is entirely a matter of style, in that it can be moved, or it can be left. To say that it is a matter of styled and not of grammar is not to say that style doesn't matter, only that they're not the same.

It's tempting to look at the fourth example sentence in the set of echo questions and say that it's already fine with no movement. This is a recurring question with wh-words in subject position. Should we say that the same movements take place in the formation of all types of wh-questions except those whose wh-NP function as subject pronouns? The answer for most theoreticians is negative. It's much more logical to expect that the same movements take place uniformly for any given part of the grammar. So what does that mean for the question, '*Who* will be hosting the after-party?'? Let's see what the normal two movements will produce:

14) Vacuous fronting of subject 'who'

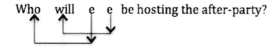

So this remains exceptional, since the arrows showing movement are not supposed to cross. We have a choice here between either graphic messiness or inconsistent grammar rules, and it's probably easier for our analysis to assume movement to work the same way in both what is visible and what is not visible or audible. So the ugliness of the arrows is the price of saying that the grammar probably is consistent, even where we don't see that. This kind of movement is called '**vacuous movement**,' since we cannot see it, and because it doesn't seem to serve any other purpose than make the grammar consistent. This is not the only grammatical phenomenon that we will need this reasoning and this consistency. We will see it again below in the section on the **vacuous movement** of **subject relative pronouns**.

Indirect Questions

Indirect questions are exact paraphrases of questions. When a question is passed from one person to another, we change it in very predictable ways, usually with any of a number of possible introductory main clauses, such as seen in these examples:

15) Indirect Questions

  (a) They asked who you want to see.

  (b) I'm wondering what you're going to drive.

  (c) No one has mentioned where you're planning to go.

  (d) Please ask who will be hosting the after-party.

  (e) Is it clear yet whose pool you'll be swimming in?

  (f) Let me see if I understand when you'll probably be home.

  (g) I'm not sure whether/if I'll let you attend.

The first six sentences are indirect wh-questions, and the final one is an indirect yes/no question. The fifth sentence is an example of an indirect question embedded inside a direct question. The sixth question has an indirect wh-question (with 'when') embedded inside another indirect question ('do I understand'). For indirect yes/no questions, the wh-word is 'whether' or 'if.' We have discussed the difference between 'if' and 'whether' earlier; only 'whether' can introduce a non-finite indirect question such as 'I'm not sure whether/*if to attend.'

The main syntactic movement that we notice in indirect questions is the fronting of the wh-word. The auxiliary inside the indirect question is not fronted. This is the main difference between direct and indirect questions. As we did in the previous section, we will assume that the subject-wh-NP in sentence four has moved invisibly ('**vacuously**') from the specifier of its IP to the specifier of its CP.

Relative Clauses and Vacuous Movement of Subject Relative Pronouns

Relative pronouns, relative adverbs, and relative determiners in general have many of the syntactic properties of other wh-words when used as interrogative pronouns, interrogative adverbs, and interrogative determiners. This is seen most easily in their fronting movement to the specifier position of their CP. A couple of examples with arrows will give us some usable visual images.

16) Empty categories in relative clauses

  (a) There's the hospital where / I was born e (there).

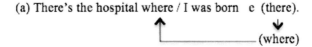

(b) This is the week (when) the big decision will be made e.

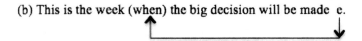

(c) There is a reason (why) I should be at home this evening e.

(d) That's the man <u>whose house</u> we visited e last week.

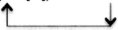

(e) Those are the people (who[m]) we saw   e yesterday.

(f) That's the dog (that/which) e greeted us so moistly today.

In each of the above relative clauses, we can determine where the wh-word was originially located by inserting a phrase which would complete the relative clause and make it into a sentence which reflects the wh-word. Here are examples of that information showing where each wh-word originated.

17) Origin of movement in relative clauses

   (a) I was born e (in that hospital).

   (b) The big decision will be made e (this week).

   (c) I should be at home this evening e (for some reason).

   (d) We visited e (that man's house – or – his house) yesterday.

   (e) We saw e (those people) yesterday.

   (f) (That dog) e greeted us so moistly yesterday.

Knowing where the wh-word originated is half of the analytic problem. We have already noticed that wh-words in questions move to the position of the specifier of CP, so that will be our working hypothesis for relative clauses also. In addition, we notice that the sixth example in each of the two sets above shows the assumption that relative pronouns which are the subject of their clause are also presumed to move – vacuously – to the specifier position of CP, just like all the other wh-words. This is the **vacuous movement of subject relative pronouns.**

Germanic Verb-second/ English Aux-second

Just as there is only one remnant of Germanic main-verb fronting for yes/no questions (the verb 'be'), so there is also only a remnant left of a rather curious Germanic phenomenon in the word order of main clauses— the inflected verb or auxiliary is always the second major constituent in the sentence. This is called 'verb second' or 'V2.' The unsurprising part of this phenomenon is a sentence like this: 'Hans leapt from the high tower last evening.' Here the verb is in second position right after the subject. No surprise. The surprising part of Germanic verb-second grammar comes when we move the phrase 'last evening' to the front of the sentence, forcing the verb to follow it in second position, and driving the subject to a position after the verb: 'Last evening leapt Hans from the high tower.' So wait a minute - are we supposed to believe that English does something like that? Well, to a limited extent, yes. Let's start by filling in the blanks in the following sentences, following the story after Hans leapt from the tower.

18) Aux-second examples

   (a) I have never been so disappointed in Hans. Never ____ done anything so stupid.

   (b) He needs to heal pretty fast, too, since the ball is coming. Rarely _____ ever seen us out together.

   (c) If he doesn't apologize soon, we're done.

   (d) Only if he apologizes tomorrow ___ ever talk with him again.

Does 'has he' fit the first blank, 'have others/has anyone' the second, and 'will I' the third? If not, your dialect has experienced a further change in English grammar as it moves away from its Germanic roots. If so, V2 is alive and well in your dialect, although it may not last for too many more generations. We notice that main verbs cannot be fronted in English, so the English version of V2 is really aux-second.

   In the first two sentences, it's quite easy to see that a single negative adverb can trigger V2/aux-second in English. The third sentence, however, reveals that sometimes the grammatical unit that triggers V2/aux-second is an entire clause.

   In order to see the movement, it's useful to write in the empty categories:

19) Movement in English Aux-second

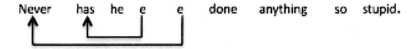

Just for the record, in Shakespeare's English, we can find examples much closer to the modern Germanic languages:

20) "... in the dark/Groped I to find out them; ..." (Hamlet, Act V, Scene II, line 16)

For non-native and early elementary speakers of English, V2/aux-second in English will definitely sound odd and unfamiliar. As speakers become familiar with **stylistic** (not obligatory) **fronting**, they will encounter V2/aux-second. Stylistic fronting is discussed in the next section.

Practice Identifying Syntactic Transformations

Identify the type(s) of transformation that have/has occurred in the following sentences.

1. Were these the international students who Jeff met yesterday?

2. He was wondering what he should do about their passport problems.

3. Actually, he was not sure if he could do anything to help them.

4. Only in the movies do you hear such an improbable tale.

5. The students who went through it, though, were very discouraged.

6. They couldn't change their money, so they needed to borrow some, but they might be deported, which made it hard to borrow money.

Eleven Stylistic Transformations

Most often, stylistic transformations are meant to move information away from the front of the sentence, so that the reader or listener has a better chance of focusing attention on it. The opposite direction is used for some few stylistic transformations: they move phrases to the front of the sentence, usually for variety and a change of pace. The reason to move information away from the front of the sentence is cognitive or psychological. In most cultures and most interactions, older information is presented first and newer information is presented after setting the stage with the more familiar information. We recognize this from longer units of discourse, such as speeches, lectures and essays. And this pattern is also normal at the sentence level. Of the seven stylistic transformations discussed in this section, five function to move the informational focus away from the beginning of the sentence. Two do the opposite, so we expect that the information fronted will be familiar or introductory.

As we mentioned earlier, these transformations are not obligatory and are used by writers and speakers according to their sense of style. In terms of linguistic analysis, we are often interested in seeing where the movement originated and where it ended up. Let's take a simple sentence with a readily identifiable focus, add in some less crucial information and see what each of the transformations will do to it.

Contraction of 'Not'

This stylistic movement function to change the formality of a sentence more than to move information to the front or back of the sentence. The negative particle 'not' can be shortened to the vowelless syllable 'nt' which attaches (technically: '**cliticizes**') to the auxiliary. We noted in the section above that 'not' always follows the auxiliary. When cliticized to the auxiliary, it can be carried with the auxiliary in a movement such as auxiliary fronting:

21) Shouldn't we e e have already arrived?

We should notice here that there is one empty category left from the movement of the negative particle onto the auxiliary, and another empty category due to the auxiliary fronting. Of all the contractions possible, only 'not' contractions front with the auxiliary. This combined movement of contracted forms of 'not' does not pattern the same as forms such as 'I'm,' 'I've,' 'you'd,' 'she's,' and 'they're.' It may be enough for now to show that the **clitic** explanation for 'not' does not work for the contracted form such as 'who's' in the echo question 'You're sure that who's winning?' In this sentence the contracted form 'who's' cannot be moved when a normal wh-question is created: *'Who's are you sure e e winning?' We will skip a discussion of the structural aspects of the contracted forms of the auxiliaries 'be' and 'have,' since that would involve elements of syntactic theory that go beyond the scope of this Guide. So our take-away from this discussion is that the contracted form 'n't' cliticizes onto the auxiliary and can move with it, but that contractions of other words do not function this same way.

'There' and 'It' Insertion

In introducing this transformation, let's start with the sentence, 'A mouse is under your chair.' The focus of our attention is pretty clearly the mouse and not the chair, but the 'mouse' is at the beginning of the sentence, where it's harder to focus on. This is because when the focus of a statement is at the very beginning of the statement, our listeners/readers may miss that information if they are even slightly distracted when the utterance or statement starts. We are well advised to move items a little away from the beginning of a statement if we want to put them more clearly in focus. In the case of our 'mouse' sentence, **'there' insertion** can move the information just far enough away from on the beginning of the sentence to allow for clearer focus, as shown here:

22) A mouse is under your chair. + 'there' insertion -> There e is a mouse under your chair.

You can verify the effectiveness of moving the focus a little away from the beginning of the sentence by (mentally?) screaming the two sentences as if the information was very shocking. The focus is more clearly on the NP 'a mouse' if it's preceded by 'there is.' We could easily insert arrows to trace this movement. It is important to note that the word 'there' here is not the same as the adverb, as in 'He's over there.' Here it is a replacement for the subject NP, so should probably be considered an odd sort of pronoun. Since it has no antecedent, it does not qualify as a normal pronoun, but in the sentence it is functioning similarly to an NP.

If the subject of the sentence is a clause or verb phrase, rather than a noun phrase, the word 'it' is used instead of 'there,' as in this example:

23) To go skiing is getting more expensive + 'it' insertion-> It e is getting more expensive to go skiing.

It-insertion moves the longish subject to the end of the sentence. There is another transformation which achieves the same purpose without inserting 'it;' please read on.

Extraposition

When the subject, or part of one, is moved toward the end of the sentence without the insertion of 'it' or 'there,' the movement is called '**extraposition**'. Extraposition is especially useful for shortening long, awkward subject Nps:

24) An article about the great sportsmanship shown by our college athletes was published in the Times last Tuesday.

+ extraposition of part of the long NP subject

-> An article e was published in the Times last Tuesday about the great sportsmanship shown by our college athletes.

In this sentence, we notice that it is also appropriate to mark the empty category resulting from the movement.

Subject-complement Inversion

Subject-complement inversion involves the reversal of the subject and complement around the linking verb 'be.' This is similar in some ways to the previous two examples of extraposition.

25) Skiing is my favorite hobby

+ extraposition of a one-word subject

-> My favorite hobby e is e skiing.

Showing this movement with arrows would be a little messy, and, more significantly, it would also violate the principle of more sophisticated versions of transformational grammar that such movement arrows may never cross one another. In this somewhat less sophisticated approach, arrows of movement will have to be allowed to cross, as subject-complement inversion would require.

Heavy Complement Shift

Up to now, we have been talking about moving the subject of a sentence. But long, awkward direct objects may also be extraposed when there is a modifying, as seen in the first pair of sentences below. The second pair of sentences gives a good counter-example:

26) (a) The police were able to run down the drug smugglers from New York, Miami, and Boston in only a week.   *heavy comp. shift*

+ heavy complement shift

-> The police were able to run down e in only a week the drug smugglers from New York, Miami, and Boston.

(b) The police were able to find Joey and Hank in only a week. + heavy complement shift

-> *The police were able to find e in only a week Joey and Hank.

The unacceptability of heavy complement shift in the second example sentence demonstrates that the heavy complement shift is only available only for truly heavy complements, and not for just any complement. This restriction on heavy complement shift is due to the basic preference in English for a direct object to immediately follow its verb. What is 'truly heavy' depends to a certain extent on the writer's native-speaker intuition and sense of style more than any hard-and-fast rule.

Clefting

Either clefting a sentence or pseudo-clefting a sentence divides it into two parts in ways that can be used to adjust the focus. Clefting is the more versatile of the two transformations, as the following example sentences show.

27) Examples of cleft sentences

(a) Jasper will be eating dinner with us today to show us his photos.

(b) It's today that Jasper will be eating dinner with us e to show us his photos.

(c) It's with us that Jasper will be eating e dinner today to show us his photos.

(d) It's Jasper who/that e will be eating dinner with us today to show us his photos.

(e) It's his photos that Jasper will be eating dinner with us today to show us e . (You're right. This one's not up to par. It had to move away from its verb 'show' and lost its context).

(f) It's to show us his photos that Jasper will be eating dinner with us today.

As we see, the construction is based on a sentence –initial 'It's,' which introduces the item that is in focus, followed by a dependent clause signaled by 'that,' or, sometimes, 'who.'

Wh-clefting or Pseudo-clefting

Wh-clefting begins with a wh-word which introduces the background information, followed by a form of the verb 'be' which introduces the item in focus, as seen in the example sentence here:

28) (a) We're looking for a black spaniel wearing a red flea collar.

(b) What we're looking for is a black spaniel wearing a red flea collar.

(c) What the black spaniel is wearing is a red flea collar.

This construction needs a noun phrase or nominal clause for the focus item, which reduces its versatility. Here's an example with a nominal clause in focus:

29) (a) That you paid for the gift in cash shocked me.

(b) What shocked me is that you paid for the gift in cash.

The way wh-clefting puts the item in focus at the end of the sentence can be seen as its main attraction as a stylistic transformation

Topicalization

In an apparent violation of the general usefulness of having new information towards the end of a sentence, topicalization allows the fronting of a direct or prepositional object into the first position of a sentence, as shown in the example sentences:

30) Beethoven, I'm not too keen on e, but Bach, I love e.

This transformation is probably most appropriate when some preceding context introduces the general topics, making this focal information a follow-up comment.

Locative, Temporal, and Causal Fronting

Another instance of moving information to the front of the sentence for variety is the fronting of prepositional phrases or adverbial clauses regarding time, place or causation.

Prepositional phrases are often fronted this way:

31) (a) In the spring, all of nature seems to come alive e.

(b) At our house, we try not to let TV interfere with meal times e.

(c) Because of the snow, we stayed home from school e.

Adverbial clauses can be fronted in the same manner:

32) (a) When we are hungry, we enjoy your cooking twice as much e.

(b) Wherever I go, I find people to be helpful and friendly e.

(c) Since we were already so late, we decided not to hurry e.

In each of the above examples of stylistic fronting, a comma marks the element that was fronted. Forgetting to mark such a moved element is the most common writing error by college students (Conners and Lunsford 400).
 Exclamatives
Exclamatives are expressions such as the following:

33) (a) What an awesome day we had yesterday!

(b) What a privilege it is to meet you!

(c) How fortunate they are to have survived the earthquake!

We notice that they are characterized by with either a fronted 'what-NP' or a 'how-AP.' Additionally, the auxiliary is not fronted. Each of these is a transformation of a related declarative statement, such as the following untransformed versions of the previous example sentences:

34) (a) We had [such an awesome day] yesterday!

(b) It is [such a privilege] to meet you!

(c) They are [so fortunate] to have survived the earthquake!

We notice in the above set that the phrases in brackets in the top two are NPs and that the third sentence has an AP in brackets. The wh-words in the exclamatives represent the qualifiers in the corresponding declarative sentences, or in this case we could easily call the wh-word an 'intensifier/qualifier' since that is its role. This fronting movement is similar in every way to the fronting a prepositional phrase.

Passivization

Passivization also moves an element, in this case a direct or indirect object, to the front of a sentence. The fronted item then becomes the subject of the transformed sentence. The original subject is either deleted or put in a prepositional 'by' phrase. Passivization is by far the most complicated of the syntactic transformations described in this section. That's why it's the last one to be discussed. First let's start with a somewhat gentle introduction. Passive sentences are always produced from transitive sentences, because the object of the transitive sentence becomes the subject of the passive sentence, as shown in this example:

35) (a) sentence in active voice: The ape has eaten the banana.

(b) sentence in passive voice: The banana has been eaten (by the ape).

Since they have no direct objects, sentences with linking verbs, prepositional verbs, and intransitive verbs cannot form passive sentences. We see in the above example how the subject of the active sentence may simply disappear, since the 'by-PP' containing the active subject is optional in passive sentences. Ditransitive sentences have two objects and each of them can become the subject of a passive transformation of the active sentence:

36) (a) active voice: My Dad gave my Mom a big bouquet of flowers for her birthday.

(b) first passive: My Mom was given a big bouquet of flowers for her birthday (by my Dad).

(c) second passive: A big bouquet of flowers was given to my Mom for her birthday (by my Dad).

Outlining the several movements, deletions, and insertions in the transformation from active voice to passive voice is actually beyond the scope of this Guide, so this will be done in a list form with very little explanation.

37) Steps in a typical passive transformation from active to passive voice

Active sentence: the ape has eaten the bananas.

Passive sentence: the banana have been eaten by the ape.

Empty categories and insertions:

The bananas$_2$ e$_1$ have been {= be+past participle} eaten e$_2$ by the ape$_1$.

Steps in the transformation:

1. The subject of the transitive sentence is deleted, leaving e$_1$.

2. (2a) The preposition 'by' is introduced at the end of the sentence.

(2b) The subject NP_1 moves to the object of the preposition 'by'(and object case is assigned), which leaves e_1. (2a and 2b are optional, since the 'by+NP' can simply be left out)

3. The object NP_2 moves to subject position (and subject case is assigned), which leaves e_2. It's unclear if e_1 still remains in our mental construct, but it should theoretically.

4. The auxiliary's number has to match the number of the new subject and the tense of the original sentence. Here, the subject of the passive sentence is plural and the tense is present, so the auxiliary also becomes plural and remains in the present tense ('have').

5. The passive auxiliary 'be' is inserted into the position after the auxiliary verb 'have,' leaving the first auxiliary unaffected.

6. The passive 'be' auxiliary matches the form of the original verb 'eaten' and also becomes a past participle, leaving no observable   trace of the original 'be.'

If the active sentence is only a little different, the process looks distinctly different, which gives further insight into the reasons for calling the structural mechanics of this transformation beyond the scope of this Guide.

38) Steps in a passive transformation with a pronoun NP

Active sentence: He did eat the bananas.

Passive sentence: the bananas were eaten by him.

Empty categories and insertions:

> The bananas$_2$ e_1 were {= be+past+plural} eaten {eat + e_3 +p.parti ciple} e_2 by him$_1$.

Steps in the transformation:

1. The subject of the transitive sentence is deleted, leaving e_1.

2. (2a) The preposition 'by' is introduced at the end of the sentence.

(2b) The subject NP_1 moves to the object of P position (and object case is assigned, turning 'he' into 'him'), which leaves e_1. It's clear that a direct object pronoun, such as 'them,' in a passive transformation would have to become a subject pronoun for the same reason.

3. The object NP₂ moves to subject position (and subject case is assigned), which leaves e₂. It's unclear if e₁ still remains in our mental construct.

4. The passive auxiliary 'be' is inserted into the position of the auxiliary verb 'did,' taking over the tense (past), person (third) and adjusting to the number (plural) of the new subject, producing 'were'. The dummy auxiliary 'do' is deleted, leaving no observable trace.

5. The main verb is replaced by the past participle form, again leaving no observable trace.

The lack of traces of movement and the wholesale replacement of some constituents of the sentence do not fit the approach to grammar outlined in the rest of this Guide, which is reason enough to leave this topic and move on to areas that we can get a better grip on. But perhaps if we ignore the empty categories, we can discover a reasonable-sounding way to explain passivization.

  39) Graphic representation of passivization (simplified)

    The ape e ate the bananas.

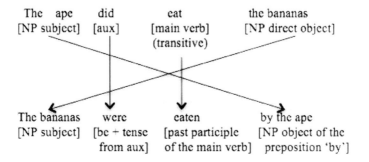

    The ape   did   eat   the bananas
    [NP subject] [aux]   [main verb]   [NP direct object]
                          (transitive)

    The bananas   were   eaten   by the ape
    [NP subject] [be + tense [past participle   [NP object of the
                 from aux] of the main verb] preposition 'by']

If we do not worry about the problem of subject and object case in pronouns and combine movements and do some sleight-of-hand insertions with 'be' and 'by,' we can describe the process as three steps:

  1) isolate the tense (by putting it on the dummy auxiliary 'do' if necessary) and move it to the newly inserted auxiliary 'be',
  2) exchange the positions of the direct object NP and the subject NP, putting the subject NP at the end of the sentence as the object of the preposition 'by'.
  3) put the main verb in its past participle form.

As we leave this topic, then, let's see what we can take away from this discussion. First, passivization can only occur when the active sentence is transitive, ditransitive, or complex transitive. Second, ditransitive sentences usually have two possible passive transformations. Third, the passive transformation is not really a two- or three-step process as it is often described in grammar books, handbooks, and textbooks.

Practice Identifying Stylistic Movement

Describe the stylistic movements involved in the following sentences

1. If the situation were simpler, Jeff would loan them some money.
2. Lack of money he considered a poor reason to get all upset.
3. What they really needed were temporary travel documents.
4. That would keep them from being deported.
5. Perhaps it is publicity in the local papers about their problem that they need.
6. It would help them to see that so many people care about them.
7. An advertisement should be published soon in the local papers about their problem.

Chapter 8: Phrase Structure Tree Diagramming

Phrase structure diagramming is closely related to the identification and labeling of phrases that we did by underlining in Chapter 4. One superficial difference is that the **phrase structure trees** (or **PS trees**), as they are called, grow upwards from the sentence being analyzed. A more substantial difference is that a PS tree more clearly shows the relationships between the various phrases (and clauses, since they are also phrases) in a sentence. Let's see how that works in an ambiguous pair that we discussed earlier: the difference between a pipe rack which is made of copper and a rack for copper pipe. Here is a PS tree of structural ambiguity:

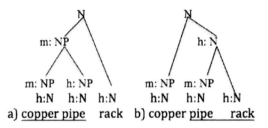

a) copper pipe   rack b) copper pipe   rack

As in the earlier analysis, the middle level of the structure tree is different, even though the top and bottom labels are identical. In the above example, the two nouns in (a) that form a modifer are first combined, while the head of the entire compound noun combines with its first modifier in (b). In the second level, the head combines with the compound modifer in (a), while the compound noun combines with the remaining modifier in (b). Especially in more complicated sentences, PS trees seem more likely to force us to recognize structural ambiguity like this. Here is a sentence-length example of structural ambiguity:

1) Sentence-level structural ambiguity: They stopped the stranger with a piece of rope.

Here we can start by noticing that 'with a piece of rope' is a PP. If we are not interested in the internal structure of that PP, we can diagram it with a triangle, and we can do the same with the NP 'the stranger'. That would give us a partial phrase structure diagram that looks like this.

Partial phrase structure diagram of a structurally ambiguous sentence

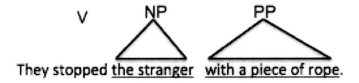

This representation of the PP and the NP seems more likely than the underlining system to lead to the question, "Does the PP modify the NP or the V?" which would lead to the discovery, "Oh, it can modify either one, but the meaning is not the same." Thus, it facilitates the recognition of structural ambiguity. That, by itself, may not be sufficient reason to prefer PS trees to the underlining system, since structural ambiguity may not occur that often, and failing to notice it may not be lead to serious lack of clarity in very many instances. A more compelling reason to prefer PS trees to underlining is that for those who are just learning to recognize phrases, the tree diagramming system seems to help them recognize every phrase in a sentence far more consistently and accurately than the underlining system does. It also shows the complexity of longer sentences with more ease than does the underlining system.

The Process of Drawing Phrase Structure Diagrams

Looking at an entire sentence will allow us to build up a tree in stages. Let's take a look at a sentence that we already analyzed in Chapter 4. As we did there, here the first step is to label each word's lexical category immediately above it. Here we need to make sure to write empty categories in as we start the process. We can even call the recognition of empty categories a step prior to the labeling of the lexical categories, since empty categories can belong to a number of different lexical categories.

2)   The first step in drawing a PS tree of a sentence – lexical categories

   D A N   N Aux V N   Adv P D   N   P   D N
Those rich business people   e   eat lunch happily at a restaurant near our beach.

One question that comes up regularly is whether 'business' here is an adjective. The short answer is that it satisfies the syntactic frame sentence for a noun but not that of an adjective, so it's a noun. The second point is that it's being used adjectivally, which is a point that we will want to include somewhere in the analysis and the diagram. You'll see NP(A) in the diagram below to identify this adjectival use of a noun. The second step is to identify any lexical items that are themselves phrases, and to combine the simplest two-word phrases (still working from right to left) by noticing that 'eat lunch' is a phrase, and 'business people' is also a phrase. The single words that are themselves phrases are 'rich', 'business', 'people', 'lunch', and 'happily'. You can check this with the short answer test for phrases: What do the rich business people do at the restaurant? A: both 'eat lunch' and 'eat lunch happily' are appropriate answers, so we need to consider those two separate phrases. And what kind of people eat at that restaurant? A: both 'business people' and 'rich business people' are acceptable short answers, so each is also phrase by itself.

3)   The most basic phrases in the sentence:

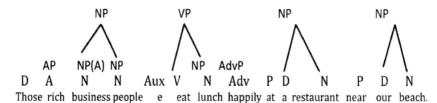

After that step, we can look to see phrases should combine with the ones on the right edge of the sentence. Here it's good to try to look ahead more than one level to avoid prematurely combining phrases. One obvious error would be to combine 'at' with 'a restaurant,' which would ignore the intermediate phrase 'a restaurant near the beach,' for the following layer of structure. Working carefully from right to left allows us to notice such intermediate phrases.

4)   Second-level phrases

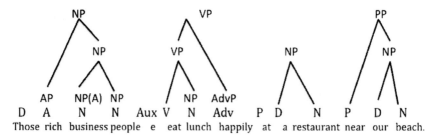

The next steps are to combine the two right-most phrases to recognize 'a restaurant near our beach' as an NP and to combine 'those' with its NP to recognize 'those rich business people' also as an NP. This latter step finishes the structure of the NP subject, divided by the 'aux' from the predicate VP. In order to finish up the predicate to the right of the second level of the VP, we need one level to show that 'at a restaurant near our beach' is a PP. After that, the two parts of the VP 'eat lunch happily' and the PP headed by 'at' can be combined to form a single, larger VP. As look back over process of forming the predicate, we notice that we needed to change direction and work from the main verb to the nearest phrases on its right: 1) eat+lunch, 2) eat lunch+happily, and 3) the entire predicate VP. Although this combining of the phrases in the VP occurred from right to left, it only arrived at the correct structure because each component phrase had been analyzed from left to right to begin with.

5) Complete subject-aux-VP structure of a simple sentence

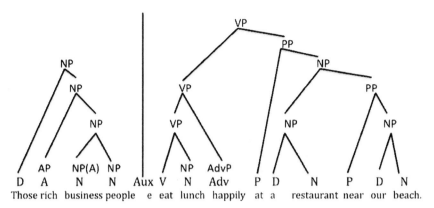

The final step in the drawing process is simply to combine, at one level higher, the three major divisions of the sentence into a single juncture (technically called a '**node**') and label this apex an 'IP.' In order to show that we also understand movement in the sentence, we also add an arrow to show the tense hopping. Our tree is complete at a second level when we label the heads, complements, modifiers, and specifiers in each phrase.

Labeling the heads, complements, modifiers, and specifiers in each phrase is done using the same initials that we used in Chapter 4 on phrase structure. Each phrase should have the same name as its head, so that should be the easiest part of the process. The next easiest part of the process should be locating the specifiers, since only NPs, IPs, (and CPs, which we don't have in this example) can have specifiers, and only one is allowed per phrase. Then the complements and modifiers are labeled. Here's what that labeling in a completed tree looks like.

6)   Complete PS tree

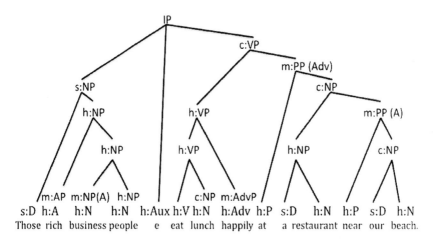

Here we have all the 'h' lexemes/words and 'h' nodes directly under a node of the same category. Three of the NP's have determiners as specifiers. The head and specifier of the IP have been added, even though we just added that node to this drawing. The specifier of IP is the NP subject, and its head is the empty auxiliary, so we can identify them easily. The only other nodes are modifiers and complements, which sometimes require a little more thinking.

One automatic step is to notice that each preposition requires an NP as its complement to form a PP. Another is that the complement of the auxiliary is the predicate VP. That leaves the somewhat stickier question about the roles of the PPs. Is the PP 'near our beach' a complement or a modifier of the NP 'a restaurant'? How can we tell? Here it's a modifier, since 'a restaurant' is complete without the PP. If it were 'the restaurant,' on the other hand, the PP would be a complement, since it's not clear how 'the restaurant' can become definite in this sentence unless we have some external context (which we don't) or unless we include the PP 'near our beach.' The prepositional phrases show another aspect of sentence grammar as well. Since 'near our beach' modifies the NP 'a restaurant,' it is being used adjectivally. Modifiers of nouns are either adjectives or adjectival, and this PP is adjectival in its role in the sentence. The larger PP 'at a restaurant near our beach' is modifying the verb 'eating' by telling us 'where' the people are eating. So it is functioning adverbially in the sentence.

Modifiers which answer the questions 'where,' 'when,' 'how,' and 'why' can be confidently identified as adverbs or adverbials. Prepositional phrases are always used either adjectivally or adverbially in English; there is no other choice. So labeling them (A) or (Adv) helps support the point made above that the PP 'near our beach' belongs under an NP node, just like the adjective 'rich' belongs under an NP node. Similarly, the PP 'at a restaurant near our beach' belongs under a VP node just as the adverb 'happily' does. Once we get used to marking PPs as either adverbial or adjectival, we will often be able to leave that marking out and rely on the higher VP or NP node to signal whether which role they have in the sentence.

This marking of grammatical roles as adjectival or adverbial is a third level of analysis that can be shown on a PS tree. The first is all the lexical and phrasal categories and their relationships. The second is the structure of each phrase in terms of its head and its modifiers, complements, or specifier. The third includes the grammatical roles of PPs (and later all CPs and some NPs).

Diagramming QPs and DPs

Taking a basic view of quantifier and determiner phrases will be sufficient to give us some background in these structures which have other, more familiar, structures embedded within them.

For the quantifier phrases, a useful variety should include one where there is no visible noun following the quantifier, as in a) below, one inside an NP with an adjective (b), and one with a PP-complement (c).

7)   Phrase structure of quantifier phrases

(a) The magnificent seven all came to the reception.

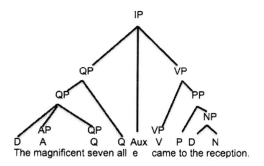

(b) We saw three majestic condors overhead.

(c) Many of the students had wonderful dreams for spring break.

For the determiner phrases, it will probably be sufficient to diagram one which is short and simple and another one which is more complicated. Since the DP can contain any kind of NP, it would, of course, be possible to construct one which has an embedded relative clause, such as 'The man who stopped by yesterday's hat is still hanging in the closet.' But we'll have to let that wait until after discussing how to diagram relative clauses. The basic principles don't change, of course, so these two examples contain enough information (although too little practice) to expand to any size DP.

8)   (a) Minimal DP

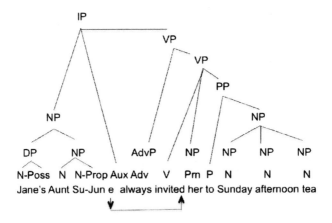

(b) DP with a layered NP inside it

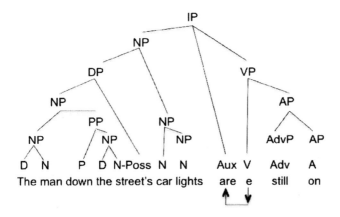

Practice Diagramming Simple Sentences

Diagram the following sentences. Please mark or describe the adverbial or adjectival function of PPs and NPs.

1. John left early with his friends for the concert on the beach.

2. He looked forward the whole year to the many bands from all over.

3. His friends went with him every year in the same old cars.

4. None of them had missed this concert since ten years ago

5. None of them had a driver's license at that time.

6. They soon bought their own cars for this kind of activity.

7. My new car got hit yesterday at the stoplight down the street.

8. A distracted driver accidentally hit my car at a speed of thirty miles per hour.

9. My parents graciously loaned me their old car in the meantime.

10. Now I have a reliable ride to the concert this year with my friends.

Diagramming Coordinate Structures

We have noticed that coordinating conjunctions are added to the front of a word or phrase to create a CCP (coordinating conjunction phrase). That is the only additional information that we need to add to what we have already discussed (in section 4.8.3 above) before being able to diagram coordinate structures, such as this sentence:

9)   PS tree containing a coordinate phrase inside a PP

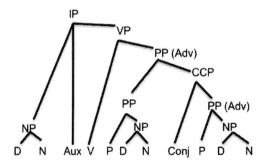

The children can run up the ladder and down the slide.

Diagramming Complex Sentences

Complex sentences are a combination of a simple sentence and a dependent clause, which might be adverbial, adjectival or nominal. Since adjectival clauses all involved a transformation and several empty categories, they will be discussed in the section on sentence transformations.

Adverbial Clauses

Adverbial clauses, like all complex sentences, are called complementizer phrases (CPs) in which the subordinating conjunction is considered to be occupying a position in the specifier of the CP. The CP node of an adverbial clause is directly under the highest node of the verb which the clause is modifying (before any movment), as we can see in the following sentence:

10) Diagram of an adverbial clause

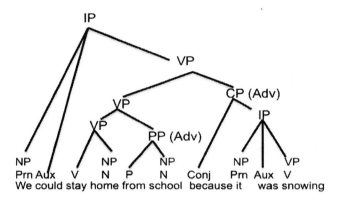

NP Prn Aux V   N   P   N   Conj Prn Aux V
We could stay home from school because it   was snowing

It may seem unnecessary to mark the CP adverbial, but that's only because we have not yet discussed any other role for the dependent clause in a sentence. Since two more will be coming soon, it is good to get used to marking the role of the dependent clause right from the beginning.

Further, the diagram has to reflect the internal grammar of the person doing the analysis. In the author's dialect, 'home from school' is not a phrase in this sentence. It may be in other sentences, but not in this particular one. If 'home from school' sounds like a phrase in this sentence to anyone else, the above diagram would need to reflect that, and it would have to be changed. The VP combining 'stay home' would have to be removed. Then we would label 'home from school' an NP. We could even mark the role as adverbial by the same convention we just used for a dependent clause: NP (Adv). The new NP would connect the NP node above 'home' to the PP node above 'from school,' and the lowest VP node would connect 'stay' and 'home from school.' The rest of the diagram would be the same. We note in passing that the IP 'it is snowing' is a complete independent clause because it has a finite verb form.

Practice Diagramming Compound and Complex Sentences

Diagram the following sentences. Please mark or describe the adverbial or adjectival function of PPs, NPs, and CPs.

1. Matt was interested in stamps and coins when he was little.

2. Now, he no longer had any time for his collections since he was so busy with sports.

3. He loved basketball and football, and he played on the varsity teams in each sport.

4. The day came, however, when his coach left the school, and a new one took his place.

5. Matt was upset at the change because he could no longer participate in

two sports.

6. Sara and her friends loved the weekend since they studied hard during the week.

7. They enjoyed their freedom from schoolwork on Saturday nights, so sometimes they just did nothing.

8. Other nights they would see a movie so that they could forget about their studies for a while.

9. Sara really liked horror films, but her best friend Eliza hated them.

10. They usually saw romantic comedies or adventure films at the theaters, but sometimes they streamed TV shows on their laptops at home instead.

Nominal Clauses

Nominal clauses serve any of the many roles that a noun can play in a sentence. Instead of an NP connecting to the next higher node, it is the CP of the nominal clause. Nothing else is affected. The first example is of a noun clause serving as the subject of a sentence. It, therefore, connects to the IP above it, just as a subject NP would. It is marked by the adverbial wh-word 'whether.' The CP here has an empty head, since it has neither complementizer nor fronted auxiliary. Here we mark the role of the dependent clause as nominal: CP (N).

11) A noun clause serving as the subject of a sentence

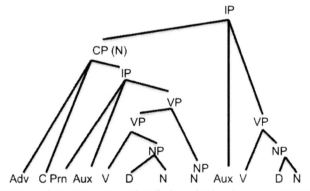

Whether e they can book another flight today has become a question.

We can also take a look at a noun clause serving as a direct object, where the CP node will connect to the highest VP node in the predicate. Here the wh-word 'how' marks the nominal clause. We can test to see if it's the direct object by asking 'figure out what?' Dependent clauses that are introduced by wh-words generally have a nominal role in the sentence.

12) A noun clause serving as the direct object in a sentence

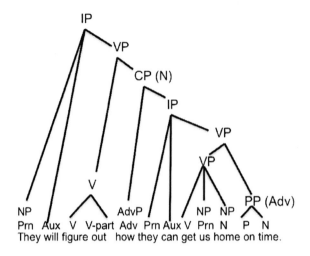

Prn Aux V V-part Adv Prn Aux V Prn N   P   N
They will figure out   how they can get us home on time.

Practice with More Complex Sentences

Please mark or describe the nominal, adverbial or adjectival function of PPs, NPs, and CPs in your phrase structure trees of the following sentences.

1. Brent 's roommate asked him if he had a surfboard with him, and he said that he did have one.

2. Before Brent started first grade, he lived with an aunt and uncle in their home by the sea.

3. The older couple loved the surf and frequently took Brent with them.

4. Brent hated sand in his hair, and he disliked layers of sunscreen.

5. Consequently, Brent would walk to the edge of the sand where he could not go any farther.

6. Now that he's older, Brent has overcome his fear of new adventures, and he has bought his own wet suit and surfboard.

7. Kacie hated the tedium of a job applications, but she needed summer job.

8. It did not help that her phone's screen shattered when she dropped in on the sidewalk.

9. Kacie knew she should have bought a case, but decided that the risk of loss was not very high.

10. Now, she really needed a job so that she could pay for her new phone.

Diagramming Reduced Clauses and Empty Categories

The main principles to notice in diagramming here is that the empty category first needs to be labeled and then it needs to be included in the over-all structure of the sentence. Its label depends entirely on the lexical category of the word or phrase that was deleted. Its place in the over-all structure depends generally on the position we assign to it as the place where the deleted item used to be. We can often check our theory of what was deleted by **lexical insertion**; we put in the categories we think are missing and see if they complete the phrase. In introducing empty categories somewhat earlier, we started with the example of a command, or imperative, which seems not to have a subject, but which turns out always to have an empty subject 'You.' It turns out that the auxiliary is also empty, making an imperative 'Wash the dishes' have the same structure as the sentence 'You should/must wash the dishes,' as is shown below.

13) Empty categories in imperatives

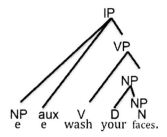

Thus lexical insertion for the above empty categories would give us 'You should/must wash your faces.'

Empty Categories from Gapping

Another kind of structure in English where we see evidence that our minds keep track of the complete structure of a sentence even when part of it is not visible (or audible) is called '**gapping.**' This is a sentence with a '**gap**' in it. Here the conjunction 'and' connects 'your sister likes cherry pie' with 'your brother peach cobbler.' The first phrase is clearly a sentence with a subject, auxiliary (which tense hopped), verb and NP complement. The second phrase is not simply two NPs 'your brother' and 'peach cobbler,' but rather 'your brother e e peach cobbler,' where the 'e's are for the missing auxiliary and the missing verb. This is our first look at a compound sentence, and we discover that it is one IP composed of two IPs.

14) Empty categories in compound IPs with gapping

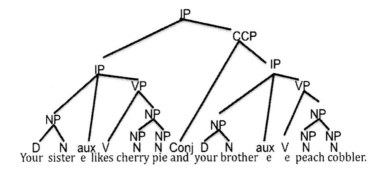

We also notice here that the embedded IP is non-finite since its aux has been deleted, giving us an IP 'your brother peach cobbler' which cannot be a sentence/an independent clause.

Empty Categories in Clauses of Comparison and Degree

15) Clause of comparison

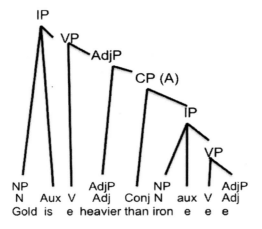

(Reed and Kellogg 102)

16) Two examples of a clause of degree

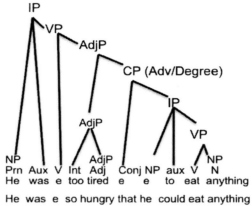

Here we see that the same structure is shared by a non-finite complement clause to the adjective 'tired' and a finite complement clause to the adjective 'hungry.' Both are clauses of degree. Looking at the two clauses in parallel may make it easier to internalize what the empty categories in the non-finite clause are. Here we notice that the CP is identified in a tradition sense as adverbial because it is modifying an adjective. This is to avoid introducing a new phrasal category such as in intensifier/qualifier phrase, which, in fact it is. We can choose to accept the phrasal category 'adverbial' as a kind of catch-all category in the tradition of the Grammarian movement, or we can use the same logic that justified introducing 'intensifier/qualifier' as a lexical category to also introduce 'intensifier/qualifer' as a role for dependent clauses.

Empty Categories in Reduced Adverbial Clauses (Non-finite)

Deleted subordinating conjunctions that introduce adverbial clauses receive the same empty category ('e') treatment.

We'll look at a phrase-structure diagram of the third sentence, just to confirm our suspicions that it isn't really that difficult. This is a complex sentence, which might give us some pause, but we'll just take the dependent clause as adverbial (since it can move), and put it under the main clause's verb 'discover' as an adverbial modifier of that verb.

17) Empty categories in a reduced adverbial clause

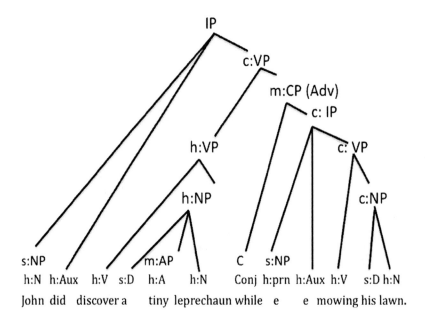

We notice that the two empty categories represent the subject NP and the auxiliary, respectively. **Lexical insertion** for these empty categories would give us 'while he was mowing…" Here again, the embedded IP is not a sentence.

Empty Categories in Reduced Nominal Clauses (Non-finite)

In non-finite nominal clauses, we often encounter the infinitive form of the verb without an apparent subject or complementizer, as in the sentence "Charlotte wanted e e to become an astronaut." We can lexicalize the empty categories as "Charlotte wanted/desired/longed *for *(her)self to become an astronaut." These empty categories must remain invisible in formal writing styles. When we want to change the subject of the infinitive verb, however, the new subject (and sometimes the complementizer, such as following the verb 'long') do appear on the surface, as we noticed earlier: "Charlotte wanted/desired/longed for her sister to become an astronaut."

    The reduced nominal clause in such a sentence is the direct object of the finite verb. We can use the sentence "Brent hated to get sandy" as an example.

A reduced nominal clause (non-finite)

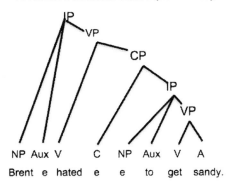

The CP is used nominally as a direct object, as in 'hated what?' Here 'get' is a linking verb, like 'become'.

Empty Categories in Gerund Clauses

Gerunds have the same form as present participles and almost the same empty categories, so that should give us a very good start in our efforts to diagram them. They seem to have all of the characteristics of a verb phrase although the auxiliary seems usually empty. As we discussed earlier, there is a difference between formal written gerunds and informal spoken gerunds in Standard American English. In formal SAE, the specifier slot left of the empty auxiliary can be filled with a possessive determiner (my, your, his, …), or a possessive noun, such as 'Mary's'. In formally, it would be filled by an object pronoun (me, you, him, …) or a noun (Mary). The specifier acts as a subject of the gerund. In sum, gerunds seem to have all the elements of an IP, but they do not seem capable of expanding further to becoming CPs. They are used nominally, so we would expect the highest node of the IP above the gerund to connect with a higher node in the same way that an NP in the same position would. This is shown in the diagram below.

18) Diagramming a gerund

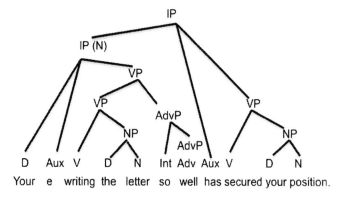

(Reed and Kellogg 66).

Practice with Gerunds and Reduced Clauses

Please mark or describe the nominal, adverbial or adjectival function of PPs, NPs, and CPs in your phrase structure trees of the following sentences.

1. We receive good by doing good. (Reed and Kellogg 66)

2. Buying and selling goods provides many with a living. (Reed and Kellogg 66)

3. More interested in sports than ever, Jeff thought living nearby would allow him to try out.

4. Recognizing this helped Jeff settle more firmly into dorm life and its challenges.

5. After dressing quickly and running out of his dorm room, Nick barely made it to class on time.

6. Alicia practiced singing two hours every day.

7. Darrel, fixing his bike, lost track of time and forgot to pick his brother up from school.

8. Excited to be interviewed, Julie was sure to be prepared by dressing sharp and arriving early.

Comparing Gerund Clauses with Gerundives

As we may recall from the section above about reduced adjectival (relative) clauses, sometimes a verb may act adjectivally in the modifier position in front of a noun, as in the sentence, 'The blushing man over there has just proposed to his girlfriend.' In this position, the verb must always be intransitive, which means it is also a VP. But there is no room in this particular VP for any modifiers after the verb, as the VP *'The blushing from ear to ear man...' Some adverbs preceding the verb seem to be allowable, as in 'The slightly blushing man...' With this information, we can expect the diagram to look very similar to an AP modifying a noun, as we see in the following diagram:

1)   Diagram of a gerundive VP modifying a noun

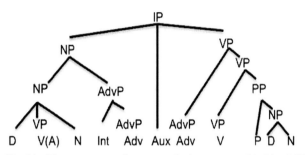

The notation (A) after the verb shows that it (and its VP, of course) are being used adjectivally. There are two ways to look at the phrase 'over there.' For those whose sensibilities are estranged by the idea of an adverb phrase modifying a noun, as shown above, it would also be possible to assume that 'over there' is a reduced relative clause with three empty categories left over from 'who is e over there.'

Now we have the foundation to show graphically what is happening in the old linguistic joke that 'Visiting relatives can be very tiring.' The joke is based on the fact that the sentence has two meanings, depending on whether 'visiting' is a gerundive or part of a gerund phrase.

Let's look at both structures.

2)   Comparing structural ambiguity between a gerund and a gerundive

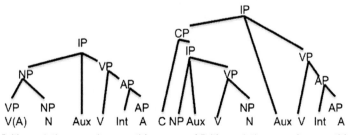

Can we see the two meanings emerging? On the left, we have a gerundive, which we remember is often the result of reducing a relative clause and then moving it in front of the head noun. So the sentence 'Relatives who are visiting...' became

'Visiting relatives…' On the right, we have a gerund, which makes a certain VP nominal, in this case, as the subject of the sentence. the right-hand PS tree is about the task of going to visit relatives. The three empty categories could be filled in lexically this way: 'for someone to be … ' where 'to be' is seen as a compound auxiliary. Perhaps the topic of this joke gives us some insight into the sense of humor that some linguists have.

Diagramming Bare Infinitives

In our earlier discussion of bare infinitives, which often follow verbs of perception, such as "I watched Toni climb the mountain," we mentioned that there is historical evidence to support the idea that bare infinitives should be considered to have a deleted 'to' as an empty category between the their NP ('Toni') and the verb ('climb'). This helps us see that a PS diagram will treat them as IPs, since the constituents NP-Aux-VP in that order are characteristic of an IP. Here, as with the gerund clauses, there doesn't seem to be any evidence or possibility that they can expand into CP structures.

3)   Diagramming a bare infinitive as an IP

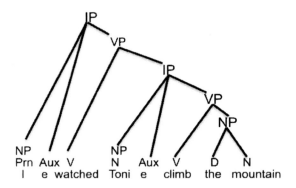

The IP here is clearly non-finite, as we would expect where the aux has been deleted. This is also seen in the fact that it cannot be an independent clause 'Toni climb the mountain.' Other sentences with a similar structure are 'I made Toni climb the mountaing' and 'I had Toni climb the mountain.'

The contrasting non-finite clause with 'climbing' instead of a bare infinitive brings us back into the more familiar territory that we explored with the story about finding a leprechaun while mowing the grass. Here we have a reduced dependent clause, as shown in this PS tree.

4) Diagramming a reduced dependent clause with an '-ing' verb form

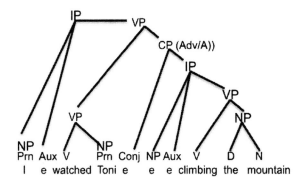

As we discussed earlier, the mind can compute this as a reduced relative clause, 'I watched the athlete who was climbing the mountain,' or as a reduced subordinate clause, 'I watched the athlete as/while s/he was climbing the mountain.' Either of these two readings preserves the contrast in meanings between the two clausal types where the bare infinitive clause tells us that the climber succeeded in climbing the mountain, and the reduced dependent clause, which is indefinite about the climber's success in climbing the mountain. In the author's dialect, the preferred reading is adverbial, so the CP is marked (Adv/A) rather than (A/Adv).

Diagramming Sentence Transformations with PS Trees

In chapter six, we discussed the locating of empty categories resulting from movement in a number of different types of syntactic and stylistic movement. One principle that will help us diagram these transformations is to remember that the empty category is part of the structure that is being diagrammed. We'll try a few sentences from chapter six to see how that works. In order to simplify the PS trees, we will not mark the roles of head, complement, modifier, and specifier, although they are important and should not be forgotten. Having simplified our diagramming in that way will allow each section to diagram a sentence representing each given structure and also to add one smaller detail which might otherwise get overlooked.

PS Trees of Tense Hopping

As we remember, tense hopping only happens for the simple present and simple past tenses, and only when there is no emphatic meaning and no negation. One typical example is from our discussion of Sentence (IP) structure above.

5)   Empty categories in tense hopping

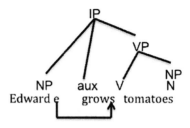

The sentence immediately above would have the exact same phrase structure, but without empty categories, if it were emphatic as in the following examples:

6)   (a) Edward does grow tomatoes.

      (b) Edward did grow tomatoes.

Negative Sentences and Contraction of 'Not'

The negative particle 'not' can be shortened to the vowel-less sequence [nt] and **cliticize** to the auxiliary. We noted earlier that 'not' always follows the auxiliary. When it cliticizes onto the auxiliary, this results in an empty category due to the movement, which is diagrammed as we would expect:

7)   An empty category left by a contraction

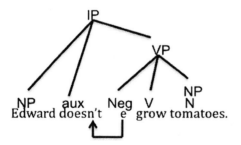

Yes/no Questions

Auxiliary fronting is diagrammed by noting that the fronted auxiliary has moved to a position to the left of the IP to the head of CP. As noted earlier, if the contracted form of 'not' is cliticized to the auxiliary, it can be carried with the auxiliary in the auxiliary fronting:

8) The empty category left by auxiliary fronting

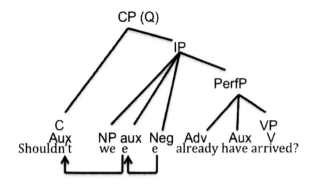

We should notice here that there is one empty category left from the movement of the negative particle onto the auxiliary, and another from the auxiliary (+n't) fronting. The two movements are seen as happening one after the other. Here we notice that we have a CP that is not a dependent clause. This seems exceptional. Perhaps we should invent a new name for this kind of phrase rather than a complementizer phrase. It doesn't even have a complementizer, but rather a fronted auxiliary as its head. The reason that no new category has been developed to label either a yes-no question or a wh-question is that they have exactly the same structure as a dependent CP, as we can see from the PS tree.

'Be' Raising

When 'be' is the main verb, it can be fronted just the way auxiliaries can, as we have seen in a question such as "Are they students?" It's the opposite of tense hopping, in that the main verb moves up to the auxiliary position: "They are e students." This sentence probably does not need a separate PS tree. In any event, it will be embedded in a yes/no question with 'be' as a main verb, which we will diagram. There 'be' has two consecutive movements which would be diagrammed in a way similar to the movement of the contracted 'not' in the previous example.

9) The empty categories left by be-raising and auxiliary fronting

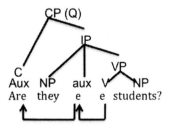

In the declarative sentence (under the IP node), the verb 'are' would be under the 'aux' node after 'be raising.' From there it moves to the head position of the CP node.

Wh-questions (Or Information Questions)

Two movements are also involved in the formation of wh-questions: **auxiliary fronting** followed by **wh-fronting**. The wh-word is fronted to a position in front of the fronted auxiliary, which we recognize as the specifier of CP. In order to see where the wh-word begins its movement, we looked at **echo questions**. We have already shown the movement by arrows in an earlier section, so there is nothing surprising about the movement:

10)   Empty categories created in wh-questions

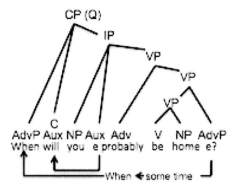

One detail is that the statement from which the question is derived might have been something like "You will probably be home on time." Then the time phrase turned into the question-word 'when,' which, in English, must be fronted. Here we again notice that the CP is marked (Q), as it was for the yes-no questions earlier.

A second detail that we can notice is that there are several layers of verb phrases. This is a reminder to work from right to left and to include each phrase separately. The empty category for 'When' is marked as an adverb, since that is its lexical category. It is marked as a phrase, since it is replacing an informational phrase, such as 'on time.' 'Be home on time' is also a phrase, which we can show by **shared string coordination**: 'they will (but we will not) be home on time.' So that phrase needs to be diagrammed. The same shared string coordination can be used to show that 'probably be home on time' is also its own phrase, which gives us the three levels of VP that are diagrammed.

Indirect Questions

Indirect questions have structures similar to direct questions, except that there is no auxiliary fronting, so the head of the CP is empty. In addition, they are always embedded, so we will always have to deal with them as complex sentences. As we did in an earlier section on questions, we will assume that the 'who' or 'what' in subject position has moved invisibly ('**vacuously**') from the specifier of its IP to the specifier of its CP. Here's an example of what that looks like in a PS tree.

Empty categories left by the vacuous movement in an indirect question (with tense hopping)

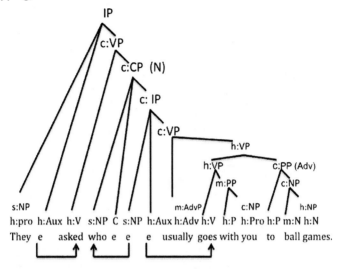

Here we notice that the two prepositional phrases at the end of the sentence do not combine to form a single PP. They each combine separately to form a separate verb phrase, though, giving us first 'goes with you' and then 'goes with you to ball games.' We could also notice that 'with you' is a modifier, while 'to ball games' is a complement because of the verb 'go.' The CP is marked as nominal because the dependent clause is a direct object, as in 'asked what?'

Exclamatives and Exclamative Movement

Exclamatives are expressions that usually begin with either a fronted 'what-NP' or a fronted 'how-AP such as moving the parenthesized phrase in the declarative statement "We had [such an awesome day] yesterday" to create the exclamative "What an awesome day we had yesterday!" Here the wh-word is functioning as an intensifer and not as a question word, so it does not signal the creation of a CP. The resulting clause has the same structure as a sentence with a fronted PP. The whole PS tree looks like this.

11) Empty categories in exclamatory sentences

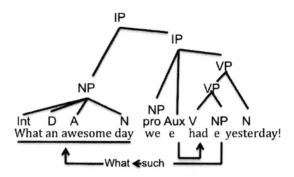

Drawing a line under the fronted NP allows easy identification of the phrase that has been moved. The replacement of the intensifier/qualifier 'such' by 'what' actually occurs before the fronting, but showing that replacement where the second 'e' now is would require a much more complicated PS tree. There is no dependent clause here.

Relative Clauses and Vacuous Movement of Subject Relative Pronouns

Relative pronouns, relative adverbs, and relative determiners in general show the same fronting movement to the specifier position of their CP as we have seen for interrogative pronouns, adverbs, and determiners. We saw several examples earlier with arrows to describe the movement. Now let's look at a typical phrase structure tree of a relative clause. We know from the start that the clause is adjectival and will have to become part of a larger noun phrase.

12) Empty categories left by the movement of a relative pronoun

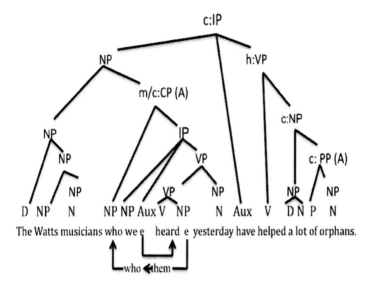

Knowing where the wh-word originated is half of the analytic problem. We mark the direct object NP as 'them,' meaning 'we saw them yesterday,' and then the direct object pronoun is replaced by a relative pronoun, which, like all wh-words in English, moves to the specifier of CP position in its clause. If we had a little more room in the diagram, we could also mark the head of CP as empty ('e'), in order to show more clearly that the relative pronoun is in the specifier position to the left of the head position. That empty position is marked in the next diagram. We should also notice that the pronoun 'them' is an object pronoun, which means that the relative pronoun could also be in its object form: 'whom.'

One important detail above is the marking of the relative clause as either a modifier or a complement. If it's a modifer ('m'), the relative clause is non-restrictive, meaning all of the Watts musicians have helped the orphans: 'The Watts musicians, who we heard yesterday, have helped a lot of orphans.' If the relative clause is a complement ('c'), it is restrictive, meaning only a restricted group of the musicians have helped orphans: 'The Watts musicians who we heard yesterday have helped a lot of orphans.'

In contrast to the above relative clause where the relative pronoun moved from the direct object position, we want to look at a relative clause whose relative pronoun is the subject of its clause, so that we can show its **vacuous** movement to the specifier position of CP. This vacuous movement (meaning you can't really follow it from one position to the position next to it, is posited so that subject relative clauses can be subject to the same kinds of movment as all the other wh-word relative markers.

13) Empty categories left by the vacuous movement of a subject relative
pronoun

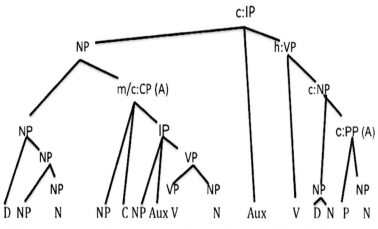

The vacuous movement changes the sentence 'They played yesterday' to the
relative clause 'who played yesterday' but the 'who' continues moving from the
specifier position of the IP to the specifier position of the CP, leaving the head of
CP empty. This is a headless CP, similar to other headless structures that we have
seen. Here we also notice that the dependent clause is adjectival regardless of
whether it is a modifier or a complement.

Practice with Relative Clauses and Vacuous Movement

Please diagram the following sentence and use arrow notation to mark any
movement. Also remember to mark or describe the relative clauses as either
restrictive or non-restrictive.

    1. Odysseus went from Lotus-land to the land where the Cyclopes, a
    pastoral people of giants, live.

    2. Among the Cyclopes, Odysseus had the adventure on which all his
    fortunes hinged.

    3. There he yelled out about having blinded the giant Polyphemus while
    rowing away.

    4. The tale of a giant-blinding hero who uses a pun to escape exists
    among peoples who never heard of Homer.

5. 'The Odyssey', which we read in high school, is a classic that seldom causes controversy.

6. Students can readily see the reasons why Odysseus is so memorable.

7. At night, Bruce Wayne disguises himself as Batman, a masked vigilante who fights crime, to save Gotham.

8. Gotham is a fictional city in which crime and corruption run rampant.

9. Only Officer Gordon and the people who are closest to Bruce know the reasons why Batman fights with a mask.

10. Many fans believe the Joker, who has clown makeup and scars on his face, is the greatest villain yet.

11. Batman's motorcycle, which fans would love to drive, is technologically advanced and fully weaponized.

Germanic Verb-second/ English Aux-second

We recall the earlier story of thoughtless Hans who leapt from a high Germanic castle tower and his fair maiden's invective and opprobrium. In English the auxiliary must be fronted to the second position, just as the main verb was fronted in Old English and still is in modern Germanic languages. This can be conveniently diagrammed:

14)   Empty categories left by English auxiliary-second movement

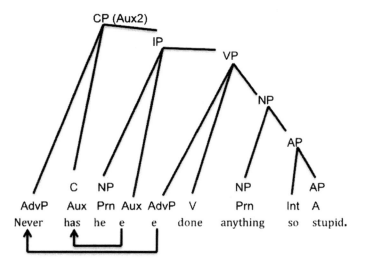

This structure is different from the usual CP structure in that the fronting of the auxiliary does not indicate a question. Nor does the fronted adverb (or adverbial) resemble a fronted wh-word, which we are accustomed to seeing in indirect questions and relative clauses (where the aux is not fronted, but which is still considered a CP. It's worth asking why this structure is not considered an IP with two layers of IP, as we have with extraposition and topicalization. The best answer for now is that the fronted aux is certain sign of a complementizer phrase in any other structure, so we'll be consistent here as well. We also mark this CP specially as 'CP (Aux2),' since it is a unique left-over from much earlier Germanic grammar in Early English and not in the same category as any other structure in English.

Practice with Aux-second

Please diagram the following sentence and mark any movement. Also note the adjectival, adverbial or nominal function of PPs, CPs. or modifying NPs.

> 1. Never will I leave him alone again.
>
> 2. Rarely are the two of them ever seen out together.
>
> 3. Only if he apologizes by tomorrow will she ever talk with him again.
>
> 4. Seldom has he visited the beach at Malibu.
>
> 5. Never have I told a lie.

Diagramming Stylistic Transformations with PS Trees

Of the nine stylistic transformations discussed in the earlier section, only five are reasonably amenable to being diagrammed with the amount of theory available to us in this Guide. In each of the transformations discussed below, it is reasonably clear how the structure of the original sentence can be preserved. We will avoid discussing the diagrams of sentences where it is not so obvious how the original sentence structure can be preserved: there-insertion, it-insertion, subject-complement inversion, and Wh-clefting or Pseudo-clefting.

Extraposition and Heavy Complement Shift

When the subject, or part of one, is moved toward the end of the sentence without the insertion of 'it' or 'there,' the movement is called **extraposition**. In diagramming, this is considered the creation of a second sentence which preserves all the structure of the first sentence and adds another layer of IP on top of the first one, as seen here:

15) Empty categories left by extraposition

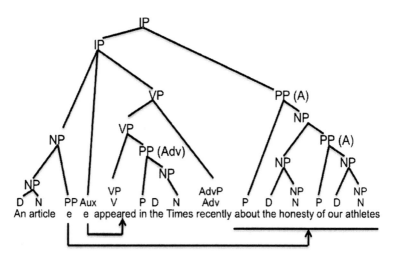

The same diagramming convention would apply to a **heavy complement shift** such as seen in the earlier example sentence, "The police was able to run down e in only a week the drug smugglers from New York, Miami, and Boston."

Clefting

With a cleft sentence, we set up a complex sentence as a shell above the original sentence, from which one element is fronted into the synthetically created focus position, as we can see will happen when we focus the word 'today' from the sentence 'Jasper will be eating dinner with us today:'

16) Diagramming a cleft sentence

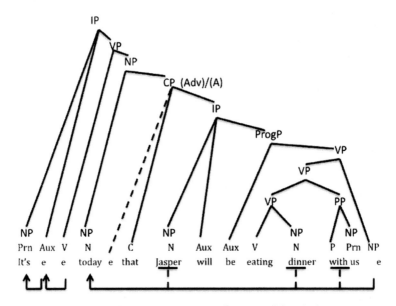

The extra structure that is used to create a focus position is here seen as an IP with and embedded CP. The embedded CP begins with the complementizer 'that.' The dotted line to the CP node shows that the specifier of CP is empty, which we generally do not need to show. It's marked here simply for the purpose of noting that that line is generally unnecessary. The dotted lines below 'Jasper,' 'dinner,' and 'with us' emphasize the ease with which any of those three phrases could be put into the focus position instead of the phrase 'today.' That would produce the following sentences, marked also to show that two of the dependent clauses are adjectival, and one is adverbial.

17) Alternative cleft sentences to vary the focus

   a) It's Jasper that/who will be eating dinner with us today [CP (A)].

   b) It's dinner that Jasper will be eating dinner with us today [CP (A)].

   c) It's with us that Jasper will be eating dinner today [CP (Adv)].

Topicalization and Fronting

In both of these optional transformations, an element is fronted. For topicalization, it's often a direct object or a prepositional object (as in, "Beethoven, I'm not to fond of"). When we say 'fronting,' we usually mean the movement of an adverb or an adverbial clause, but with topicalization, the fronted phrase is generally an NP. Structurally, the two look very similar, since the empty category in each case is nearer the end of the sentence, and the original sentence structure is easily preserved.

18) Diagramming a sentence with stylistic fronting

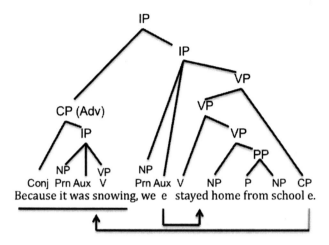

One of the most characteristic features of this kind of transformation is that the end result is an IP and not a CP. We can reason this out by saying that the fronting of an auxiliary in question formation changes a declarative sentence (which is an IP) to a question, but the fronting of an adverbial leaves a declarative sentence a declarative sentence.

Passivization

It is always with a feeling of apprehension that one acknowledges one's own limitations, and that is no less true in attempting to discuss passivization, which has earlier been shown to be beyond the limitations of the approach (or analytical framework) that has been presented up to this point. Because passive constructions are so common in English, however, a non-theoretical approach may be helpful to those whose careers may some day require that they have god-like answers to questions on messy elements of English grammar. It should be noted that the following section on Reed-Kellogg diagramming is so atheoretical that it has no difficulty whatever in describing passive constructions. Something of that simplicity will eventually be adopted in the following discussion.

First, though, let's describe the malady before declaring the disease incurable with the given technology. So far, we have seen so far that the original structure of any given sentence before all transformations is preserved by the mind. Let's see graphically what that would produce for a passivized sentence:

19) Passivization transformations seen to overwhelm PS diagramming

To start with the positive aspects of the above PS tree, we see that the movements and insertions can be marked rather clearly at the bottom of the diagram, and we can see how the three empty categories under the lower IP node preserve the original active sentence. The two insertions initially look quite acceptable with the theory of grammar that we have developed so far. We've seen 'do'-insertion as legitimate for the two simple tenses, so inserting an aux is something that modern English is known to do. For the tense to move from the original aux to the new aux is somewhat new but not particularly surprising, since we have seen tense-hopping earlier. And the fact that the 'by'-PP is optional and could be deleted helps us accept that as part of the normal grammatical apparatus of English because optional PP modification is very normal in sentence-final position.

If we stopped there, the transformations would be recorded and summarized fairly. The passive transformations do not do anything that we have not seen elsewhere in English grammar. The problem is not with the transformations, but with the limitations of the theory that we are using. We notice first that the aux 'be' was cleverly inserted to the left of the original active sentence, although there is no theoretical reason to chose that placement. It simply works, which would not be true if it were placed elsewhere, but we don't know why that should be.

The change of the verb form from a finite verb to a past participle is not explained either; it's simply noted. The real reef on which the phrase structure ship sinks, however, is seen at the top of the diagram. The higher IP connects nicely to a subject NP, followed by a (fortuitously placed) finite aux, which is exactly as we expect, but then it falls apart. Looking to the right, where there should be a VP, we find the IP of the original active sentence followed by the optional 'by'-PP. If only we could say that the verb 'eat' was the head of the hypothetical 'VP??'-node for some reason, like erasing the two empty categories to its left, the diagram would follow the pattern of all the sentences we have discussed so far.

So it's clear what direction we need to go if we are willing to abandon part of the analytical apparatus that has served us well up to this point in order to produce a simplified, atheoretical PS tree for emergency use – ignore the three empty categories belonging to the original active sentence. This is also the Reed-Kellogg approach of the following section. If we decide to do that, though, let's leave one symbolic reminder of the disappearance of the active sentence by marking the aux as 'passive.'

Here's what the result would look like:

20) PS tree of a passivized sentence as if there were no transformation

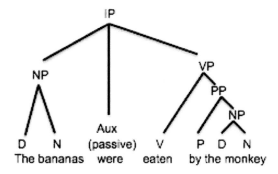

The simplicity that this achieves is marvelous to behold. That is the aspect in which it succeeds. This example should make the advantages and disadvantages of both a data-driven approach and a non-theoretical one more evident.

Practice with Stylistic Transformations

Please diagram the following sentence and mark any movement. Also note the adjectival, adverbial or nominal function of PPs, CPs. or modifying NPs.

1. If the situation were simpler, Jeff would loan them some money.

2. Lack of money he considered a poor reason to get all upset.

3. Perhaps it is publicity in the local papers that they need.

4. It would help them to see that so many people care about them.

5. Someone should publish an advertisement soon about the seriousness of their plight.

6. As the DJ turned up the volume, the crowd screamed louder and danced faster.

7. It is in Texas that the championship game will be held next week.

8. What the police officer wanted was James' license and registration.

9. At the end of the term, college kids often eat hotdogs, mac and cheese, and ramen noodles for dinner.

10. They posted flyers all over the school about the upcoming election.

Summary Phrase-tree Diagraming Practice

Diagram your choice of the following sentences. Please mark any movement and note the adjectival, adverbial or nominal function of PPs, CPs. or modifying NPs. For several of them, you should also be able to mark all the parts of each phrase as head (h), complement (c), modifier (m), or specifier (s).

1. Mitch was shocked that his grades improved dramatically from last semester. ('That' marks an adjective complement clause. Diagram the clause as if it were an appositive to the adjective).

2. Anna knew Brian wanted to marry her.

3. That they could arrive on time was now a certainty.

4. I wondered if/whether they would arrive on time

5. I didn't know whether to donate money to that campaign.

6. I didn't know whether to wake up and exercise or sleep in.

7. I am hoping you will come home soon.

8. I found the place to which you referred (Reed and Kellogg 96).

9. They that work hard will be rewarded..

10. We react when temptation rears its head.

11. He did what was considered right

12. When we leave the A.C. on, the utility bill gets way too expensive.

13. When my gait slows down and my eyes dim, then I will need help from others.

14. A gym is a place where people can keep in good shape.

15. My dad weighs less than your dad.

16. My Dad always eats faster than my Mom.

17. The new orbiter flies faster than any plane has ever flown..

18. That's the fastest computer any company has ever built.

19. They were so exhausted that they could not swim another ten feet

20. Our roommates thought that we were wise enough not to take such a risk.

21. Rich to the point of embarrassment, Warren Buffet announced his support for a special tax on the wealthy

22. For us to stay at home when wild fires are approaching would be insane. This is similar to #24 is section 9.2.1 above.

23. Going anywhere safe would be wiser than staying here.

24. Brent's college roommate asked him to go surfing with him.

25. As a child, Brent had had to live with an aunt and uncle in their seaside home.

Chapter 9: Reed-Kellogg Diagramming

Reed-Kellogg diagramming is still used in some elementary and secondary schools, which is only one reason to spend time learning this century-old system of diagramming. It is relatively unsophisticated compared to modern phrase-structure diagramming in that it does not account for empty categories due to movement, and it ignores most deletions. These simplifications also recommend it as an introductory way to begin diagramming. It does have the advantage over phrase-structure diagramming that the adjectival, adverbial, and nominal roles of modifiers need to be carefully distinguished. This last aspect is another reason to spend the time necessary to master basic Reed-Kellogg diagramming.

Basic Reed-Kellogg Diagramming

Reed-Kellogg diagrams are built on a subject-predicate split for all IPs. These two parts are put on a horizontal line which is split by a bisecting vertical line, like this

1)   The basic Reed-Kellogg subject-predicate split ('They are sleeping.')

So we see immediately that there is no special role for auxiliaries in this system. The string of auxiliaries and the verb are treated as a single unit. Soon we will notice that Reed-Kellogg recognizes only a few empty categories resulting from deletion and none at all resulting from movement. In these respects, Reed-Kellogg is less sophisticated than phrase structure diagramming. One area where Reed-Kellogg diagramming requires more attention than the phrase structure trees do is the grammatical roles: subjects, direct objects, indirect objects, complements and appositives all need to be specifically identified because they are treated separately in the Reed-Kellogg system. Attention also needs to be paid for the same reason to the distinctions between noun clauses, adjective clauses and adverb clauses.

Determiners, Quantifiers, Qualifiers, Adjectives, and Adverbs

Modifers are added to this basic skeleton on slanting lines below the word or phrase that is being modified. No distinction is made between adjectives, quantifiers and determiners. Manner adverbs are treated in the same way and placed under the verb that they are modifying. Qualifiers/intensifiers are put on a slanted line attached to another slanting line, as seen below. The one exception to this uniform treatment of modifiers is that nouns modifying nouns are treated as a single unit: one after another on a horizontal line. All compound nouns are written out together.

2) Determiners, quantifiers, qualifiers, adjectives, and manner adverbs

The two tired children are sleeping very soundly.

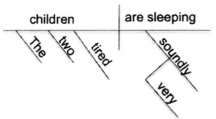

Sentence adverbs, on the other hand, are not treated as part of the sentence and are consigned to float above it on their own lonely platform, sort of where one might imagine the disembodied author or speaker to be expressing an opinion from.

3) A sentential adverb

Fortunately, our soldiers are not sleeping.

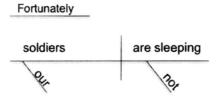

Practice Diagramming Simple Sentence in Reed-Kellogg Style

Diagram the following sentences.

1. Sam's tennis is improving rapidly.

2. Our delighted host opened the champagne bottle very carefully.

3. Indignantly, the host laughed and walked around nervously

4. Interestingly enough, no one reacted.

5. The star forward could only rest very infrequently. (hint: compound noun).

Prepositional Phrases

Adverbial and adjectival prepositional phrases use a slant combined with a horizontal line for the NP object and are also place below the word or phrase that they are modifying.

4)   Adverbial PP

The children are sleeping in their crib

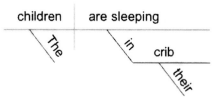

This diagram would also represent a prepositional verb, such as in the sentence, "They are living in Phoenix." This diagramming system does not distinguish between a prepositional phrase which is a modifer, such as in the above diagram, from one which is a complement, such as "living in+NP."

5)   Adjectival PP

The soldiers on duty are not sleeping

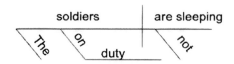

Practice Diagramming Prepositional Phrases in R-K

Diagram the following sentences

1. They are living in Phoenix.

2. In March, many students travel during a week of vacation.

3. They waited for ten minutes at the entrance to the theater.

4. At noon, they met in the coffee shop.

Subject Complements

Subject complements of linking verbs are indicated by a slanted line on top of the main horizontal which separates the complement from the verb string. This system does not distinguish between adjectival and nominal subject complements.

6)   Adjective subject complement

The mosh-pit was really overcrowded

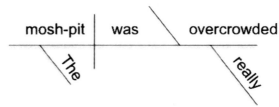

Note that possessive nouns are treated like determiners. A compound noun, or any adjectival noun, is also treated as a noun and not an adjective modifying a noun.

7)   Nominal subject complement ('Sam's cousin is becoming a fire
     fighter')

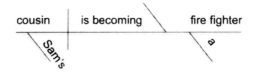

Practice with Subject Complements

Diagram these sentences

1. The jacket is green.

2. This is a green jacket.

3. The satin jacket felt incredibly smooth.

4. Because of that insult, he got very angry. (hint: 'because of' is a phrasal preposition.)

Direct Objects

Since it matters so much in this system, it is worth reviewing how to recognize a direct object. In sorting out transitive verbs from other kinds, it usually helps to ask the question, "What are they doing?" and try to answer it without a noun object. If the answer is acceptable grammatically, the verb is intransitive, if not, the verb requires an object or a complement. Testing the verb 'consider' will give us an example. "What are they doing? *They are considering." The answer is not acceptable, so the verb is not intransitive. Filling a noun object in helps us see if it's a direct object. 'They are considering my proposal.' That works. So if the subject 'they' and the object 'proposal' have different antecedents or referents (that is, they refer to different objects or ideas), then 'proposal' is a direct object. The direct object is placed next to the verb, which is appropriate because of their complementary relationship. It is separated by a half vertical line.

8)   A diagram of a transitive verb

That Claire has already finished her term paper.

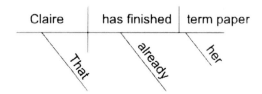

Practice with Transitive Verbs

Diagram these sentences.

1. She has read her history assignment.

2. Would you put your shoes in the corner? (hint-make it a statement)

3. He just bought a fresh pair of shoes.

4. Blake heard a new song on the radio.

5. Jonathan can throw a baseball incredibly far.

Indirect Objects

Indirect objects are treated in a way that is doubly unusual: first, they are placed below a verb string, rather than on the main horizontal line with the direct object or subject complements. This seems counter-intuitive until we notice that the shape of the line is that of a prepositional phrase that is missing its preposition. This is clever in the sense that it recognizes the optional transformation of an indirect object to a prepositional object in a "to"-phrase or a "for"-phrase. There is no difference in meaning and the two diagrams are almost exactly the same, as shown in the following two examples.

9)   A sentence with a ditransitive verb

   Barack is reading his children a bedtime story

10) An indirect object structured as a prepositional object

   Barack is reading a bedtime story to his children.

A transitive prepositional sentence, such as "They put the horseshoes around the stake" would also be diagrammed in the same way as the above diagram. Again, Reed-Kellogg makes no distinction between prepositional phrases which are complements and those which are modifiers.

Practice with Indirect Objects

Diagram these sentences

   1. He is writing his niece a letter.

   2. They gave the neighborhood children a warning about Halloween.

   3. They will make the school new banners for the next track season.

4. Tim always buys his younger brother lunch.

5. He made me an offer on the refrigerator.

6. Laura loved saving her family time and money

Noun Phrases Used Adverbially

The indirect object gives us an example of a way that a noun phrase can be shown to modify a verb. There are two other instances where this is useful and Reed and Kellogg were consistent in their use of an indirect-object-like shape for each of them. The first one consists of time references, indicating "when," such as "today," "yesterday," or "last month." The second consists of noun phrases that indicate "how often," such as "five times."

11) A sentence showing the adverbial use of NPs

Last evening, Jack fell down three times.

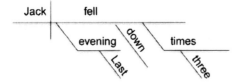

Complex Transitive Verbs

Complex transitive verbs look similar to linking verbs in the use of a slanted line above the horizontal one. As is true of the linking verbs, the diagram looks the same whether the complement is an adjective or a noun phrase.

12) A complex transitive sentence with a nominal object complement

Several students considered the course a challenge.

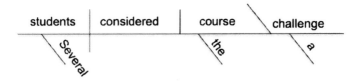

13) A complex transitive sentence with an adjectival object complement

Several students considered the course easy.

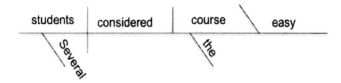

Practice with Complex Transitive Sentences

Diagram these sentences

1. The populace elected her president.

2. We never called him dishonest.

3. Jonathan named his car 'the beast.'

4. Many people considered the Captain America movie a success.

Coordinate Nouns, Verbs, Adjectives and Their Phrases

Coordinate structures are entertaining in Reed-Kellogg diagramming because of the visual effect created by the parallel lines with a connecting line for the conjunction(s). In order to give an impression of Reed and Kellogg's original work, sentences from their 1877 work "Higher Lessons in English" are reproduced for the following two examples of coordinate structures. For a coordinate NP subject, verb, direct object or subject or object complement, the main horizontal line is split among as many nouns, verbs, or adjectives as the coordinate structure includes, theoretically without any limit. The coordinating conjunction is placed on a dotted line. If one modifier modifies all of the members of the coordinate structure, as in the first example below, it is attached to a single extension of the compound array. The coordinate NP subject also shows the treatment of an interjection.

14) A sentence with a coordinate NP subject (and an interjection)

Ah! Anxious wives, sisters, and mothers wait for the news.

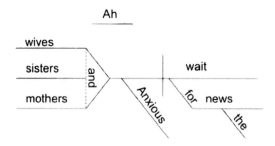

The following example also shows how a sentence with a passive verb is treated. The compound modifiers are adjectives, but the same principle would apply to compounded adverbs or prepositional phrases or quantifiers (such as "four or five"). Here an "x" has been used to signify the lack of the coordinating conjunction between "mental" and "moral," even though this was not done in the example above. Either way was apparently deemed acceptable.

15) Coordinate structures for adjective phrases

Many mental, moral, and muscular powers are improved by exercise (Reed & Kellog)

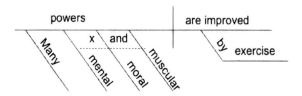

Practice with Coordinate Structures

Diagram these sentences

1. They washed and dried the dishes.

2. The wheel and axel was invented millennia ago. (hint: a postposition!)

3. Their school colors are black and yellow.

4. They like their pizza with pepperoni and bacon, but no cheese.

5. Austin usually goes to the gym or to the pool for exercise.

Prepositional Phrases Used Nominally or As Complements

Prepositional phrases are sometimes used nominally, such as when they are the object of another preposition. This usage allows us to see another shape which we can refer to as a 'stilt.' When a clause or phrase is functioning in the place of a specific grammatical category, such as a nominal clause acting as the subject, the whole clause goes up on stilts. It is used for many nominal structures, including all nominal clauses. Although the Reed-Kellogg system does not distinguish between adjectival and nominal complements, it does force us to recognize one unique feature of the linking verb 'be:' it can, in addition to adjectival and nominal complements, also have a prepositional phrase as a complement, as in the following sentence, which also shows a PP as the object of a P:

A prepositional phrase as the object of a preposition or subject complement:

The children from across the street are still in the family room

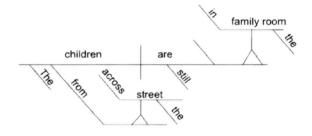

Practice with Prepositional Subject Complements

Diagram these sentences

1. My friends are all in really good shape.

2. At this speed, we will be on time.

3. Parker looks on the top of his game tonight.

4. Jillian and Jackson seemed beyond the point of friendship.

Appositives

The reflection-like appositive at it's simplest is simply a noun phrase that adds information about a previous noun phrase. In more complex situations, it's a full noun (nominal) clause. The NP form of appositive sis put in parentheses immediately next to the initial noun phrase, such as in the following sentence:

16) A sentence containing a simple (NP) appositive

Dr. Smith, our archeology teacher, looks like Indiana Jones.

Here we notice that 'look like' is a phrasal verb, so 'like' is not diagrammed as a preposition. This make 'Indiana Jones' a direct object.

Diagramming Sentences with Dependent Clauses

Nominal Clauses

Nominal clauses use the same stilt shape that was devised for the prepositional phrase in nominal or complement position. This allows us to see the CP in the position where the noun of an NP would be expected. The complementizer 'that' and interrogative adverb 'whether' float on a line above the verb and are connected to it by a dotted vertical line.

17) A nominal clause functioning as the subject

Whether they can book a flight today is a question. ('whether' marks the subject CP(N) in this example)

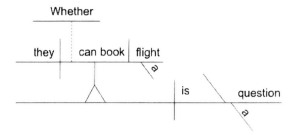

When wh-words are used as the specifiers of CP, they occupy the position of an adverb, noun, or determiner in the nominal phrase itself, as seen in the two examples below

18) A nominal clause functioning as a direct object

They discussed how they could get home on time.

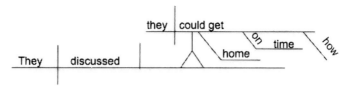

For **non-finite nominal clauses**, Reed and Kellogg recycled familiar forms to mark the infinitive form of the verb. The infinitive looks like a prepositional phrase with 'to' in the position of a preposition.

18) A non-finite nominal clause functioning as the object of a preposition

They wondered about where to get good information. ('where' is the complementizer introducing a prepositional object CP(N))

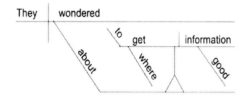

Appositive clauses are signaled in the same way that appositive NPs are, that is, by using parentheses around the appositive and placing it next to the NP that it is modifying, as seen here.

19) a nominal clause functioning as an appositive

The message that El Al had open seats cheered them up.

('that' marking an appositive CP(N))

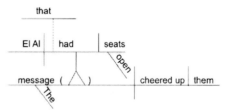

Indirect object clauses, in an analogous treatment to indirect object NPs, are placed in the noun position of a prepositional phrase.

20) A nominal clause functioning as an indirect object

They gave whomever they were sitting next to a big hug.

('whomever' marking an indirect object CP(N))

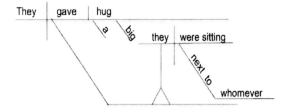

The treatment of **subject complement clauses** is also done in an analogous way to the diagramming of a subject complement NP.

21) A nominal clause functioning as a subject complement

The reason for joy was that they could leave very soon.

('that' marks a subject complement CP(N))

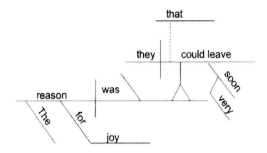

The complementizer 'for' in non-finite clauses is not diagrammed in the same way as the complementizer 'that,' but rather as if it were a preposition. This is similar to the way the auxiliary 'to' is treated in infinitives.

22) A non-finite nominal clause functioning as a subject

For them to be at home for Granma's funeral was a comfort.

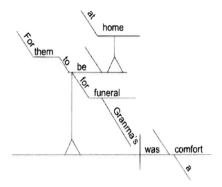

A final note here should focus briefly on **adjective complement clauses**, as in the earlier example 'They were amazed that things worked out.' The Reed-Kellogg approach consider all such clauses nominal. But the 'that' clause is shown under the adjective as a modifier of the adjective. The modifier line is the same shape as an indirect object – as if the clause were the object of an invisible preposition. There, it goes up on a stilt, as all nominal clauses do, like this.

25) An adjective complement clause: They were amazed that things worked out.

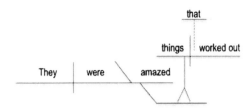

In this case, the stilt stands on the horizontal line of the prepositional-phrase shape, just as 'home' in the PP 'at home' stands on the prepositional-phrase shape of the previous diagram.

Practice with Nominal Clauses

Diagram these sentences.

1. That Odysseus' fate had changed in the land of the Cyclops was not clear to him or his sailors yet.

2. Homer describes that it was ten days' sail from Ithaca to his next destination: the Isle of Aeolus, the king of the winds.

3. Odysseus was very grateful the king gave him a bag with all the winds in it except the one favorable one. (The position of the deleted 'that' should be marked with an 'X') (Diagram the adjective complement clause as described in the text.)

4. For Odysseus' foolish sailors to open the bag and release the other winds meant that their twelve ships were blown back to the Aeolian Isle.

5. Their next adventure with the cannibal Laestrygonians confirmed Odysseus' fear that few of his crew would survive and return with him.

6. Odysseus next struggled on the Isle of the witch Circe for his crew to metamorphose back from pigs to men.

7. Whether they will call me for an interview remains to be seen.

8. I do hope I can get a job this summer.

9. They sent me a discouraging email that no positions were available at this time.

10. However, for me to be rejected once again did not break my spirit.

11. I sent whoever looked promising my next batch of applications.

12. I am still hoping that some opportunity will come my way.

Gerunds

Although a more modern view of **gerunds** is that they are a part of a clause, that was not the case in the nineteenth century, and gerunds were treated as a combination of a noun and a verb. They are put on a broken horizontal line since "Nouns and verbs are both written on horizontal lines" (Reed and Kellogg 66).

26)   A gerund used as a subject

Your writing the letter so neatly secured the position (Reed and Kellogg 66).

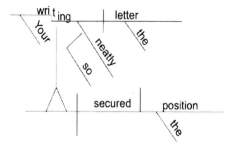

Practice with Gerunds

Diagram these sentences

1. We receive good by doing good.

2. Buying and selling goods provides many with a living.

3. Visiting relatives can be very tiring.

4. Swimming too soon after eating gives a person stomach aches.

5. Her working extra hours caught the boss's attention and got her a raise.

6. Speaking to yourself in public is bad for a person's reputation.

Participial Clauses or Phrases

When they are **gerundives**, both past and present participles are treated the same way: as a type of adjective which can turn into a verb if it has an object. In the simplest case, the participle is derived from an intransitive verb, and it precedes the noun. Here it looks just like an adjective. We'll use an example that contrasts with the gerund interpretation of the structurally ambiguous third sentence in the exercise set above.

27) A present participle (gerundive) used as a simple adjective

Visiting relatives can be tiring

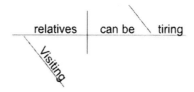

If the participle is derived from a transitive verb and follows the noun, on the other hand, the adjectival line grows to show its verbal characteristics.

28) A present participle representing a reduced relative clause

The man washing his car over there is Terry's uncle.

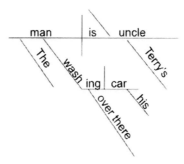

Practice Diagramming Participles

Diagram these sentences

1. The blushing man standing there has just proposed to his girlfriend

2. Pushed by the crowd, the young demonstrator fell.

3. Realizing they could succeed, the students studied hard.

Sentences with Subordinate and Relative Clauses

Subordinate and relative clauses are both diagrammed as separate sentences below the main clause. For subordinate clauses, a dotted line connects the two verbs with the subordinating conjunction on the dotted line.

29) An adverbial clause

It looks as if it'll rain.

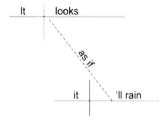

Relative clauses are different from adverbial clauses in that the relative marker has grammatical role within the dependent clause, and thus is not written on the connecting line. The connecting line in relative clauses is also different in that it connects the head noun in the higher clause to the relative marker in the relative clause.

30) A relative clause

Those are the people (who(m)) we saw yesterday.

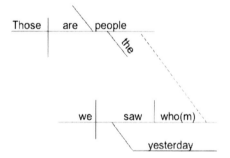

If the relative pronoun is deleted, as is optional in the above diagram, the missing pronoun is marked by an "X" in a way analogous to the "e" in phrase structure trees.

The original system set up by Reed and Kellogg is inconsistent in terms of where the relative marker was placed: relative pronouns were placed in their position within the relative clause, but relative adverbs were placed on the connecting line in the same way as subordinating conjunctions. Although this approach to grammar recognizes the original system, it prefers to treat all relative markers consistently and to allow only subordinating conjunctions and coordinating conjunctions to occupy a place on the connecting line. In this way, the diagram shows a clear difference between the use of relative adverbs which might be confused with subordinating conjunctions, such as 'when.'

31) An adjectival clause using a relative adverb

This is the week when the big decision will be made.

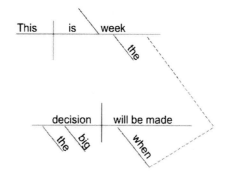

Practice with Subordinate and Relative Clauses

Diagram the following sentences.

1. We listen when pleasure calls (Reed and Kellogg 101).

2. Because they were so excited, they missed the announcement.

3. That's the dog (that/which) we saw yesterday.

4. Those are the people who invited us out.

5. That's the dog that/which ran away from home yesterday.

6. I found the place to which you referred (Reed and Kellogg 96)

7. They that play with tar will get stained.

8. There is no logical reason why I should stay at home this evening.

9. When my Facebook wall gets nasty comments, then an electronic solution will be useful.

10. A hard drive is a place where documents and graphics are stored.

In the case of subordinating conjunctions of time, the only way to distinguish their use to mark adjective clauses is that the line they are on leads to a head noun, rather than a verb in the higher clause.

32) An adjectival clause with a subordinating conjunction of time

The day after they finished their final exams was devoted to moving everything out of the dorms.

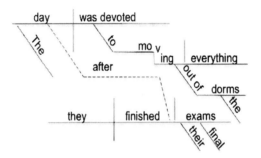

Compound Sentences

In distinction to their use in coordinate structures in smaller phrases, coordinating conjunctions in compound sentences are placed on a line connecting the verbs, as is done with subordinating conjunctions.

33) A compound sentence

Light has spread and darkness retreats (Reed & Kellogg)

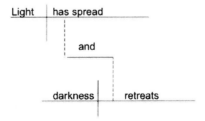

Clauses of Comparison and Degree

In clauses of comparison, Reed and Kellogg recognized the empty categories for both the verb and its complement, marking each of them with an "X," as is seen in this example from their 1887 text book.

34) A clause of comparison

Gold is heavier than iron (Reed and Kellogg 102)

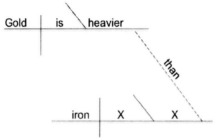

Superlative constructions recognize the deleted direct objects if the relative marker is an empty category. Here is an example with both e's marked.

35) A clause with a superlative
That was the most frightening movie e they had ever seen e.

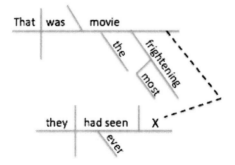

Clauses using the 'so....that...'' construction should treat 'so' as a qualifier/ intensifier (read 'adverb' for the nineteenth century), and the 'that' clause as a nominal complement to the adjective, as in the example below.

36) A clause of degree with 'so'
The classroom aircon was often so cold that everyone brought a sweater.

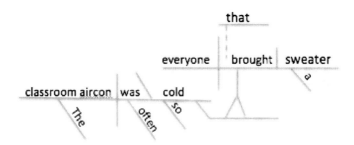

An example is included in the practice set below. Infinitive CPs following 'enough' should be treated as an infinitive phrase modifying 'adjective+enough'.

37) A clause of degree with 'enough'
They were strong enough to escape from the burning car.

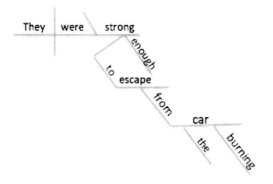

This type is also included in the practice set below.

Practice Diagramming Clauses of Comparison

1. My dad is stronger than your dad.

2. My dad can run faster than your dad.

3. The experimental plane goes faster than a plane has ever traveled before.

4. That's the fastest plane anyone has ever been built.

5. They were so exhausted that they could not walk another mile.

6. Our roommates thought that we were wise enough not to take such a risk.

Transformed Sentences

Transformed sentences in the Reed-Kellogg system are treated as if no movement had taken place. This requires the same skill as analyzing where the 'e' for an empty category would go, except that it is not empty in Reed-Kellogg but contains the moved element as if it had not moved. The only empty categories that are customarily marked are the deleted subject in imperatives, the deleted relative marker in some complex sentences, and the deleted verb and its complement in clauses of comparison.

Summary Reed-Kellogg Diagramming Practice

Diagram your choice of the following sentences, but don't look back at the answers in the previous section.

1. A bystander was amazed that things worked out. ('That' marks an adjective complement clause)

2. All the relatives knew they would be glad to get home.

3. That they could arrive on time was now a certainty.

4. I wondered if/whether they would arrive on time

5. I didn't know whether to donate money to that campaign.

6. It was not too late for you to start a new life.

7. I am hoping you will come home soon

8. My GPS found the place about which you wrote.

9. They that curry favor will be disappointed.

10. We react when temptation rears its head.

11. He did what was considered right.

12. This is the time when the election for president will be held.

13. When my gait slows down and my eyes dim, then I will need help from above.

14. A school is an institution where students can be challenged and taught.

15. My Dad weighs less than your Dad.

16. My Dad always eats faster than my Mom.

17. The new orbiter flies faster than any plane has ever flown.

18. That's the fastest computer any company has ever built.

19. They were so exhausted that they could not swim another ten feet.

20. Our roommates thought that we were wise enough not to take such a risk.

21. Rich to the point of embarrassment, Warren Buffet announced his support for a special tax on the wealthy.

22. For us to stay at home when wild fires are approaching would be insane.

23. Going anywhere safe would be wiser than staying.

24. Shane rested under a tree where he often went as a child.

25. They ordered Dominoes again even though they ate pizza last night.

26. Mike slowly jogged home after he hit the game winning homerun.

27. Whenever the temperature rises above 100 degrees, they jump in the pool to stay warm.

28. If I don't drink coffee in the morning, my head hurts

Chapter 10: Tools for Analyzing Writing

Several analytical tools are available for a sometimes-revealing look at writing. Two of them, a T-score calculation and a Corbett profile, are potentially useful to anyone, no matter whether the writer is in first grade or in a publishing house. The other analytic technique, contrastive analysis, is most useful for writers whose home language is a non-standard variety of English. For writers whose first language is standard American English (SAE), or any other standard variety, the technique should not work at all, in theory.

Using contrastive analysis to analyze writing done by writers whose first language is not English is possible, but less practical because the writer's second-language grammar may still be developing and changing, which would require continuing re-analysis. Below, contrastive analysis is paired with a short introduction to code-switching as a pedagogical technique. The term 'contrastive analysis' in this context is not the same as the usage of the same term in a second-language ('L2') learning context where it was applied (unsuccessfully) as a way of predicting which areas of L2 grammar would give students the most difficulty.

T-score Calculation and Flesch Readability Indices

T-scores are simple statistical measures that can be used for innumerable purposes. The term 'T-score' is not a technical term for grammatical analysis. Arithmetically, T-scores are simply averages, and so provide no computational complexity. Conceptually, in this context, a T-score is a measure of syntactic maturity that was invented for the purpose of analyzing a writer's syntactic maturity or syntactic complexity (Hunt 4). It measures the growth of syntactic maturity in younger writers, and it measures the growth of restraint in more mature writers. It favors complex sentences over compound sentences, and it favors simple sentences with adverbial modifiers that can be fronted over simple sentences without such modifiers. The only theoretical knowledge required for this sort of analysis is the ability to distinguish an independent clause from every other type of grammatical structure, so it is by far the simplest of these tools to use.

A T-score for any given written text is computed by counting the number of words and dividing that by the number of independent clauses contained in the text. For a text with fragments, one has a choice of not counting the fragments at all, or counting them as independent clauses, depending on the purpose of the analysis.

Here is a paragraph and its analysis:

1)   Example paragraph for T-score computation using the above paragraph

T-scores are simple statistical measures that can be used for innumerable purposes. [one independent clause] Arithmetically, they are simply averages, and so provide no computational complexity. [one independent clause] Conceptually, in the present context, a T-score is a measure of syntactic maturity that was invented for this purpose. [one independent clause] It measures the growth of syntactic maturity in younger writers, and it measures the growth of restraint in more mature writers. [two independent clauses connected by 'and'] It favors complex sentences over compound sentences, and it favors simple sentences with the kind of adverbial modifiers that can be fronted over simple sentences without such modifiers. [two independent clauses connected by 'and'] The only theoretical knowledge required is the ability to distinguish an independent clause from every other type of grammatical structure, so it is by far the simplest of these tools to use. [two independent clauses connected by 'so'] (123 words) [9 indep. clauses] T-score: $123/9 = 13.7$.

What does a T-score of 13.7 tell us? Research done at Florida State University in the 1960's indicates that the average T-score of the fourth graders in the study was 8.6; eighth-graders averaged 11.5, twelfth-graders averaged 14.4, and authors published in two national literary magazines averaged 20.3 (Hunt 6). We can conclude, then, that the sample paragraph was written at the syntactic maturity of a junior or senior in high school. One other point deserves to be mentioned, namely that more complexity is not necessarily more mature. T-scores higher that 21 can indicate a level of syntactic complexity that is a burden to the reader who has to keep track of multiple dependent clauses.

This simple analysis gives different results from the commonly used Flesch Readability Index and the Flesch Reading Ease Index. [1] These two, related, indices weigh not only the number of words per sentence, but also give important weight to the average number of syllables per word. Thus they would show short sentences with morphologically complex words to be quite difficult to read, in contrast to the simpler T-score analysis[2]. The two Flesch indices for the above text calculate it to be at the 16.13 grade level, or that of a new college graduate, with an ease of readability at 22. 79. The readability scale classifies numbers in the 0-30 range to be at a college graduate's level, those in the thirties and forties to be at a college level and those in the fifties and sixties to be at a high school level[3]. Thus the two Flesch ratings are consistent with one another in classifying

---

[1] The program can be downloaded as freeware for either a Macintosh or PC type of operating system: (*www.macupdate.com/app/mac/15848/flesh*) or *enable it in the word program:*   http://office.microsoft.com/en-us/word-help/test-your-document-s-readability-HP010148506.aspx: (accessed most recently 23 August 2012).
[2] The computational formula is this: Flesch Reading Ease Index = 206.835 – 84.6 x (# of syllables ÷ # of words) - 1.015 x (#of words ÷ # of sentences)
[3] adapted from Flesch. R. *The art of readable writing.* New York: Harper 1949.149.

the text to be comfortable for a college graduate, and rather difficult for a college student. It is up to the reader to see which calculation seems closer to her or his experience in reading the text. This experiential factor is important in deciding which index to use for what purpose.

Corbett Profile

Edward P.J. Corbett, a well-respected rhetoritician and writing teacher, developed a number of different ways of profiling writing for the purpose of analyzing and improving style. One of his profiles which has been further developed in other research counts the number of simple, compound, complex, and compound-complex sentences, and a larger number of other variables which add sophistication to the analysis. For the sake of simplicity these further variables will be ignored for now.

This stripped-down version of the Corbett profile gives important insights into a writer's sentence variety. Theoretically, one only has to be able to distinguish the four sentence types. Computationally, one only needs to be able to divide the total number of sentences in a writing sample by the number of each sentence type in order to calculate the percentage of sentences of that type in the sample. The following text on "Fairness" comes from a Wikipedia entry. Although Wikipedia is not considered reliable for use as a source of information for academic use, its entries are excellent sources of texts for stylistic and other analyses. Here is an example calculation.

2)   Sample Corbett computation and profile of a short text

In his *A Theory of Justice*, John Rawls used a social contract argument to show that justice, and especially distributive justice, is a form of fairness [complex]. It is based on an impartial distribution of goods [simple]. Rawls asks us to imagine ourselves behind a veil of ignorance that denies us all knowledge of our personalities, social statuses, moral characters, wealth, talents and life plans, and then he asks what theory of justice we would choose to govern our society when the veil is lifted, if we wanted to do the best that we could for ourselves [compound-complex]. We don't know our own specific characteristics, and therefore we can't bias the decision in our own favor [compound]. So, the decision-in-ignorance models fairness, because it excludes selfish bias [complex]. Rawls argues that each of us would reject the utilitarian theory of justice that we should maximize welfare because of the risk that we might turn out to be someone whose own good is sacrificed for greater benefits for others [complex]. Instead, we would endorse Rawls's two principles of justice [simple]. Each person is to have an equal right to the most extensive total system of equal basic liberties that is compatible with a similar system of liberty for all [complex]. Social and economic inequalities are to be arranged so that they are both to the greatest benefit of the least advantaged, consistent with the just savings principle, and

---

(http://www.utexas.edu/disability/ai/resource/readability/manual/forcast-versus-flesch-English.html) (accessed most recently 1 September 2012).

attached to offices and positions open to all under conditions of fair equality of opportunity [complex].

This imagined choice justifies these principles as the principles of justice for us, because we would agree to them in a fair decision procedure [complex]. Rawls's theory distinguishes two kinds of goods – (1) liberties and (2) social and economic goods, i.e. wealth, income and power – and applies different distributions to them [simple]. For the first there would be equality between citizens[simple]. For the second the standard would be equality unless inequality improves the position of the worst off [complex] (Anonymous).

3) Computation and profile (total number of sentences = 13):

Simple sentences - 4 out of 13 = 4/13 = 31%

Compound sentences - 1/13 = 8%

Complex sentences – 7/13 = 54%

Compound-complex sentences - 1/13 = 8%

(rounding up produced a 1% error): = 101%

The one percent error from rounding up is not a problem for the analysis, since what we are looking for is the relative frequency of different sentence types. The above profile can be seen as an example of good sentence variety. It shows a majority of complex sentences, which is generally considered a mature, effective style for most purposes since complex sentences show the relation between the ideas in the main clause and the subordinate clause(s). The low frequency of compound sentences is also considered effective style for most purposes for the opposite reason that coordinate conjunctions show little or no relationship between the ideas in their coordinate clauses. A equally small number of compound-complex sentences is often praised as an attempt to keep the reader from having to process too many ideas in a single sentence.

A relatively large number of simple sentences is often appropriate in order to give a mental counter-balance to the longer sentences and give the reader a smaller processing burden between the longer sentences. Saying 'often' and 'for most purposes' here reflects the need to make stylistic choices that are designed to accomplish the specific purpose of the piece of writing, so there are no hard and fast rules about what an ideal profile should look like. There should be clear reasons for the choices that are being made, however. One factor not yet mentioned is that the density of the complex and simple sentences also matters in that they should usually be fairly evenly mixed, rather than having all of one type clumped together. Again, this depends on the writer's purpose.

If the complex sentences (or any of the other types for that matter) were too long and complicated, we would be able to notice that with a T-score calculation or the Flesch indices. So the two types of analytical tool complement each other.

Contrastive Analysis and Code-switching

For those actively helping student writers whose home dialect is non-standard, certain non-standard features ('errors', or – better - 'anomalies') occur with predictable regularity. These dialectal forms are obvious to speakers and writers of the standard language. Such regular patterns can form the basis for a pedagogical technique called code-switching which has been shown to be more effective than the traditional correction technique where the teacher marks the errors and returns the writing to the writer for corrections.

The first step is the process called contrasitive analysis, which starts by listing the patterns of non-standard grammatical features. Contrastive analysis then moves from recognizing student writing errors to cataloging and categorizing them. The listing of non-standard features can then be put into charts, first for the teacher's use, and later, for the student's use. After the teacher has set up charts contrasting the student usage with standard American English ("SAE"), it's important to try to conceptualize the reasons for the non-standard usage, which usually reside in the student's non-standard cognitive grammar. This involves the same analytical tools that we have worked through in the previous eight chapters.

As mentioned above, this is most appropriate for writers who speak a non-standard English dialect, rather than those whose second language is English, and almost never for native speakers of SAE. The reason is that non-standard English dialects are first languages whose grammar remains a stable part of the writer's cognition. So a teacher's careful analysis can remain useful to the writer for a lifetime. Second-language writers, in contrast, generally have grammars which are subject to change as they learn more about English. Their cognitive grammars of English are in flux, making a careful analysis of today's writing patterns less relevant at some future time when a more accurate grammar has been acquired. These techniques still work for some second language ("L2") speakers and writers of English, but the results are less stable, and usually require on-going reanalysis.

Research has shown that this approach to standardizing a student's grammar is effective. At Aurora University, near Chicago, urban AAE speakers in high school were taught the linguistic differences between their dialect and SAE in a writing class. Over an 11-week period, their use of AAE features in writing dropped 59% (Rickford). A parallel control group was taught writing in a traditional way by simply pointing out non-standard usage and telling the students to replace it with standard usage. No reference was made to the students' home dialect AAE. The control group's use of AAE features increased 8.5% during the same period (Rickford). The conclusion is that students learn better when they are taught to recognize the existence of two different dialects and to make an effort to help students develop bidialectal abilities with a sensitivity to when each dialect is appropriate. Bidialectalism does not apply the same way to L2 English writing.

Below is a short look at the contrasts between Shakespeare's English and Standard American English. Shakespeare's English has been chosen as the guinea pig for this analysis so that this technique can be applied to other non-standard dialects as a classroom or research experience. If the following sample analysis were to use Hawaiian Pidgen, Appalachian English, or African American English, texts in those dialects would not be as fresh and new for students to try to exercise their own understanding and to learn by practicing these techniques. An overview of the basic process has three main steps: 1) mark the differences, 2) group differences (or anomalies) that are similar and put them into chart form, and 3) explain the reasons for the non-standard usage.

Contrastive Analysis Exercise

What morphological and syntactic structures in Shakespeare's English are different from SAE? First, set up a list, then a table, of comparisons. Here is a sample from the writer of non-standard English that we will look at briefly.

4) Writing Sample featuring Early Modern English (EME) as the home dialect

    "Whether had you rather lead mine eyes, or eye your master's heels?" (Mistress Page in The Merry Wives of Windsor, III, ii, 3).

    "Belong you to the Lady Olivia, friends?" (Duke Orsino in Twelfth Night, V, i, 9)

    "Signior Hortensio, come you to part the fray?" (Petruchio in Taming of the Shrew, I, ii, 22)

    "But died thy sister of her love, my boy?" (Duke Orsino in Twelfth Night, II, iv, 105)

    "…pure surprise and fear/Made me to quit the house." (First Gentleman in Pericles, Prince of Tyre, III, ii, 24)

    "I had rather hear you to solicit that/ Than music from the spheres.." (Olivia in Twelfth Night, III, i, 72)

    "I go, sir; but I would not have you to think that my desire of having is the sin of covetousness:" (Clown in Twelfth Night, V, i, 27)

    "Blood hath bought blood, and blows have answer'd blows." (King John, II, i)

    "First he denied you had in him no right." (Comedy of Errors, IV. 2. 7.)

    "You may deny that you were not the cause." (Richard III, I. 3. 90.)

    "Forbade the boy he should not pass these bounds. " The Passionate Pilgrim IX. 10

The anomalies in Early Modern English (EME) can be charted in the following way:

Table 4: Writing sample by Shakespeare in contrastive analysis to SAE

Early Modern English text	EME syntactic feature	Standard American English equivalent
"Whether had you rather lead mine eyes, or eye your master's heels?"	1) Whether+perf. aux+ subj...? (conditional y/n Q	1) Would you rather...? Modal aux+subj...? (no wh-)
"Belong you to the Lady Olivia, friends?"	2) main V+subj...? (indicative y/n Q)	2) Do you belong to.. do+subj+V...?
"Signior Hortensio, come you to part the fray?"	3) V+subj...? (indicative y/n Q)	3) Have you come to ...? have+subj+V...?
"But died thy sister of her love, my boy?"	4) V+subj...? (indicative y/n Q) (a reminder of thou/thee/thy forms)	4) Did your sister die...? do+subj+V...?
...pure surprise and fear/Made me to quit the house.	5)made+obj.prn+to+V ('made'+ +infinitive)	5) fear made me leave.. made+obj.prn+V (made+ + bare infin.)
I had rather hear you to solicit that/ Than music from the spheres.	6) hear+obj.prn+to+V ('hear'+ +infinitive)	6) hear you request ... hear+obj.prn+V (hear+ +bare infin.)
I go, sir; but I would not have you to think that my desire of having is the sin of covetousness:	7) have+obj.prn+to+V	7) have you think... heav+obj.prn+V (have+ +bare infin.)
"Blood hath bought blood, and blows have answer'd blows."	8) morphology of 'have' 3S pres. 'hath'	8) morphology of 'have' 3S pres. 'has'
"First he denied you had in him no right."	9) denied (that)+ subj.prn+have+no right	9) denied you had any right to him denied (that)+ subj. prn+ have+any right
"You may deny that you were not the cause."	10) had+PP+d.o. 11) denied (that)+ subj.prn+be+not NP	10) had+d.o.+PP 11) denied you were the cause. subj.prn+be+NP
"Forbade the boy he should not pass these bounds. "	12) forbid+NP+(that)+	12) forbid the boy to pass..

	subj. prn+aux+not+V	forbid+NP+to+V

So far, this not only lists the differences, but it also gives a structural outline of the divergent grammatical structures. The previous eight chapters should be useful in making these analyses, starting with lexical categories. Explanations can be derived directly from this sort of chart. These explanations are most useful if seen from the student/writer's point of view, so they will be discussed in the following section as part of the process of teaching a student to 'code switch.'

Code Switching

The purpose of teaching code switching as an academic exercise is to show respect for the student's non-standard home dialect. It moves the student through the same comparative exercise that the teacher has already worked through in analyzing the student's non-standard usage. The teacher can show the student examples of his/her own work and show the corresponding SAE usage, helping the student to set up a chart of numerous usages of the same type and grouping them together, while separating out other non-standard usages for a separate chart. It is helpful to show the student that the code-switching can work both ways: that it is possible to predict non-standard usage from standard usage just as readily as to predict standard usage from non-standard usage. This is the foundation for allowing the student to appreciate bidialectal code-switch both orally and in writing. Respectfully done, this chart creation can also help L2 English writers.

Code Switching Applied

Looking at the chart that was created by contrastive analysis, we want to be able to explain each divergence of the home dialect (EME) in the writing sample(s) from the standard language (SAE in this case).

First, we use the structural description to separate the data set into structurally similar groups:

5)   "Belong you to the Lady Olivia, friends?"

"Signior Hortensio, come you to part the fray?"

"But died thy sister of her love, my boy?"

The grammatical structures above (writing sample items 2-4) all relate to yes-no questions. The explanation of these examples should produce a single set of procedures for code switching from EME to SAE for yes-no questions.

6)   "Whether had you rather lead mine eyes, or eye your master's heels?"

The grammatical structure in the item above becomes a yes-no question in SAE, but its EME structure needs its own explanation; its structural description is different enough to need an explanation after the issue of yes-no question formation is resolved.

7)   …pure surprise and fear/Made me to quit the house.

I had rather hear you to solicit that/ Than music from the spheres. I go, sir; but I would not have you to think that my desire of having is the sin of covetousness:

The sentences in item 7 above (grammatical structures 5-7 in the chart) should be useful in producing a single set of procedures for code switching for some of the verbs that introduce bare infinitive structures in SAE ('make,' 'hear', and 'have' in this data set, which also suggests other possibilities such as 'watch' and 'help.'). Notice that SAE still requires verbs like 'force,' 'require,' and 'ask' to use complete infinitives with 'to'. In this respect, EME was thus much more consistent than is SAE. [4]

8)   "Blood hath bought blood, and blows have answer'd blows."

Grammatical structure 8 is simply a reminder of the EME conjugation of verbs in the third person singular forms (and, inferentially, second person singular 'thou' form with –st: hast, goest, wantest…).

9)   "First he denied you had in him no right."

"You may deny that you were not the cause."

"Forbade the boy he should not pass these bounds. "

The grammatical structures in 9 containing 'deny' should allow the production of a single simple rule for code switching for verbs such as 'deny' whose complement clauses normally don't contain a negator like 'not'. The sentence with 'forbid' is different in that SAE usually uses a non-finite VP in addition to the code switching needed to remove a negator.

10)   "…you had in him no right."

Grammatical structure 10 should produce a rule defining the order of verb-direct object NP-modifying PP.

Following the grouping of the structures in the writing sample, an explanation should be created which creates a procedure for moving from the home dialect

---

[4] This lack of consistency in SAE in comparison to other dialects is also seen in some particular instances in home dialects today. One such instance is the home dialect use of 'hisself' and 'theirselves.' (These two non-standard forms are consistent in having he same morphology of determiner [like 'my-,' 'your-,' and 'our-,'] +self, which are the acceptable forms. The forms 'himself' and 'themselves' are inconsistent in combining an object pronoun [like 'me-,' 'you-,' and 'us-'] which normally cannot combine with '-self'.

grammar to the SAE grammar. This can be put in a list or a chart, whichever is more helpful to the student-writer.

Explanatory Procedures for Code-switching from Early Modern English to SAE

The following explanatory procedure is based on the above writing sample. There are sometimes pedagogical reasons for preferring to discuss the syntactic anomalies first and others later, and that is a matter of judging the student's learning style and comfort level.

Code Switching for Yes-no Questions

When introducing these non-standard structures to the student writer, the mentor, tutor, or teacher should have an exercise set up that will allow the writer to discover for himself or herself the principles involved.

For the anomalous yes/no questions above, two or three sentences from the student's writing would be contrasted with the appropriate translation into SAE. Another two or three anomalous structures would be listed without any such translation, so that the student could derive the SAE forms for herself or himself. Since we only have three items to work with, we'll use the first one as the opportunity for the student to discover the principles of the translation (or transformation), perhaps with a little help. The second one can be used to help the writer gain confidence using the principles involved, and the third one to show off his or her newly-gained skill. As mentioned before, it's better to have several sentences for each of these steps, rather than only one. This is represented by the numbers with no sentence to work on.

Example of a transformation (translation) exercise chart for 'yes/no' questions

The student writer's home dialect (Early Modern English)	Standard American English
1. "Belong you to the Lady Olivia, friends?"	1. Do you belong to the Lady Olivia, friends?
2. ...	2. ...
3. "Signior Hortensio, come you to part the fray?"	3. "Signior Hortensio, _____ to part the fray?
4. ...	4. ...
5. "But died thy sister of her love, my boy?"	5.But _____ _____?

In introducing this translation sequence to the writer, we'll start with the question "Belong you to the Lady Olivia, friends?"

First, we would like the writer to see that the verb needs to be moved back into its normal post-NP declarative position, giving us "You belong to the Lady Olivia, friends"

Then we will help the student see that it's useful to make the statement emphatic, producing "You do belong to the Lady Olivia, friends."

Finally, we can show how front the auxiliary 'do' to the position that 'belong' had in the original data and restore the question mark , giving us "Do you belong to the Lady Olivia, friends?" This is the SAE form.

Next we would lead the writer through the code-switching procedure using data structure 2., starting with the new position of the main verb, then the addition of the auxiliary 'do', and finally the fronting of the auxiliary. The third stage would be to let the writer work independently to gain practice with this element of code switching.

Continuing on to the next strucuture, we see the data sentence, "Whether had you rather lead mine eyes...?" It is a reminder that 'whether' no longer functions in direct yes-no questions in SAE and needs to be deleted, giving "Had you rather lead mine eyes...?"

Once the wh-word 'whether' is removed, we notice that 'rather' in SAE is used with the auxiliary 'would' and not with 'have.' This is simply a matter of different vocabulary or lexical choices than in EME. The structure 'aux+rather' is exactly in both dialects. Such differences in lexical preference are unrelated to grammatical structure and completely unpredictable. They can only be memorized.

The substitution of SAE 'my' for EME 'mine' requires making the distinction between the possessive determiners (my, your...) and the possessive pronouns (mine, yours, ...). These categories were not so distinct in Shakespeare's dialect as in SAE.

Code Switching for Modern Bare Infinitives

We'll use the clause "I had rather hear you to solicit that than..."
Before starting, we'll borrow the lexical difference or preference that 'had rather' becomes 'would rather' in SAE from the above procedure for yes-no questions, giving us "I would rather hear you to solicit that than ..."

The **first** step in the bare infinitives procedure is to recognize the verb 'hear' is one of those in SAE that introduces a complement clause with a bare infinitive.

The **second** step is to delete the 'to' from the infinitive, giving us "I would rather hear you solicit that than ...". This is the SAE form.

Then, after having explained the code-switching procedure using data structure 6, the EME speaker could be led through the same procedures with the sentences from structures 5 and 7 to gain practice with this bit of code switching.

At this point it's potentially useful to add reverse code-switching to this discussion. One reason to encourage reverse code switching from SAE to the home dialect is to validate in the student's mind both the method as one that can work for any two dialects. A second reason is also to validate the home dialect, which is rule-governed and predictable in the way all human languages are. This does not apply to L2 English. There is another benefit to working through a reverse code switching exercise with a student-writer. S/he will notice that the exercise does not produce a perfect version of the home dialect. Just as the reverse code switching does not create a perfect version of the home dialect, so the student's code switching will initially not create a perfect version of the standard dialect. This realization should lead to a number of teachable moments where the student can be helped to better appreciate her/his own need to continue learning the skill of code switching to the standard language.

Reverse code switching can be shown most easily by teachers or tutors who are bi-dialectal in the sense that they can accurately predict what a given sentence or grammatical structure in SAE will be in the home dialect. For teachers of SAE who are helping students whose home dialects they are not so familiar with, reverse code switching poses some risk to their position of authority, since the student knows more than they do about what the home dialect version of any given SAE sentence is.

Where potential loss of face would be a significant burden to the classroom dynamic, reverse code switching should, clearly, be avoided. But where there are several students whose writing shows the same grammatical effects from the same home dialect, it is possible to avoid the potential of loss of face by using one student's sentences in the reverse code switching exercises for another student, thus guaranteeing an accurate version of the home dialect.

In the case of reverse code-switching from SAE to EME, the teacher could easily make up another sentence or two for code switching from SAE into EME. This was not mentioned for the code-switching procedures with yes-no questions because they are somewhat more complex. That would be an exercise to return to later. The bare infinitives provide a simpler environment in which to initiate a discussion about code-switching from SAE to the home dialect.

This is a useful principle to carrying into any reverse code switching situation – begin with the simplest examples possible. Here the possibilities of 'watch' and 'help' which were mentioned above would allow an affirming dialog about code switching, using a sentence like "Olivia helped her friends learn about the dangers around them." The reverse code-switching rule is simply to insert the auxiliary 'to' in front of the bare infinitive, giving us "Olivia helped her friends to learn about the dangers around them." This is not only correct in EME, but it's also acceptable in SAE, showing that the language change which over the centuries has created bare infinitives is not complete in the case of the verb 'help.' Using a sentence with the verb 'watch' would bring out this difference more clearly.

Code switching for Verbs like 'Deny' and 'Forbid'

We'll use the sentence "You may deny that you were not the cause" as the basis for a code-switching procedure. We notice as a matter of structure that the complementizer 'that' is optional in both EME and SAE for the verb 'deny', so code-switching is not needed to determine whether to include the complementizer or not. It is helpful to the student writer, though, to mention that 'that' can be optional in both EME and SAE.

First. There are several ways to approach this explanation. One would be to distinguish verbs that allow a negator like 'not' in the complement clause, such as 'think' or 'say,' as in 'I thought/said they would not come.' But then we notice that these two verbs also allow negation in both clauses, such as "I didn't think/say that they would not be coming.' So a more direct approach here is to focus on multiple negation.

The main point here may be to show that verbs like 'deny' and 'forbid' already contain a negator: 'deny' means something like 'say that .. not,' and 'forbid' means something like 'not allow...' Home dialects often allow multiple negation in ways that SAE does not, so this issue is an important one for code switching. The difference may be, as here, whether the basic interpretive principle is additive (like this: -1 + -1 = -2) or multiplicative (like this: -1 x -1 = +1). Under an additive principle, the two negatives remain negative or become more negative.

A typical example is a sentence like, "We won't never save enough money to go to Six Flags." Under a multiplicative principle, two negatives become positive, three negatives are again negative, and so on. Where verbs have an implicit negative meaning, several of them may appear in the same sentence in SAE, and they are grammatically acceptable under a multiplicative interpretation, even though they are stylistically frowned on because the combinations are difficult to interpret. One example sentence would be "We refused to forget to neglect to fast." In order to answer the question "Are we eating or not?" each of the four verbs containing a semantic negative has be be multiplied by the next one. In all, they become a positive, giving the answer, "Yes" to the question. If one of the verbs were removed, the answer would be "No."

The two negatives in the EME sentence are meant to produce a negative interpretation. So, we see that the EME speaker is using an additive principle to interpret 'deny ... not.' SAE speakers, in contrast, would most likely use a multiplicative principle to interpret the same sentence if they didn't simply reject it as unacceptable. This difference needs to be made clear to the EME speaker.

Second. After understanding the difference in interpreting multiple negation in SAE and EME, the EME speaker would need to practice removing multiple negators from sentences where a negative meaning is intended. The most helpful examples should come from the student's own writing. But other examples can be constructed if one is willing to run the risk of being laughed at by the student for an example that does not sound like the home dialect.

Third. Such examples might be similar to these. We begrudged him that he didn't crash the party. We disallowed that he might not go to the party. They contradicted us that there was no party that evening. They disproved that they didn't go to the party. They all doubted that they couldn't speak freely. We withheld that they couldn't go to another party the next day.

Fourth. The writing sample's grammatical structure in the complement clause to the verb 'forbid' is more complex because its verb is non-finite. This is a matter of lexical distinctions and can only be solved by memoring a list of such verbs or by reading a great deal. None of the verbs in the example sentences in c) above, with the possible exception of 'disallow,' permit the infinitive form of the verb in the complement clause. The verbs 'forget,' 'neglect' and 'refuse' are similar to 'forbid' in SAE.

Contrastive Analysis Practice

The following is from the Prologue to Geoffrey Chaucer's "Canterbury Tales" which is older than Shakespeare's works by more than two centuries. The reason for the choice of this particular textual source is that it is more familiar to present-day readers than almost any other Middle English text. For the sake of clarity, vocabulary is explained briefly in the margin, and somewhat longer, numbered footnotes below the text[5].

Choose 20 or so lines and set up a contrastive analysis of Chaucer's non-standard usage (according to present-day standards) and SAE.

1)   A Middle English text for contrastive analysis

THE CANTERBURY TALES

THE PROLOGUE (Chaucer)
WHEN that Aprilis, with his showers swoot*, *sweet
The drought of March hath pierced to the root,
And bathed every vein in such licour,
Of which virtue engender'd is the flower;
When Zephyrus eke with his swoote breath
Inspired hath in every holt* and heath *grove, forest
The tender croppes* and the younge sun *twigs, boughs
Hath in the Ram <1> his halfe course y-run,
And smalle fowles make melody,
That sleepen all the night with open eye,
(So pricketh them nature in their corages*); *hearts, inclinations
Then longe folk to go on pilgrimages,
And palmers <2> for to seeke strange strands,
To *ferne hallows couth* in sundry lands; *distant saints known*<3>
And specially, from every shire's end
Of Engleland, to Canterbury they wend,
The holy blissful Martyr for to seek,
That them hath holpen*, when that they were sick. *helped
Befell that, in that season on a day,
In Southwark at the Tabard <4> as I lay,
Ready to wenden on my pilgrimage
To Canterbury with devout corage,

---

[5] Notes 1. Tyrwhitt points out that "the Bull" should be read here, not "the Ram," which would place the time of the pilgrimage in the end of March; whereas, in the Prologue to the Man of Law's Tale, the date is given as the "eight and twenty day of April, that is messenger to May." 2. Dante, in the "Vita Nuova," distinguishes three classes of pilgrims: palmieri - palmers who go beyond sea to the East, and often bring back staves of palm-wood; peregrini, who go the shrine of St Jago in Galicia; Romei, who go to Rome. Sir Walter Scott, however, says that palmers were in the habit of passing from shrine to shrine, living on charity -- pilgrims on the other hand, made the journey to any shrine only once, immediately returning to their ordinary avocations. Chaucer uses "palmer" of all pilgrims. 3. "Hallows" survives, in the meaning here given, in All Hallows -- All-Saints -- day. "Couth," past participle of "conne" to know, exists in "uncouth." 4. The Tabard -- the sign of the inn -- was a sleeveless coat, worn by heralds. The name of the inn was, some three centuries after Chaucer, changed to the Talbot.

At night was come into that hostelry
Well nine and twenty in a company
Of sundry folk, *by aventure y-fall *who had by chance fallen
In fellowship*, and pilgrims were they all, into company.* <5>[6]
That toward Canterbury woulde ride.
The chamber, and the stables were wide,
And *well we weren eased at the best.* *we were well provided
And shortly, when the sunne was to rest, with the best*
So had I spoken with them every one,
That I was of their fellowship anon,
And made forword* early for to rise, *promise
To take our way there as I you devise*. *describe, relate

Supplemental Contrastive Analysis Practice

The following is from the Wycliffe translation of the book of Acts (chapter seventeen) in the New Testament. It, too, is older than Shakespeare's works by more than two centuries. The same reason applies to the choice of this text as did to Chaucer's. Its content is more familiar to present-day readers than perhaps even Chaucer's, just in case Chaucer's world is too unfamiliar. This text is easier to read than is Chaucer's and can also be used for contrastive analysis.

Choose ten verses and analyze the differences between Wycliffe's translation and SAE. The following version is modernized to the extent of using more standard spelling, which allows us to focus on grammatical differences and not be too distracted by the choice of vocabulary items or the spelling conventions.

2) A Middle English text by Wycliffe for contrastive analysis
   [18] And some Epicureans, and Stoics, and philosophers disputed with him. And some said, What will this sower of words say? And others said, He seemeth to be a teller of new fiends; for he told to them Jesus, and the again-rising.
   [19] And they took and led him to Areopagus and said, May we know, what is this new doctrine, that is said of thee?
   [20] For thou bringest in some new things to our ears; therefore we will know, what these things will be.
   [21] For all men of Athens and comelings harboured gave attention to none other thing, but either to say, either to hear, some new thing.
   [22] And Paul stood in the middle of Areopagus, and said, Men of Athens, by all things I see you as vain worshippers.
   [23] For I passed, and saw your maumets, and found an altar, in which was written, To the unknown God. Therefore which thing ye unknowing

---

[6] 5. In "y-fall," "y" is a corruption of the Anglo-Saxon "ge" prefixed to participles of verbs. It is used by Chaucer merely to help the metre. In German, "y-fall," or y-falle," would be "gefallen". "y-run," or "y-ronne", would be "geronnen." [from the Project Gutenberg Etext of The Canterbury Tales and Other Poems by Geoffrey Chaucer (http://www.gutenberg.org/cache/epub /2383/pg2383.txt)].

worship, this thing I show to you.

[24] God that made the world and all things that be in it, this, for he is Lord of heaven and earth, dwelleth not in temples made with hand,

[25] neither is worshipped by man's hands, neither having need of any thing, for he giveth life to all men, and breathing, and all things;

[26] and made of one all the kind of men for to inhabit on all the face of the earth, determining times ordained, and terms of the dwelling of them,

[27] to seek God, if peradventure they feel him, either find, though he be not far from each of you.

[28] For in him we live, and move, and be. As also some of your poets said, And we be also the kind of him.

[29] Therefore since we be the kind of God, we shall not deem, that godly thing is like gold, and silver, either stone, either to graving of craft and thought of man.[b]

[30] For God despiseth the times of this unknowing, and now showeth to men, that all every where do penance;

[31] for that he hath ordained a day, in which he shall deem the world in equity, in a man in which he ordained, and gave faith to all men, and raised him from death.

[32] And when they had heard the again-rising of dead men[c], some scorned, and some said, We shall hear thee again of this thing.

[33] So Paul went out of the middle of them.

[34] But some men drew to him, and believed. Among which Dionysius Areopagite was, and a woman, by name Damaris, and other men with them.

(www.biblegateway/passage/?search=acts17&version=WYC)

Appendix

Answers to Practice Exercises

Answers to Chapter 1

1 and 2. Writing without double negatives or sentence-final prepositions helps a student or other person make an impression that can be useful in this society. Certain kinds of double negatives and sentence-final prepositions are grammatical, though. So students need to understand when to use a more or less formal style of writing.

3. Of the twelve verb forms in Table 1, only two are technically called tenses: the simple present and the simple past. The other ten forms are more correctly called aspects. But all twelve forms are informally called tenses.

Answers to Chapter 2

Answers to Practice Recognizing Adjectives, Qualifiers/Intensifiers, and Seterminers in 2.3.1

Distinguish adjectives, qualifiers and determiners. Decide if any of the underlined words belong to any of the three categories. If it's not one of our three target categories, please don't worry about figuring out at this stage what it might be.

1.<u>quite</u> a <u>balmy</u> <u>summer</u> evening

This is a phrase about the evening, so it's a noun phrase (more on phrases later). 'A' is a determiner. 'Quite' stacks with the determiner 'a,' but cannot be modified by 'very,' or fit in the adjective frame sentence, so it's a qualifier, and not a determiner or an adjective. 'Balmy' stacks with the determiner 'a,' and can be modified by 'very,' and does fit in the adjective frame sentence, so it's an adjective. 'Summer' also stacks with the determiner 'a' and the qualifier 'quite,' so it's neither of those. It cannot be modified by 'very,' or fit in the adjective frame sentence, so isn't an adjective either. That should be the end for this exercise, but we'll take it one step further. When we test it in the noun frame sentence it works, though, so it's a noun, which sounds acceptable for now.

6. From a great distance, his father saw him <u>several</u> times during <u>his</u> <u>upward</u> climb. 'His' is a determiner. 'Upward' would stack with another adjective, such as 'his heroic upward climb,' but it only fits the first half of the frame sentence, so it could be non-gradable, attributive only, or a noun. It's not a noun, so it is an adjective. It would fit the second half of the frame sentence if the word 'very' were not present, so it is non-gradable. None of the other words is an adjective, a qualifier, or a determiner.

Quick answers without explanations:

2. Spreading <u>his</u> <u>white</u> light across the bumpy path in front of him, he tried to move look <u>a</u> <u>bit</u> to his <u>left</u>. 'His' and 'a' are determiners; 'white' is an adjective; 'bit' and 'left' are not adjectives, qualifiers, or determiners.

Answers to Practice Testing for Nouns

Which of the following are acceptable in the frame sentence for nouns?

1. singer The frame sentence "They had no singer" sounds fine. It's a noun

2. lettuce The frame sentence "They had no lettuce" sounds fine. It's also a noun

3. stupendous The frame sentence *"They had no studpendous" sounds awful. It's not a noun. We would need to test it further.

4. buying The frame sentence *"They had no buying" also sounds awful. It's not a noun. We would need to test it further as well.

Quick answers without explanations: 5-6 both pass as nouns under some meaning of the word.

Answers to Practice Testing for Adjectives

a) Which of the following words pass the frame sentence diagnostic for adjectives?

1. glossy : The glossy print is very glossy. Passes easily - adjective

2. absent : ?The absent student was very absent. 'very absent' is odd so it's a noun or an attributive-only or a non-gradable adjective. Testing for non-gradabilty: all possible things that can be referred to with this word are either absent or they're not (then they're 'present') – so it's a typical non-gradable adjective.

3. umbilical: ?The umbilical cord was very umbilical. 'very umbilical' is odd – so it's a noun or attributive-only adjective or non-gradable adjective. Not all things referred to by this word are either umbilical or not umbilical, so it fails the test for non-gradability. Test for noun: "They have no umbilical" leads to the question, 'umbilical what?,' so it's not a noun, but an attributive-only adjective.

4. plastic: Passes the test for a noun: "They have no plastic." So it's a noun in its most common meaning. If we mean its very limited meaning of 'malleable' as in 'the plastic arts,' it's an adjective, such as "This clay is very plastic." At this point, we start noticing that testing some words individually, without the context of a sentence, leads to several pos sible answers. The only way to avoid this problem is to test words in the context of a sentence. For frame sentences, we put words into a sentence, but it may turn out that we have to take them out of another sentence in order to know which of several possibilities we're interested in testing.

N.B. Here we can test 'stupendous' from the previous noun practice set above. 'The stupendous accomplishment was very stupendous.' It's acceptable, even though 'really' would make it sound better than 'very.' It's an adjective.

b) Identify the nouns and adjectives in the following sentence:

> The helpful foreigner standing near the bicycle accident gave his un used blanket to a homeless beggar among a group of others who all belonged to the poorest of the poor.

Quick answers: nouns: foreigner, bicycle, accident...adjectives: poorest (used as a noun!), and poor (also used as a noun). ... The forms of 'poor' are modifying an invisible noun 'people.' One way to test this is to ask whether 'poor' could be talking about some other noun which could possibly be modified by 'poor,' such as a neighborhood or a country. It couldn't in my dialect, which is the reason to posit that it is still an adjective, even though used nominally. We have already seen that nouns can be used adjectivally. We will see later that verbs can also be used adjectivally, so the nominal use of an adjective fits within the range of English grammar. The last bit of analysis (substituting words with other meanings for 'people') is not syntactic but semantic and will not be significantly developed in this textbook.

Answers to Practice Testing for Adverbs

Which of the following words pass the frame sentence diagnostic for adverbs?

1. rarely Both sentences "They handle the matter (very) rarely" and "They told the story (very) rarely" sound reasonably good if we are answering the question 'when...?'. So we'll say it passes as an adverb.

2. excellently "They handled the matter (very) excellently."

Check. It's an adverb.

3. elderly "They handled the matter (very) elderly." Yuk. Can it move? "The elderly couple took a walk." ?"The couple took an elderly walk. Well, it might move, but the sentence changes meaning completely, which we're not interested in. Nope, it's not an adverb. It turns out to be an adjective

4. nervously "They handled the matter (very) nervously." It sounds a little odd, but only because of semantic factors. So let's check its mobility. "They entered the house (very) nervously." "They (very) nervously entered the house." That works. It's an adverb.

Quick answers without explanations: 'savagely,' passes the tests as an adverb. 'Very,' ..., and 'hardly' do not. We'll have to reconsider 'hardly' later.

Answers to Practice Testing for Verbs

a) Which of the following words pass the frame sentence diagnostic for verbs?

1. revelation *"They could/should revelation (something)" sounds no good. Neither does *"The patient revelations healthy." It's not a verb.

2. landscape "They could/should landscape (their yard)" sounds fine, so it's a verb and we don't need to try the second frame sentence. The fact that 'landscape is also a noun does not keep it from being a verb, too, but this again tells us that we really need to test words from a sentence context and not from a list like this.

3. repeat "They could/should repeat (their answer)" sounds fine, so it's a verb.

Quick answers without explanations: 'Shot' does not pass the tests because it is the past tense of a verb, but it's still a verb form.

Please Read the note below for more clarity on that issue.

N.B. Here we can test the word 'buying' from the noun set above. "They could/should buying (their food)" sounds odd, but the same test would show that 'repeating' and 'landscaping' are not verbs, when we already showed that they are, so we have a conundrum. What we need to do is use this test on the dictionary form of the verb (the 'bare infinitive' form): buy. Thus "They should/could buy (their food)" shows that 'buy' is a verb. The same is true for 'shot.' The sentence "They should shoot (only enemy combatants.)" shows that 'shoot' is a verb. Therefore, its past tense form 'shot' is also a verb.

Here we should also add the fact that verbs with '-ing' endings can also be tested with some form of 'be' instead of 'could/should...' So we can ask how we like the sentence 'They are buying (their food),' and we can say that 'buying' – as well as 'repeating' and 'landscaping' are verbs. But words with '-ing' endings can also be adjectives, such as '(very) interesting,' or nouns , such as '(holiday) greetings.' So the bare infinitive forms are the most reliable for these tests.

b) All the adverbs and verbs in this sentence:

After they had been working hard all day, the laborers could not easily suppress their longing for a refreshing change of pace.

Quick answers: the adverbs are 'hard,' and 'easily.' One verb is 'suppress.' 'Longing for ... ' fits in the frame sentence for a noun, and so 'longing' should be considered one. In another context, it could be a verb, but here it is a noun.

Answers to Chapter 3

Answers to Practice with Verb Subcategories

Identify the sub-category of each of the following verbs (and verb forms).

1. rescue – transitive; enjoy - transitive

2. consider – transitive; make – linking

3. tell – ditransitive

4. look - prepositional; rock –intransitive

Answers to Practice with Phrasal Verbs

a) Identify the phrasal verbs in the following sentences.

1. Molly was sick of sitting around every day; she felt like she was going to break down.

1a. We first identify the verbs: was, sitting, felt, was, going, and break . Then we look for possible verb particles associated with the verbs: was – none, sitting - around, felt - none, was - none, going - to, and break – down. 'Going to' is a construction meaning 'future time' and has no other lexical meaning, so it doesn't qualify as a phrasal verb. 'Sitting around' and 'break down' both have the characteristics of a phrasal verb: the verb 'sit' in the first one doesn't necessarily mean just 'sit,' and 'around' has little to do with direction or surrounding anything.

2. She didn't come up with the ideas to open the blinds or work out, but a friend brought it up in conversation.

The same process applies. Verbs: did, come, open, work, brought. Possible particles: did –none (besides, it's an auxiliary here, and not a verb), come – up with, open -none, work - out, brought -up. 'Come up with' clearly has a new meaning not related to 'come' or 'up,' so that's a phrasal verb.

Quick Answers:

3. 'going to' a modal substitute similar to 'will' (not phrasal with a meaning in the normal sense); carry out (phrasal, meaning 'accomplish'), live up to (phrasal meaning 'fulfill')

6. She'll be going upstairs (not phrasal verb+adverb), to throw out (phrasal, meaning 'dispose of' or 'throw away'). feel (not phrasal), take on ((phrasal, meaning 'accept')

b) Identify the types of verb particles in the following sentences.

1. Thomas the tailor was tired of letting out people's pants.

We recognize 'let out' as having its own idiomatic meaning, so we need to ask whether it can move: 'letting people's pants out' sounds fine, so it is a movable verb particle.

2. He wanted a change of life-style - a chance to mix things up, and decided a trip to Paris was exactly the right solution. 'Mix things up' has its own idiomatic meanings, and the same question needs attention; how does 'mix up things' sound? The meaning is clearly different, so 'up' in 'mix things up' is a non-adjacent verb particle.

Quick answers for 3b)

3. listen to (prepositional, not phrasal), fall back on (phrasal as 'rely on'), work out (phrasal as 'succeed'), hope (not phrasal).

Answers to Practice Distinguishing Qualifiers and Adverbs

1a. 'Sometimes I wish' ... and 'I sometimes wish...' both sound fine, so it can move, and it's an adverb. The second instance given here is inside the predicate, and it's not any of the other adverbs, so it's a predicate adverb.

1b. 'that I could just go...' and 'that I just could go ...' both sound fine, so 'just' can move, and it's an adverb. The first instance is inside the predicate, so it's a predicate adverb. If we ask about 'go just outside...,' the meaning of 'just' changes, we notice it's modifying an adverb (see 1c.), and we recognize it as a qualifier.

1c. go outside and jump around. 'outside' answers 'go where?' and 'around' answers 'jump how?' so they should both qualify as adverbs. The only extra consideration is whether 'jump around' is a phrasal verb with an idiomatic meaning. But 'walk around,' and 'look around' seem to both have the same, unidiomatic meaning for 'around,' so 'around' turns out to be an adverb and not a verb particle.

2a. 'It's a feeling I often get…' and 'It's a feeling I get often …' both sound all right, so it can move, and it's an adverb.

2b. The word 'late' fits the frame sentence 'The late evening was very late,' so it qualifies as a gradable adjective. The word 'very' in 'very late at night' is a typical qualifier modifying an adjective, so it's still a qualifier. It would be different in a context like 'That's the very man I was talking about,' where it's modifying a noun, and not an adjective.

2c. when I'm typing my most challenging papers. 'My' does not fit the frame sentence for adverbs, cannot become 'my-er,' and cannot move so is not an adverb. It's modifier, not one word 'most,' but the whole sequence, 'most challenging papers, so it cannot be a qualifier either. We'll discuss it soon. 'Challenging' needs to be analyzed first, just like 'late' did in 2b, so we can see what 'most' is modifying. The sentence 'the challenging paper was very challenging' tells us that it's an adjective. 'Most' is modifying an adjective, so it could be an qualifier or an adverb. We find that we can stack it with 'very,' as in 'my very most challenging papers,' so we'll label it an adverb in this context.

Quick answers

3. Tomorrow is a noun, as is morning. 'really' is an qualifier. 'along' is a verb particle. 'incredibly' is a qualifier and 'well' is an adverb describing 'move along'.

Answers to Practice with Types of Nouns

a) Identify the nouns and the types of nouns in the following sentences:
We'll start by looking closely at #6 this time:

6. He recently heard a talk about honesty in communication, so he's started sharing his insight with those around him.

a. We can run a number of the words through the noun frame sentence and discover that four of the words are clearly nouns:

They have no *he/*recently/talks/honesty/communication/?sharing/ insights/*those/*him (to speak of).

b. It turned out that using plural forms of 'talk' and 'insight' increased the clarity of this diagnostic test. Having a plural form is also a characteristic of certain nouns in English, and helps us identify those two nouns as common count nouns.

c. 'Honesty' and 'communication' seem not to have plural forms, so could be either non-count nouns or abstract ones. The sentences ' (*The) honesty/communication between people is important' help us see that they're functioning as abstract nouns here. That leaves 'sharing' which we'll have to put off discussing until we talk about gerunds, which are verb forms ending in '-ing' that are used as nouns.

Quick answers; the following are the nouns in each sentence:
    1. Sam (proper), decisions (common, count)

    2. block (common, count), cheese (common, non-count), workers (common, count), deli (common, count), department (common, count).

    3. income (common, count), foods (common, count), protein (common, non-count), products (common, count)

    b) Identify the types of nouns in the following sentences (Butcher and Lang): Odysseus (proper) was the King (common, count) of Ithaca (proper), a small and rugged island (common, count) on the western coast (common, count) of Greece (proper).

Answers to Practice with Pronouns

a) choose the correct pronoun form in these sentences:

    1. There was one person who/whom I wanted to address in the arena.

We take the relative clause starting with the word 'I' and make a statement out of it: 'I wanted to address her/him/them in the arena.' The 'her/him/them' tells us that we're dealing with an object pronoun here. so 'whom' is fine. In informal writing and speech 'who' is also acceptable here.

2. She was the one that/which I hoped to interview.

Here again, we start with the relative clause, again beginning with 'I.' and make the statement 'I hoped to interview her/him/them.' So again, 'who' or 'whom' are both fine, depending on the context. 'That' is used in casual conversation to refer to persons, but is frowned on in formal writing. 'Which' is not acceptable in any context, since it seems to still refer only to head nouns without a personality.

Quicker answers:

    3. Unfortunately there was no way to find out who/whom her manager was.

b) Identify the quantifiers and pronouns in the following sentences; we'll start with a close look at #2.

    2. As always, he listened first to his stomach and delved into the several white expanses of the appliance, searching for as many worthwhile items as possible.

We see a couple of candidates for pronoun status: he, and his. 'He' is a subject pronoun, but 'his' is a possessive determiner since it is followed by the noun 'stomach.' It would have to stand alone to qualify as a pronoun.

Looking for possible quantifiers, we see 'first,' 'several,' and 'many.' 'First' here modifies 'listen' (answering 'listen when?'), so its an adverb here. 'Several' follows 'the' and precedes the noun phrase 'white expanses,' which is exactly where we'd expect to find a quantifier. 'Many' is also followed by the noun phrase 'worthwhile items.' Both of these are therefore quantifiers.

Quicker answers:

1. It (Prn) was the third (A) fantastic morning of vacation when Draper arose from his bed and walked a couple of steps to his refrigerator.

2. above

3. Like most great explorers and archaeologists, he (Prn) took some time to closely exam all (Q) its contents before he (Prn) found a two (Q) -day-old Danish hidden behind the one (Q) container of vegetable curry he (Prn) had made the night before.

c) Identify the types of determiners, quantifiers and pronouns in the following sentence:

That (demonstrative D) young prince, whose (relative D) uncle was among the (article D) many (indefinite Q) heroes that (relative Prn) there are in their (possessive D) family, had himself (intensive Prn) watched his (D) uncle defeat ....

Answers to Practice with Auxiliaries

a) Identify the auxiliaries in the following sentences, where they appear.

1. The children were doing their homework when the lightning struck.

1a. If we look for the verbs, we're most likely to find the auxiliaries right before them. The verbs we see are 'doing' and 'struck.' Right in front of 'doing' is 'were,' which is an auxiliary here. The word right in front of 'struck,' however, is not an auxiliary, since 'lightning' here is a noun.

2. No one had any time to think about what they should do.

Looking again for the verbs, we see 'had,' 'think,' and 'do' and we see 'should' right in front of it, so we recognize 'should' as an auxiliary. 'Had' is a verb here and not an auxiliary, as is 'think.'

Quicker answer:

> 3. None of them was used to needing to think so quickly.

Verbs: was ('be'), 'used,' 'need,' and 'think.' 'Used' here has become an adjective, since you can be more or less used to something. The other three are verbs.

b) Identify the types of prepositions, conjunctions, and auxiliaries in the following sentence:

> As far as (phrasal conj.) the young prince was concerned, it was time for (conj.) them to (aux.) honor a man to (prep) whom they all owed a great debt and (conj.) who not only (correl.conj.) could (aux.) have (aux.) been (aux.), but (correl.conj.) almost was (aux. – passive), killed, and had (aux.) thereby increased the tribe's reasons for (prep.) pride.

Answers to Practice with Several Lexical Categories

a)   Identify the types of verbs, verb particles, prepositions, and auxiliaries in the following sentences:

> 1. Samuel needed to tell someone; he hadn't felt really and truly inspired for several years.

1a. We can start with the verbs: need, tell, had, felt, inspired. Auxiliaries- had (here we see that it isn't being used as a verb at all, but a signal of the perfect aspect). Then we can look for verb particles and prepositions – to, for.

1b. types of verbs – need: transitive (needed what? 'to tell...'), tell: ditransitive (tell who? – someone, tell what? – (that) he hadn't...), feel: transitive ? (feel what? – 'really inspired,' where 'really' is a qualifier, which shows that 'inspired' here is not a verb, but an adjective. The frame sentence confirms this (try it). So 'feel' is discovered not to be intransitive, since the answer to 'feel what?' is an adjective. This makes 'feel' here a linking verb. We can confirm this by checking to see that 'inspired' modifies the subject 'Samuel.' Click; done with the verbs. Types auxiliaries: 'had' was identified in 1a as an aspectual auxiliary.

1c. types of prepositions, and auxiliaries. 'To' is followed by a verb (tell), so it is not a preposition at all, but an infinitive marker. More about that later. 'For' is followed by 'several years,' which is a noun phrase or a quantifier phrase. Either are fine objects for a preposition, so that works. It's therefore a simple preposition.

2.He knew that he could easily become an expert in art and languages and exceptional music, but really he'd just been giving in to whatever made him happy.

2a. verbs: knew, become, giving, made. Aux: could, 'd'('had').

Prepositions and possible verb particles: in, to. 'In' joins 'giving' to create a new meaning, so it's a verb particle, and 'giving in' is a phrasal verb.

2b. verb types: knew – transitive (knew what? 'that…'); become – (become what? 'an expert'). So it's transitive, right? Wrong. Here the subject 'he' and the word 'expert' refer to the same person, so it's a linking verb; giving in – (giving in what? – no good, but 'giving in to what?' shows that the 'to'- prepositional phrase is required for the meaning). So the phrasal verb is a prepositional verb. 'Made' is followed by 'him' and 'happy.' And they answer the question 'made what?' which has a transitive feeling to it. Moreover, 'happy' modifies 'him.' So the verb is complex transitive.

3. He thought that he must be missing out on his artistic opportunities; he had to wear a hat now just to pen a few creative lines.

Verbs: thought, missing, wear, pen; Verb particle: (missing) out; Preposition: on

Auxiliaries: must, be, had to, to.

Answers to Practice with All Categories and Subcategories

1. As (subordinating conjunction) Menelaus (proper noun "pn") was (linking verb) the (article determiner "ad") brother (countable common noun "ccn") of (simple preposition "sp") Agamemnon (pn), who (relative pronoun) was (passive auxiliary) recognized (transitive prepositional verb in its passive voice) as (sp) the (ad) chief (ccn) of (ditto) the (ad) petty (gradable adjective) kingdoms (ccn) of (sp) Greece (pn), he (personal subject pronoun) could (modal aux) call (transitive phrasal verb) on (verb particle) the (ad) whole (attributive only adjective) force (ccn) of (sp) these (demonstrative determiner) kingdoms (ccn).

2. No (indefinite determiner) prince (ccn) signed (prepositional phrasal verb) on (verb particle) with (sp) the (ad) league (ccn) of (sp) Troy (pn) from (sp) a (ad) home (ccn) more (qualifier) remote (gradable adjective) than (sp) that (demonstrtative pronoun) of (sp) Odysseus (pn).

Answers to Chapter 4

Answers to Practice with Phrasal Typology

a) Identify and name the phrases in the following sentences:

7. He turned things around and asked others the reasons for their personal criticism of him at this time.

7a. Let's start with single words that are also phrases. It doesn't matter whether we do this left-to-right or right-to-left. 'He' we recognize as a pronoun, which is always an NP. What's he turning around? -'things,' so it's phrase, as we expect from a plural count noun. And 'others' is a plural noun, too, and answers the question, 'who did he ask?'. What did he ask for? 'reasons' and reasons for what 'criticism.' So those two are also NPs. And finally, we first ask, 'Is 'time' a phrase? What are they discussing? 'time' – that sounds good as a short answer, but it's a different meaning of 'time,' so we notice that this usage is a common count noun, which needs a determiner to become a phrase.

b. Looking at combinations of words that are phrases, we start at the right edge of the sentence. 'this time' then is recognizable as a phrase as an answer to the question 'Are they discussing criticism from this time or another time?. It's an NP. Criticism of him when? – 'at this time,' so that's a phrase – a PP. Criticism of who(m)? 'of him' – another PP. But notice that 'of him at this time' is not a PP. What kind of criticism? 'personal' – call it an AP. Another answer to the same question – 'personal criticism' – an NP. Another answer to that questions – 'personal criticism of him at this time' – a bigger NP containing the smaller ones. And whose personal criticism of him at this time? 'their personal criticism of him at this time' – that's also an NP. Notice that 'their' does not stand by itself. 'reasons' we said will stand by itself, but 'the reasons' will not. So the answer to 'what did he ask others?' is the whole following phrase, 'the reasons for their personal criticism of him at this time'. It's an NP. What did he do? 'asked others the reasons for their personal criticism of him at this time' is one answer – a VP. A second answer is 'turned things around and asked others the reasons for their personal criticism of him at this time,' which is also a VP. In between those two, we can also see another phrase that will stand by itself as a response to the question 'What did he do – turn things around?' response: 'and asked others the reasons for their personal criticism of him at this time'. It's a CCP outside the VP from 'asked'. The only bigger phrase than these is the whole sentence – an IP.

Quick Answers
1.

Samuel had not felt very inspired for several years

Samuel	had	not	felt	very	inspired	for	several	years
N	Aux	Neg	V	Qual	A	P	Q	N
NP					AP		QP	NP

```
                          _____AP_____        _____NP_____
                                                  ___PP_____
                          _____VP_____
          _____IP_____
```

2.

```
He knew a    lot about the different kinds of artistic expression.
Prn V  Det N  P    D    A       N    P    A       N
NP                                        AP
       _NP_                               _NP_____
                                          PP_____
                                 _____NP_____
                          _____NP_____
                    _____NP_____
               ____PP_____
          ____NP_____
       ___VP_____
   ___IP_____
```

4.

```
He thought about his  many opportunities as an   artist.
Prn V       P   Det   Q       N          P Det   N
NP                    QP      NP
                                                 NP_____
                                                 PP_____
                              _____NP_____         |
                      ___PP_____
               ___VP_____
          __IP_____
```

Answers to Practice with Adjective Phrases

a) Identify the adjective phrases in the following sentences and label their heads, complements, and modifiers.

> 2. As he focused his intense, white light on the strangely curvy path in front of him, he moved his blood-shot eyes from left to right.

2a. First, we need to find the adjectives. The words 'intense,' 'white,' 'curvy' and 'blood-shot' fit the frame sentence "the ____ [noun] was very ____ " with 'light,' 'path,' and 'eyes'. 'Strangely,' 'left,' and 'right', in contrast, do not. Each of the four adjectives is also an AP, and it is the head of its own AP. Only 'curvy' has a modifier, which is 'strangely,' making 'strangely curvy' also an AP headed by 'curvy.' The others become immediately incorporated into an NP at the next phrasal level.

Quick answers
a) Identify the adjective phrases in the above sentences and label their heads, complements, and modifiers (adjectives are always the head of an AP).

> 1. Adjective phrases: 'balmy,' 'servant-hearted,' and 'oppressive.' If it had read 'a quite balmy...', then 'quite balmy' would also be an AP.

> 2. (above)

3. Adjective phrases: 'small,' 'similar to a second birth' (h:similar, c:PP)

b) Identify the verb phrases in the above sentences and label their heads, complements, and modifiers.

1. 'emerged slowly' is the shortest VP, with 'emerged as its head and 'slowly' as its modifier. 'emerged slowly from some sort of oppressive darkness' is the entire VP with the same head and 'from some sort of oppressive darkness' as a PP modifier. That takes care of the VP in the dependent clause. The shortest VP in the main clause, with 'was' as its head, is this 'was quite a balmy summer evening.' The NP 'quite a balmy summer evening' is a complement to the head V. The longest VP includes the entire dependent clause, like this: 'was quite a balmy summer evening when our servant-hearted hero emerged slowly from some sort of oppressive darkness.' Here the 'when'-clause is an adverbial modifier modifying the verb 'was' in the main clause.

2. In the main clause, the shortest VP begins with its head 'moved': 'moved his blood-shot eyes' where the NP 'his blood-shot eyes' is a complement (direct object) of the head verb. The next longer VP in that clause is 'moved his blood-shot eyes from left to right' where the PP 'from left to right' is a modifying PP. The full VP in that clause is thus 'cautiously moved his blood-shot eyes from left to right' where 'cautiously' is a modifying adverb (and AdvP). In the dependent clause starting with 'As', the head of the VP is 'focused'. The shortest VP is 'focused his intense his intense, white light' where the NP 'his intense white light' is a complement (direct object). The next longer VP is 'focused his intense his intense, white light on the strangely curvy path in front of him.' Here the PP 'on the strangely curvy path in front of him' is a modifier.

3. This sentence is similar to #2 in having a form of the verb 'be' as the head of the VP in the main clause. Its shortest VP is this 'was similar to a second birth'. Here the AP 'similar to a second birth' is the complement of the head verb. Surprisingly, and for reasons that we'll discuss in more detail later, there is a longer VP in the main clause: 'was similar to a second birth in several small ways.' The PP 'in several small ways' is a modifier to the AP similar. The short explanation at this point is that the PP 'in several small ways' is considered to have moved from the end of the sentence to the front, but the trace of the PP is still in final position and still functions as a modifier in that position.

Answers to Practice with Adverb Phrases

Identify the adverb phrases in the following sentences and label their heads and modifiers.

> 6. It's raining harder outside now, which will help me concentrate completely intensely.

6a. Identifying the adverbs is the main part of this exercise, since they have so little structure. Questions about the verb's when/where/how/why should help us find adverbs. Raining how? – harder; raining where? – outside; raining when? - now. 'Outside' and 'now' fit the frame sentence (if we put the verb into a present tense to accommodate the meaning of 'now'), but 'harder' doesn't: 'They are telling the story outside/now /*harder.' We have to notice, then, that 'hard' doesn't fit the semantics of the frame sentence, but that it's clearly modifying the verb 'raining,' so it must also be adverbial. Let's call it exceptional, but still an adverb.

6b. The second VP, after the word 'and' is headed by 'feel,' which we recognize as a linking verb. We then expect a complement that is either a noun or an adjective, and find 'trapped' looking very much like an adjective. It also fits the frame sentence for an adjective. What about the words 'almost' and 'completely'? Only one fits the frame sentence: 'They told the story completely/*almost.' If the sentence were 'they almost told the story,' we would recognize 'almost' as an adverb modifying 'told.' But here it's not; it's modifying 'completely,' which we have just shown to be an adverb. So the simplest adverb phrase is 'completely,' and the next level of the AdvP is 'almost completely,' where 'almost' serves as a qualifier.

Quick Answers (the adverbs themselves are always the heads of the AdvPs).

1. AdvPs: 'sometimes', 'just,' 'outside,' and 'around.' (no modifiers). 'Just' is like 'simply' and says 'how' the verb will happen.

2. AdvPs: 'often,' 'late,' N.B. 'late at night' is a PP and the adv is its modifier. The adverbial PP fits the frame sentence for an adverb 'told the story PP.'

6. (above)

Answers to Practice with Noun Phrases

First, a) identify the noun phrases in the following sentences, and then b) identify the relative clauses in the following sentences and determine whether they are restrictive or non-restrictive.

2. He was upset about his current state of health that prevented him from moving from his chair on the porch.

2a. In order to find noun phrases, we need to find either nouns or pronouns to be their heads. So we have 'he' (Prn), 'health,' 'him (Prn),' 'chair,' and 'porch' as pretty clear ones. The pronouns we simply memorize if we need to, since the lists are fairly short. 'That' can be a pronoun in certain contexts, but here it means the same as 'which,' so it's not functioning as a pronoun. The nouns fit the frame sentence, 'They have no health/chair/porch.' What about 'current' 'state' and 'moving'? 'Current' fits the adjective frame sentence, so need not concern us further. 'State' can be a noun because it can follow a determiner 'his state,' and we recognize 'of health' as its complement, since 'state' needs such a PP to complete its meaning. 'Moving' looks very noun-like as the object of the preposition 'from,' but it doesn't fit the noun frame sentence, except to sound adjectival, in need of a noun. In checking the adjective frame sentence, we find that it changes meaning to fit in: 'The moving story was very moving.' So we won't call it a noun or an adjective, which only leaves the verb form ending with '-ing' as a possibility. More about this type of verb when we discuss 'gerundives.' 2b. Having identified the NPs, we'll move on to the relative clauses. Noticing that 'that' means the same as 'which' is our key here, since they are only similar when they are relative pronouns. Here we notice that the sentence would be ungrammatical if we wrote it with a comma, 'He was upset about his current state of health, that prevented him from moving from his chair on the porch.' That is because 'that' cannot introduce a non-restrictive relative clause. So if 'that' fits, the relative clause is restrictive. The relative pronouns 'who' and 'which,' in contrast, can introduce either a restrictive or non-restrictive relative clause. So we got off easy here. But correct usage of commas is also a helpful signal, so we only need to really analyze such clauses when we doubt the correctness of the punctuation.

Quick answers:
    1. NPs: George, George who had rescued many from a burning inferno, a burning inferno, the clear bay. Relative clause ('RC'): who had rescued many from a burning infrerno.

    2. above

    3. NPs: the methods, us the methods which enabled you to survive the 1999 earthquake, you, the 1999 earthquake, 1999. N.B. '1999' is not quantifying anything here, since we seldom think of the number as a certain number of years since a certain event. So it is an NP here, not a quantifier. RC: which enabled you to survive the1999 earthquake

    4. NPs: the man, the man whom George was facing, George. RC: whom George was facing

Answers to Practice with Phrasal Structure in Simple Sentences

a) Identify and name the phrases and their **heads**, <u>complements,</u> modifiers, and *specifiers* in the following sentences (identified by the various typefaces). The scanning for phrases is most efficient and accurate when done right to left, so the answers will reflect that procedure.

    1) The two boys, and their mom, were fed up with ropey play dough between their toes.

    NPs: *toes, their* **toes,** play **dough,** ropey play **dough,** *their* **mom, boys,** *the* two *the* two **boys** and their mom. If 'play' is seen as an inseparable part of the compound noun 'play dough,' then both should be bolded. It is here treated as a modifier which could be deleted without destroying the grammaticality of the sentence.

    CCP: *and* <u>their mom,</u>

    PPs: **between** <u>their toes,</u> **with** <u>ropey play dough between their toes.</u>

VP: **fed up** <u>with ropey play dough between their toes.</u>

2) Then they found out about a new kind of modeling clay without fiber.

AdvP: then

NPs: **fiber,** modeling **clay,** *a* new **kind** of modeling clay, **they**

VP: **found out** <u>about a new kind of modeling clay without fiber.</u>

PP: **without** <u>fiber,</u> **of** <u>modeling clay without fiber,</u> **about** <u>a new kind of modeling clay without fiber</u>

3) Their mom was grateful for this new idea for their afternoon playtime.

NPs: afternoon, *their* afternoon **playtime,** *this* new **idea** for their afternoon playtime, *their* **mom. N.B.** the 'for-PP' is not a complement if we take the previous sentence into consideration as the context for 'this new idea.' Without that context, the PP would be a complement.

VP: **was** <u>grateful</u> for this new idea for their afternoon playtime.

b) Identify and name the phrases and their **heads,** <u>complements,</u> modifiers, and *specifiers* in the following sentence (adapted from Butcher and Lang): Odysseus' personal narrative to the Phaeacians of his adventures in the previous ten years, however, takes up two nights of the six weeks in the narrative of the Odyssey.

NPs: *the* **Odyssey,** *the* **narrative** <u>of the Odyssey,</u> *the* six **weeks,** two **nights,** two **nights** <u>of the six weeks,</u> **years,** *the* previous ten **years, adventures,** *his* **adventures** <u>in the previous ten years,</u> *the* **Phaeacians,** *Odysseus'* personal **narrative** to the Phaeacians of his adventures in the previous ten years.

PPs: **of** <u>the Odyssey,</u> **in** <u>the narrative of the Odessey,</u> **of** <u>the six weeks in the narrative of the Odyssey,</u> **of** <u>the six weeks in the narrative of the Odyssey,</u> **in** <u>the previous ten years,</u> **of** <u>his adventures in the previous ten years,</u> **to** <u>the Phaeacians</u>

VP: **takes up** <u>two nights of the six weeks in the narrative of the Odyssey</u>

AdvP: **however**

Answers to Practice with Structural Ambiguity

Identify structural ambiguity in the following sentences and tell what the two possible meanings are.
1. Police Alert on Stolen Drugs

The funny meaning is that the police are alert because they are using ('on') stolen drugs. The serious meaning is that the police have issued an alert warning about stolen drugs. The structural ambiguity comes from the possibility that 'alert' is an adjective in the funny sense and a noun in the serious sense. 'On stolen drugs' is modifier of the word 'alert' in either case.

> 2. Lord to Decide Future Next Month

The funny meaning comes from the capitalization of the word 'lord' in the headline, which could be taken in its biblical meaning that God is going to decide the future of the world next month, which would be quite a scoop. The serious meaning is that a member of the British House of Lords will decide about his own future (probably continued participation in some function) this coming month. The ambiguity comes both from the lack of a determiner to specify 'the Lord' or 'a lord' (normally 'Lord + last name') and from the missing determiner specifying either 'the future' or 'his future.'

Answers to Practice with Singular–plural Agreement

Decide in the following sentences whether the verb form should be singular or plural

> 1) " 'The Leaves' are climbing up the top 100 song list." Assuming that 'the Leaves' is the title of a song, it should be singular. The context of the following sentence indicates that it's the name of a song.

> 2) "I believe it was The Desks who wrote the song." Assuming that 'The Desks' is a group, U.S. speakers would use a singular verb, and British speakers would probably use a plural verb.

> 3) "The song is not that good, but the lyrics have drawn positive reviews for their interesting imagery." The singulars and plurals here are correct.

Answers to Practice with Correlative CCP

Evaluate the following sentences and correct them if necessary. This exercise produces the same kind of responses that one would expect from an exercise in prescriptive grammar. Sometimes the two overlap like this.

> 1. "Neither eggs or broccoli has touched Nick's lips in the last few weeks." Neither... or' is not acceptable, and it should be 'Neither ... nor...'

> 2. "He thinks he is slowly wasting away either from mental exertion with grammar or all the repetitive music he's been listening to."

Here we have 'either from + NP' followed by 'or +NP,' which is not parallel, so we can move 'either' to a position between 'from' and its NP object or we can add a second 'from' right before the word 'or.' Both options are grammatically acceptable. Since the second option has unnecessary repetition of 'from,' the first option is better style: 'from either mental exertion ... or all the ...' .

3. "Really, it's not that big of a deal since he ate both his own lunch and somebody else's several hours ago."

'Both…and…' is correct as given here since each is followed by an NP.

Answers to Practice with Phrase Structure in Complex Sentences

For each of the following sentences identify all of the phrases contained in the sentence and label each phrase's head, and if there are such elements, the phrase's complement(s), modifier(s), and its specifier.

1. "Although a bit rough on shoes, couches, and cats, she is the best dog in my family."

Looking for words which are themselves phrases, we see 'shoes,' 'couches,' 'cats,' and 'family.' We also see the pronoun 'she.' All five are NPs. 'Rough' and 'best' are adjectives, but only 'rough' can stand by itself to qualify as a phrase (AP).

1b. Beginning on the right edge, we see that 'my family' will stand as a short answer to the question 'in whose family?' It's an NP whose head is 'family' and for which 'my' is a specifier. Another answer to the same question is 'in my family,' which is a PP with 'in' as its head and for which the NP is a complement. Moving left and combining parts, the smallest addition we can make is 'the best dog in my family,' which is an NP. Its head is 'dog'; 'the' is its specifier, and the PP is a complement because of the word 'best.' Further left, we have the entire independent clause (an IP) with 'she' as its specifier and 'is' as its head, and the rest of the sentence is a complement. In the dependent clause, we also start at the right edge and see that 'and cats' is a short response to 'What's she rough on – shoes and couches?' It's an NP with 'cats' as its head and 'and' in its specifier position. Then we can ask 'What's she rough on – shoes and what else?' A short answer is 'couches and cats,' which is an NP with 'couches' as its head and 'and cats' as a CCP modifier. Another phrase is 'shoes, couches, and cats,' which is a short answer to 'what's she rough on?' It's an NP with 'shoes' as its head and the following NP as its modifier. 'On' seems unable to head an independent PP which will stand alone as a short response. We do see 'on+PP' as the complement to the adjective 'rough.' The PP is not a modifier, but rather a complement since it's needed for that particular meaning of 'rough.' 'Although' is a subordinating conjunction and the head of the CP. The CP is missing part of the IP that has to be embedded inside it. We can easily fill in the empty categories 'Although she is' and the discussion on this sort of 'reduced clause' will be in the following chapter.

Not so quick answers (again using different type faces to designate the various structural roles: **head**, and if there are such elements, the phrase's complement(s), modifier(s), and its *specifier*.). The scanning is most efficient when done right to left, so the answers will reflect that procedure. The main IP at the end of the procedure is always the entire sentence. Individual words are always the head of their own phrase, so they need not be marked any more. They should be easy to distinguish from the modifiers, which are also unmarked, since a modifier is never the only word in its phrase.

> 1. Although a bit rough on shoes, couches, and cats, she is the best dog in my family. (above)
>
> 2. Every time I leave her in my friends' back yard while we talk, she will sit by the door and wait for me.
>
> NPs: me, *the* **door**, she, *my friends'* back **yard**, her, I, *every* **time.**
>
> PPs: **for** <u>me</u>, **by** <u>the door</u>, **in** <u>my friends' back yard</u>
>
> VPs: **wait** <u>for me</u>, **sit** <u>by the door</u>, talk, **leave** <u>her in my friends' back yard</u>
>
> CCP: **and** <u>wait for me</u>
>
> IPs: *she* **will** <u>sit by the door and wait for me</u>, *we* **e** <u>talk</u>, *I* **e** <u>leave her in my friends' back yard</u>
>
> CPs: **while** <u>we talk</u>, **every time** <u>I leave her in my friends' back yard</u>, **every time** <u>I leave her in my friends' back yard while we talk</u>.

N.B. 'every time' here looks for now like it is functioning as a subordinating conjunction. The NP 'every time' functions the same as 'when' or 'whenever' would. We can see that 'every time I leave her in my friends' back yard' will not stand alone as an IP, but that 'I leave her in my friends' back yard' will stand alone as an IP. So 'every time' has acted to make the IP into a dependent clause (CP). We will reanalyze this using a different approach in the following chapter, so you'll have a chance to compare the two and decide which one you like better.

Main IP: the entire sentence

> 3. Once she found a squeaky toy, and she didn't let go of the thing for weeks.
>
> NPs: weeks, *the* **thing**, she, *a* squeaky **toy**, she
>
> PPs: **for** <u>weeks</u>, **of** <u>the thing</u>
>
> VPs: n't **let go** <u>of the thing</u> for weeks, **found** <u>a squeaky toy</u>
>
> IPs: *she* **didn't** <u>let go of the thing for weeks</u>, *she* **e** <u>found a squeaky toy</u>
>
> CCP: **and** <u>she didn't let go of the thing for weeks</u>
>
> AdvP: Once

Answers to Practice Recognizing CP Modifiers in 4.10.2

> 1. "When the children first awoke in their vacation lodge, the flowers were slowly opening in the summer sun."

The word 'when' catches our attention immediately, and we notice that the when-clause is correctly marked by a comma as having been fronted. Its original position was at the end of the sentence. Its movement shows that it's an adverbial clause. It is modifying the main verb 'opening.' In its fronted position, it's part of the IP structure of the main clause. The clause itself is a CP, as we expect.

> 2. "The sunlight was streaming through their window as well, which woke them from their slumber."

We notice the word 'which', which is a relative marker here. The clause has not moved, so we just want to know what it is modifying. The relative clause, however, is not modifying any noun in the main clause, but rather, it's modifying the entire main clause, which only the word 'which' can do. This makes it part of the main clause's IP structure.

> 3. "What had been two lumps under the bedcovers was transformed into two people who were ready to meet the day."

Here there is no phrasal movement. "X was transformed into Y" shows no phrasal movement, even though both X and Y are CPs. The first What-CP is the subject of the sentence and therefore not modifying anything but rather serving as the specifier of the entire IP. The second who-CP is a relative clause modifying its head NP 'two people.' Since it is modifying an NP, it is functioning adjectivally.

This discussion does remind us that 'you have lived' is a clause in its own right. It happens to be a CP without any kind of complementizer or conjunction to introduce it. Why? Because the complementizer 'that' has been deleted for stylistic reasons. 'that you have lived' is functioning as a direct object, which makes it nominal, so it is not modifying anything in the sentence.

Answers to Chapter 5

Answers to Practice Identifying Clauses

Identify the dependent clauses in the following sentences and label them adjectival, adverbial, or neither.

> 6. Hours later, she wearily lifted the last of the boxes she'd packed up, and she limped out the door with it.

The sentence begins 'hours later,' which is composed of a noun followed by an adjective. This is a noun phrase, and not a clause of any kind. Clauses must generally have a visible verb to qualify as clauses. So we'll take the next string of words which clearly contains a verb, namely 'she wearily lifted the last of the boxes,' which is a complete clause. It's an independent clause, so it is neither adjectival nor adverbial. Then follows 'she'd packed up,' which is reduced from 'which/that she had packed up.' This is a reduced relative clause, which is always a type of adjectival clause. The final string of words with a verb is 'and she limped out the door with it.' This is a coordinate main clause, as we expect from the 'fanboys' connected with the coordinating conjunction 'and.' So it is neither adjectival nor adverbial,

Quick answers (AdjCP = adjectival clause, AdvCP=adverbial clause, CP=neither)

1. Ashley decided CP [to move] AdvCP [before she was supplanted by the next tenants.]

2. AdvCP [Although she was usually very tolerant,] the neighbors had gotten to her.

6. above

Answers to Practice with Nominal Clauses

Identify the dependent clauses in the following sentences and label the grammatical role of the nominal clauses.

2. Since we were going to be there for a while, we decided that it would be fun to play some games.

This sentence has two dependent clauses, the first marked by 'since,' and the second marked by 'that.' The first could be moved to the end of the sentence, so we recognize it as adverbial. The second answers the question 'decided what?' and this helps us recognize it as a direct object, which is one role that nominal clauses can have.

Quick Answers with [square brackets] for dependent clauses and {curly brackets} to indicate embedding within another dependence clause. Only full infinitival clauses will be marked, since we have not yet introduced reduced infinitival clauses. We'll get to them in the following sections.

1. . Because of the storm, it had become dangerous for us to travel, so we just stayed in our cabin with the small tour group.

The question 'dangerous what?' is hard to understand, but the for-clause is still best seen as nominal in the sense that it is a complement to an adjective. It answers the question 'dangerous in what situation?' This is not the same as 'dangerous how?' meaning that it is not adverbial. We can then agree with the more traditional view that uses 'nominal' as a term for clauses that give more information about an adjective. We can say then that clausal names are still restricted to one of only three types. We will wrestle with this question again when we discuss clauses of degree, such as 'too dangerous (for us) to travel.'

2. above

3. AdvCP [While some of the group thought of games {AdjCP (that) we liked}], others called the emergency information center to ask NomCP [how long we would be stuck] [direct object – ask what?].

Answers to Practice Identifying Clausal Types

Identify all the subordinate clauses – adverbial, adjectival, nominal whether finite or non-finite. Identifying verbs should help locate the clauses. In the quick answers 'MC' stands for 'main clause' AdvCP, NomCP, and AdjCP stand for 'adverbial,' 'nominal,' and 'adjectival' dependent clauses, respectively. CPs embedded inside other CPs are marked with curly brackets {}. Some reduced clauses are not marked below. They have not yet been discussed in the material we have covered so far.

1. AdvCP [After Troy fell,] MC [Odysseus touched at Ismarus, the city of a Thracian people,] AdjCP [whom he attacked and plundered], but AdjCP [by whom he was at last repulsed].

2. MC [The north wind then carried his ships to Malea, the extreme southern point of Greece,] AdjCP [which, AdvCP {if he had rounded safely,} would probably have allowed him to reach Ithaca in a few days], AdjCP [where he would have found Penelope unvexed by wooers and Telemachus a boy of ten years old].

3. MC[But this was not to be.]

Answers to Practice Identifying Reduced Relative Clauses

Identify the adjectival clauses in the following sentences as either reduced or not.

1) Flying between storm clouds is one of the most memorable experiences some travelers ever have.

Here we can best identify all the clauses by looking for the verbs. They are 'flying,' 'is,' and 'have'. 'Flying' is a gerund, which we'll discuss in the next chapter. It is a verb form in a reduced clause. Here the reduced clause is the subject of the sentence, so it's nominal. 'Is' is the verb in the main clause. 'some travelers ever have' is a reduced form of 'which some travelers ever have, ' which is a reduced relative clause modifying 'experiences.'

2) The air rising inside the clouds creates strong up-drafts that can jolt the plane and lift a passenger out of his or her seat.

Verbs: 'rising,' 'creates,' 'jolt, and lift.' This time we have found three clauses, not four. The first is a reduced clause, which can be restated as 'which is rising inside the clouds.' This follows an NP immediately and describes it, so it is adjectival. 'Creates' is the verb in the main clause.

'Jolt' and 'lift' are coordinate VPs that both belong to the clause 'that can jolt the plane and lift....' Since 'that' is its marker and the subject of the clause, which follows and describes the NP 'up-drafts,' it is also an adjectival clause, but it is not reduced.

Quicker answers:

1) above

2) above

3) Some pilots choose a route the passengers cannot fathom and fly deftly around each succeeding cloud.

Verbs: choose, fathom, fly. Here we again have a pair of coordinate VPs and have only two clauses for the three verbs. 'Choose ... ' and 'fly' is a pair of coordinate verbs in the main clause. 'Fathom' is inside a reduced relative clause '(which) the passengers cannot fathom' and is adjectival.

Answers to Practice with Reduced Adverbial Clauses

a) Identify and categorize the reduced adverbial clauses in the following sentences. Here it may be helpful to use 'e' to identify the missing lexical items.

1. While e e digging up flowers, I decided that I should apply some sunscreen. Reduced adverbial CP: 'While (I was) digging..' Since this clause is introduced by its subordinating clause, it is not referred to as any kind of participial clause. N.B. The that-CP is nominal.

2. e e Still enthusiastically learning to garden, my cousin from the city discovered this outdoor truth a little late and got a bit of a burn. Reduced adverbial CP: ('Since/ Because she/he was') still... This is a present participle clause.

3. We both paused later in the afternoon, e e e warming up from the sun, and got a big drink of water. Reduced adverbial CP: (since/because we were) warming.... Without a comma, it could be interpreted (since it was) warming up... Either way, this is a present participle clause.

b) Distinguish the reduced adverbial clauses from the reduced adjectival clauses in the following sentences. N.B. the abbreviation 'xyzCP' marks the end of that clause.

1. Although e e (she was) a bit rough on shoes, couches, and cats [AdvCP], she was the best dog I had ever known. This is a reduced adverbial CP with the main verb 'be' deleted, leaving an AP. This sort of structure was discussed in the previous exercise.

2. Every time e (that) I left her in my friends' back yard [AdjCP] while e e (we were) talking [AdvCP], she would sit by the door, e e e (while/where she was) waiting for me to come play with her [AdvCP/AdjCP]. The first reduced clause is the reanalysis of the NP 'every time' which was mentioned in the previous chapter. We now can look at the fronted CP as a reduced relative clause. It's odd to see that a relative clause can be fronted, since we have seen in the text that relative clauses cannot move without losing their adjectival trait. Here not only the relative clause but also the head NP 'every time' was moved as an entire unit. That is enough to preserve the adjectival clause as adjectival. This movement is then similar to fronting any time NP as an adverbial (yesterday, today, every month…). 'While we were talking' has a subordinating conjunction which marks it as adverbial, even though it cannot move. The 'while/where she was waiting' clause could be either adverbial if one reads the clause as 'while' and modifying the verb 'sit' or adjectival if one reads it as 'where' and modying the NP 'the door.' My preference is to read it adverbially, but this is structurally ambiguous, so both interpretations are theoretically acceptable.

3. Once she found a squeaky toy e (which) another friend's dog owned [AdjCP], and she didn't let go of the thing for weeks. The AdjCP is a reduced relative clause.

Answers to Practice with Dangling Participles

Identify and correct the dangling participles in the following sentences.

4) Still holding their candy, the store manager chased after the young shop-lifters.

4a. The fronted clause has a main verb 'holding' which has no explicit subject, so the empty category finds its identity in the first noun phrase in the following clause, namely 'the manager.' The sentence thus means, 'while he was still holding their candy, the manager chased…,' which is unlikely. Corrected, the sentence could read, 'Still holding their candy, the young shop-lifters ran from the store manager.

Quicker answers:

1) e e_i e Walking by the lake, the stars$_i$ twinkled in its reflection. The second empty category is the subject of the verb 'walking' which is co-indexed with the NP 'the stars,' meaning that the stars were walking. Correcting the main clause can be done this way (among others): '…lake, we enjoyed how the stars…'

2) e e_i e Running as fast as he could, his classmates$_i$ cheered Jeremy on with all their enthusiasm. The second empty category is the subject of the verb 'running' which is co-indexed with the NP 'his classmates,' meaning the classmates are running. The pronoun 'he' in the participal clause makes this impossible, so the sentence is not only anomalous, it is

also ungrammatical. One way of correcting it would be '…could, Jeremy heard his classmates cheering…'

4) above

Answers to Practice with Empty Categories

a) Identify the empty categories in the following sentences and label them or find a lexical replacement. Include tense hopping and be-raising.

   Some pretty quick answers

> 1. e e e Opened sixteen weeks and three days ago, the situation at Tilly's Candle Shop now e looked critical. The empty categories can be replaced with the lexical items 'Since it had.' We should notice that 'the situation' did not open 4+ months ago, so 'opened' is a dangling past participle, and the sentence needs to be re-written. The 'e' after 'now' represents tense hopping and can be lexicalized with the word 'did,' which would take the past tense morphology away from the verb 'look.'

> 2. Tilly's wife e (did) finally convinced her husband e (that) this great adventure was e (be-raising0 too risky e e (for them) to keep investing their savings in e (co-indexed with 'this adventure'). The co-indexing of the 'e' after 'savings in' is because the preposition 'in' would otherwise not have an NP object.

> 3. She had immediately said 'yes' when he e (did) knelt down on his denim-clad knee and (no e) offered her the largest diamond e (that) she'd ever seen.

> It seems logical to add a subject before the verb 'offered' but, traditionally and in transformational practice, compound VPs do not require the marking of the same subject a second time. A different approach would be to mark the position of the subject and co-index it with the visible one.

b) Just for fun: which of the following is ambiguous in terms of its empty categories? Why is only one ambiguous?

> 1) They loved adventure more than job security.

> 2) Joan loved the Beatles more than her husband.

> The first sentence can only be read as

> 'They loved adventure more than e e (they loved) job security' because the second possible structure is not semantically possible:

> 'They loved adventure more than job security e '(VP: 'loved adventure')'

'Job security' cannot love anything, which makes the second interpretation impossible. This shows how semantics can have a role in the syntactic process of analyzing empty categories. We will not return to this topic in this textbook because it is far too large (for us to do).

Answers to Chapter 6

Answers to More Practice Identifying Empty Categories

Identify the empty categories in the sentences below and suggest possible lexical replacements.

> 1. e e e Not used to life on campus, Jeff considered e moving back home and commuting again.

There are three empty categories before 'Not.' These can be represented by the conjunction, NP, 'be-'verb sequence, 'Since/Because he was.' If we see 'used to' as a verb form, those three are sufficient. If we see 'used to' as an adjective with an obligatory PP-complement (like 'allergic to'), however, 'be' would have to be seen as the main verb. This view would require a fourth empty category to represent 'be-raising. The single 'e' before 'moving' marks it as a gerund which requires a subject or specifier, such as 'his' 'his own,' but no complementizer. The lexicalization might sound odd because it refers back to the NP subject of 'consider.' The need for this specifier is clearer if we think of Jeff considering someone else's moving back home, as in 'Jeff considered John's moving back home." For the sake of consistent analysis, the 'e' meaning 'Jeff' is best lexicalized by the word 'self' even though that also sounds odd.

> 2. e e e e More interested in competitive sports than e e during his high school years, he e thought e e living on campus would allow e him to try out as a walk on.

The first four empty categories can be lexicalized as 'Since/Because he was' in exactly the same way as the first example. The fourth empty category represents be-raising, since 'interested' here is also seen as an adjective. The empty categories following 'than' represent 'he was.' The following two are tense hopping and poss-ing gerund structure. These can be lexicalized as '…did think that his/self living …' Here the gerund can be introduced by a complementizer since it is serving as an IP in a nominal CP ('that') construction.

> 3. e e e e (Since/Because he was) Unable e e to resolve the issue clearly, he e went to the counseling center. The first four have been explained above. 'To resolve' is an aux-verb combination that is missing a CP head ('for') and an IP specifier ('self' or 'himself'). We have tense hopping before 'went' (did go).

Answers to More Practice Identifying Clauses and Empty Categories

Identify the empty categories in the following sentences and explain whether the clauses (both finite and non-finite) are adjectival, adverbial or nominal.

> 1. Brent 's roommate e asked e him to go surfing with him and he e thought it might be interesting e e to try e.

We first look for infinitive verb forms and see 'to go' and 'to try.' Then we ask whether the conjunction and subject NP have been deleted. For 'to go,' we see that the subject NP is present in the word 'him,' but for 'to try' we see that it is missing. Next we test to see if a range of NP subjects is possible. We see that '...asked others to go...' or '..asked Jerry to go...' are possible for the first infinitive, so that infinitive has the characteristics of belonging to a non-finite clause. The complementizer 'for' seems a little awkward in the structure: ?'...asked for others to go...' or '..asked for Jerry to go...,' but we'll accept it unless there's a good reason not to.

We have seen that the subject NP of the infinitive 'to try' has been deleted, but it the complementizer 'for' fits easily into the construction and allows other subjects as well: '...it might be interesting for others to try' or 'it might be interesting for Jerry to try.' Since it means 'for himself to try,' the NP subject must be deleted, as we have seen earlier. The still unresolved empty category is 'try what?' which indicates that the direct object of 'try' has also been deleted. We could represent it with the word 'surfing,' to complete the clause. We recognize that as a poss-gerung and would therefore consider the empty category a VP used nominally.

The first reduced non-finite clause answers the question 'asked what?' which tells us that it is a nominal clause functioning as a direct object of the main verb. The second reduced non-finite clause is modifying the word 'interesting.' We can look at this either of two ways. First, it can be viewed as any modifier of an adjective - either it's a qualifier or it's an adverb. The second way is to say that the structure 'it might be interesting e e to try e' is derived from the sentence 'e e to try e might be interesting,' where we could see the reduced non-finite clause as the subject of the sentence. This would also lead us to consider it a noun clause. But when a clause moves, that tells us usually that it is adverbial. Both views give the same answer, though, so we'll call the second non-finite clause adverbial.

Quicker answers (N.B. the curly brackets indicate the boundaries of a clause embedded inside another clause marked by square brackets.)

> 2. [Before Brent e started {e e to go to school NomCP} AdvCP], he e had to live with an aunt and uncle in their home by the sea.

The 'e's before 'started' and 'had to' represent tense hopping. The 'before'-CP is adverbial, and the 'to go'-reduced CP is nominal. It's empty categories are complementizer ('for,' even though we would never say it, and 'self'). If the 'for' seems to distort the sentence too much in your dialect, then you'd have to consider the infinitive an IP, rather than a CP. 'Had to' is something different – a type of phrasal auxiliary with the same meaning as 'must.' It is followed by a 'live'-VP.

3. The older couple e loved [e e to surf NomCP] and frequently e encouraged [e Brent to go with them NomCP].

Again, two instances of tense hopping ('did love' and 'did encourage'). The non-finite clause has an empty complementizer.

Answers to Chapter 7

Answers to Practice Identifying Syntactic Transformations

Identify the type(s) of transformation that have/has occurred in the following sentences.

1. Were they the international students who Jeff met yesterday?

1a. We notice first that 'were' begins the sentence, which means that it was fronted in a yes/no question transformation. In order to be in the auxiliary position to be so fronted, the verb 'be' had to undergo be-raising from the main verb position to the auxiliary position, were it got tense and number information and changed into 'were.'

1b. Next we notice the word 'who,' which in this case is marking or introducing a relative clause. It has been fronted within the relative clause from the direct object position after 'met,' as in 'met the international students.'

1c. Finally we see that the verb 'met' is carrying the past tense, which means that tense hopping occurred from the (now empty) auxiliary position to the main verb 'meet.'

Quicker answers

2. He was wondering what he should do e (what) about their passport problems. 'What' moved to the front of the nominal clause.

3. Actually, he was not e sure e if he could do anything e e to help them.

First 'was' underwent 'be raising.' The other three empty categories represent deletions, not transformations.

Answers to Practice Identifying Stylistic Movement

Describe the stylistic movements involved in the following sentences

1. If the situation were simpler, Jeff would loan them some money.

1a. The sentence begins with a dependent clause whose original position was after the word 'money.' This is an example of the fronting of an adverbial clause. It's certainly not locative or temporal, and may not fit so comfortably into the category 'causal,' but it's the same kind of stylistic transformation.

Quicker answers

2. Lack of money (topicalized NP) he considered a poor reason to get all upset.

3. What they really needed (pseudo clefted CP) were temporary travel documents.

4. That would keep them from being deported (passivized VP).

Answers to Chapter 8

Answers to Practice Diagramming Simple Sentences

1. John left early with his friends for the concert on the beach.

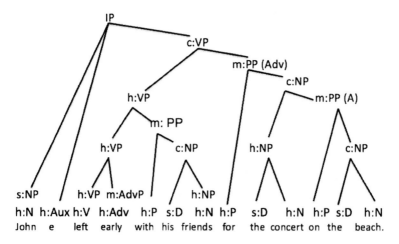

Things to observe in this phrase structure tree are the NP 'the concert at the beach,' separate VPs for 'left early,' 'left early with his friends,' and the entire predicate. The on-PP is functioning adjectivally and the other two PPs are functioning adverbially.

2. He looked forward the whole year to the many bands from all over.

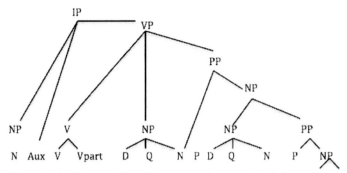

He e looked forward the whole year to the many bands from all over

Notable features of this PS tree are the AdvP 'all over' and the phrasal verb 'look forward to.' It is clear from the connecting lines that the to-PP and the year-NP are both functioning adverbially.

Answers without drawn lines. N.B. It should be possible to imagine (or draw in) the lines connected from the head of each phrase on the line below with its modifier(s), complement(s), and/or specifier to the appropriate higher node with the correct label. Please note that every IP connects to three nodes below it – an NP (or nominal CP), an Aux, and the highest VP. That should help the branchless PS trees take shape.

3. His friends went with him every year in the same old cars.

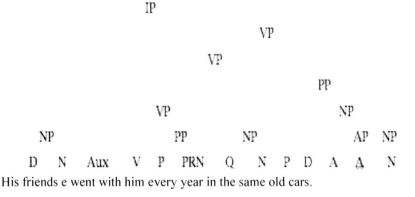

His friends e went with him every year in the same old cars.

This phrase structure tree shows separate VPs for 'went with him,' 'every year,' and the in-PP. The PPs headed by 'with' and 'in' are functioning adverbially, as is the NP 'every year.'

Answers to Practice with Complex Sentences (1)

1. Matt was interested in stamps and coins when he was little.

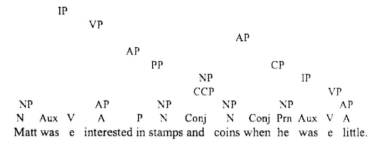

Two instances of be-raising are not too subtle in this sentence, but they are important. Both the when-CP and the in-PP are acting adverbially, since each is modifying an AP. From the word 'interested' to the end of the sentence is one big AP.

2. But he no longer had any time for his collections since he was so busy with sports.

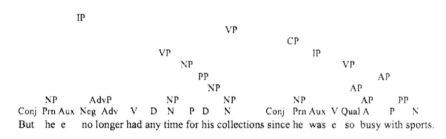

The with-PP is functioning adverbially, as a modifier of the adjective 'busy'.

3. He loved basketball and football, and he played on the varsity teams in each sport.

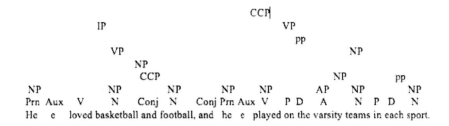

One interesting aspect of this PS tree is that each of the strings 'teams in each sport,' 'varsity teams in each sport,' and ' the varsity teams in each sport' seem to test out as acceptable NPs.

Answers to Practice with More Complex Sentences

1. Brent 's roommate asked him if he had a surfboard with him, and he said he did have one.

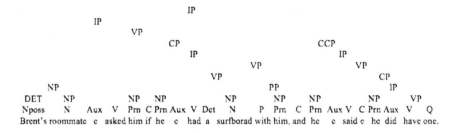

Here, the top IP connects the left-hand IP with the CCP. The left-hand IP connects the higher NP, Aux, and highest VP. This VP connects the V, NP, and CP below it. The VP below the IP connects the lowest left-hand VP with the PP. Under the CCP, the IP connects its NP, Aux, and VP

2. Before Brent started first grade, he lived with an aunt and uncle in their home by the sea

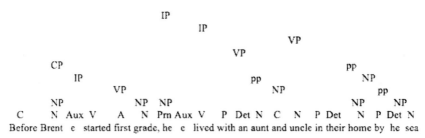

```
                        IP
                   IP
                                      VP
                             VP
      CP                                        pp
         IP                pp                 NP
            VP                   NP                pp
      NP              NP  NP                   NP      NP
  C      N  Aux  V    A   N  Prn Aux  V   P  Det  N   C   N   P  Det   N   P  Det N
Before Brent  e  started first grade, he  e  lived with an aunt and uncle in their home by  he  sea
```

The before-CP is connected to the top IP node directly, and each lower IP connects to the subject NP, the Aux, and the highest VP below it. The main-clause IP is quite straight forward with only a reminder that 'their home by the sea' is an NP that needs to be connected before the PP 'in their home by the sea' can be finished. There is, thus, no such PP as 'in their home.'

Answers to Practice with Gerunds and Reduced Clauses

1. We receive good by doing good. (Reed and Kellogg 66)

```
         IP
              VP
                        pp
                             IP
              VP                   VP
      NP              NP                   NP
  Prn Aux  V        N   P  NP  Aux    V      N
  We   e  receive good by  e    e   doing good
```

Both adjectival forms 'good' are used as nouns here and could be modified by adjectives such as 'absolute good.' An adjective would require a form like 'absolutely good.' 'By doing good' could be 'by ourselves…' or 'by others doing good,' which shows the existence of the empty NP category. The empty aux cannot be shown as easily, except that all English clauses seem to have a slot for one between the NP subject and the verb.

2. Buying and selling goods provides many with a living. (Reed and
Kellogg 66)

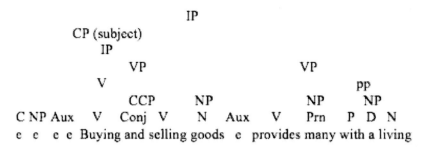

```
                              IP
           CP (subject)
              IP
                  VP                              VP
               V                                              PP
                  CCP        NP                   NP     NP
      C NP Aux  V  Conj  V    N   Aux    V     Prn    P   D   N
      e  e    e  e  Buying and selling goods  e  provides many with a living
```

If we interpret this as an accusative gerund, the lexical substitutions would be
'For many to be buying and selling goods provides many/them...' The compound
gerund is then seen as the verbal heart of a CP, and that CP is functioning
nominally as the subject of the sentence. 'Buying and selling' is transitive and
therefore remains a V until it combines with its NP object 'goods' to become a
VP. The VP 'provides many with a living' does not seem to be divisible into two
VPs, since 'provides many' does not pass any test as a constituent (=XP). 'A
living' is seen as an NP and not a gerund.

3. More interested in sports now than ever, Jeff thought living nearby would
allow him to try out.

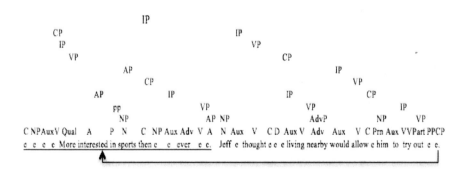

It will probably help to lexicalize all of the empty categories to see what has been
left out. In the following sentence, the items in parenthesis are ones that sound
odd if we pronounce them out loud, but they are still considered part of the
structure: "Since he was (be-raising) more interested in sports than he had ever
been (interested), Jeff (tense hopping) thought that his being (this is the aux)
living nearby would allow (for) him to try out for the ___ team"
At the top, we see that the main IP is composed of an adverbial CP and the main
clause IP. We notice that the 'more'-CP is built up from a complex AP that has a
CP embedded inside it. The main clause IP has a CP inside its VP ('thought
that...'). The CP is functioning nominally as a direct object. The that-CP is
interesting in that its subject is not an NP, but an IP (from the gerund functioning

nominally, of course, as the subject). At the end of the sentence, 'try out' is considered transitive. This could be debated, and in dialects where it's intransitive, there would be no empty PP at the end of the sentence.

Answers to Practice with Relative Clauses and Vacuous Movement in 8.5.9

In diagramming the following sentences, please used arrow notation to show any movement and note whether the relative clauses are restrictive or non-restrictive.

1. Odysseus went from Lotus-land to the land where the Cyclopes, a pastoral people of giants, live.

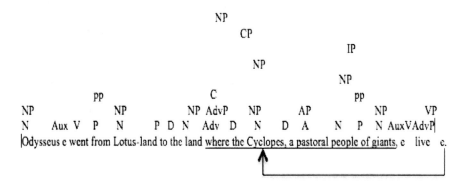

When we first look for empty categories in this sentence, it looks like there might be another relative clause like this 'the Cyclopes, e e e (who e are) e a pastoral ....' This is a reasonable approach, but traditionally, an NP which follows another NP and gives further details about it is not called a reduced relative clause but an appositive. The NP 'a pastoral...' is then called a non-restrictive appositive. In a different approach, it could also be seen as a reduced relative clause, but this time around it's diagrammed as an appositive, just for the sake of consistency and a little bit of review.

From the arrow, we notice that the final phrase 'a ... people of giants (do) live there' allows 'there' to become a relative marker 'where.' This relative adverb can move to the specifier of CP position of the relative clause, which is restrictive in that it defines what 'the land' is. This CP then becomes part of the NP 'the land where...' which in turn becomes part of the large PP 'to the land...' The word 'where' is not in the head of CP position, so it should not be marked 'C.' But the head of CP is always empty in relative clauses, so this Guide has simplified and allowed the head and specifier positions of CP to merge in relative clauses.

2. Among the Cyclopes, Odysseus had the adventure on which all his fortunes hinged.

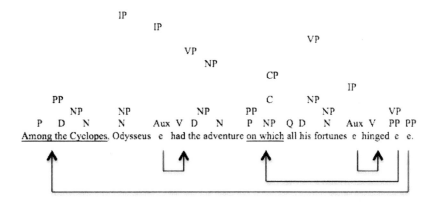

We see that the top IP node joins the fronted PP to the main clause. This is indicated by the longest arrow. In the following sections, we will discuss how to mark this movement. The relative clause is restrictive since it defines what 'the adverture' is about. One longer, bolded, arrow shows the movement of 'on which' and the two short ones show tense hopping for 'did have' and 'did hinge.' If only the relative marker 'which' had moved, stranding the preposition 'on' at the end of the sentence, the NP 'which' would occupy the specifier of CP slot alone and 'on' would remain at the end of the sentence. The rest of the PS tree would be the same. As it is, the PP 'on which' is in the specifier of CP slot. It is not in the head of CP position, so it should not be marked 'C.' But the head of CP is always empty in relative clauses, so this Guide has simplified and allowed the head and specifier positions to merge in relative clauses.

3. There he yelled out about having blinded the giant Polyphemus while rowing away.

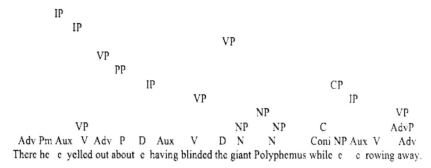

```
        IP
            IP
                                        VP
                    VP
                        PP
                            IP                              CP
                                VP                              IP
                                          NP                          VP
                VP                  NP   NP      C              AdvP
    Adv Pm Aux  V  Adv  P  D  Aux   V   D   N    N       Conj NP Aux  V   Adv
    There he  e yelled out about e having blinded the giant Polyphemus while e  e rowing away.
```

The top IP again connects a fronted adverbial to the main clause. The top VP connects the adverbial while-CP to the main-clause yelled-out-about-IP. 'Out' does not seem to be a verb particle since the meanings of verb and adverb have not changed, but for some strange reason 'out' does not seem to qualify as a phrase, so there is not 'AdvP' marking above it. The NP 'Polysemous' is a restrictive appositive in this approach. The while-CP could be ambiguous except for the fact that the story of Odysseus is so familiar. It is diagrammed to modify 'yelled out,' so Odysseus yelled out while rowing. The other possible interpretation is that he blinded the giant while rowing. In that case, the CP node would be under a second, higher, VP node above 'blinded the giant.' In this sentence, we also see a visible auxiliary in the gerund IP 'having blinded...'

Here the 'C' above the conjunction does really mark the head of the CP because this is not a relative clause, but a subordinate clause.

Answers to Practice with Aux-second

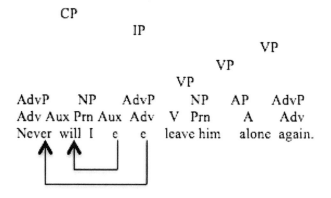

```
            CP
                IP
                                        VP
                                VP
                            VP
    AdvP      NP     AdvP      NP    AP     AdvP
    Adv Aux  Prn   Aux  Adv    V   Prn     A    Adv
    Never will  I    e    e    leave him  alone again.
```

Here the top CP node connects to the AdvP 'Never' as the specifier of the CP and the Aux 'will' as the head of CP and to the IP node. The IP node connects to the NP 'I', the 'e' from the fronted Aux, and the highest VP node. The highest VP connects to both the empty AdvP position from the moved 'never,' and to the VP 'leave him alone,' as well as the AdvP 'again'.

2. Rarely are the two of them ever seen out together.

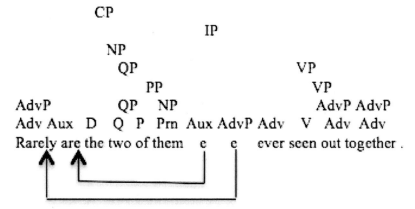

The top CP again connects to the fronted AdvP, the Aux, and the IP. The highest NP connects to D and QP. In more advanced approaches, the top NP would be called a DP, but this Guide has not moved into that area of syntax. The IP connects the NP, Aux, and VP, as expected.

This analysis also simply ignores the fact that the verb is functioning in a passive form. The complications of passive forms are introduced and discussed in the following sections and are beyond the scope of this Guide. So we pretend we didn't notice.

Answers to Practice with Stylistic Transformations

1. If the situation were simpler, Jeff would loan them some money.

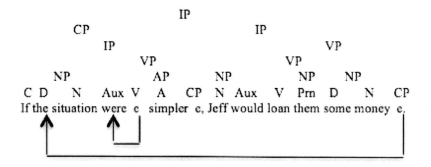

Here the adverbial CP is fronted. The top IP connects the fronted adverbial CP with the main clause (IP). The lowest AP connects with 'A' and the neighboring CP ('than it is [simple]'). 'Loan them' doesn't pass muster as a phrase, so the lowest VP has to include 'loan them some money.' The next higher one includes 'loan them some money CP ('if..')'

1.   Lack of money he considered a poor reason to get all upset.

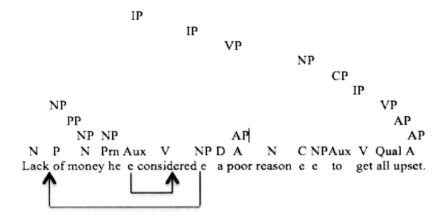

The topicalization of the NP 'lack of money' does not create a CP, but simply extends the IP, similar to other fronting movements. The top VP connects with the V 'consider' and two NPs as in 'to consider X Y' in complex transitive verbs.

3. Perhaps it is publicity in the local papers that they need.

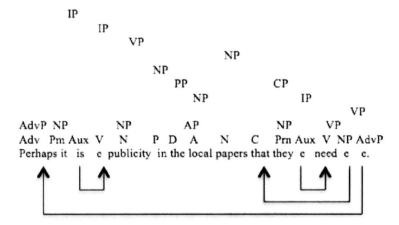

This sentence shows a clefted sentence with a focus position after 'it is.' There is a second IP to account for the fronted AdvP 'perhaps.' There are two VPs in the that-CP so that the top one can connect to the AdvP 'perhaps' separately.

Analysis of Summary Phrase-tree Diagramming Practice

1. Mitch was amazed that his grades improved dramatically from last semester. 'That' marks an adjective complement clause. Our discussion concluded that the

primary question is whether a 'what'-question can be answered by the 'that'-clause. Here it can, so the adjectival complement clause is a NomCP .

2. Anna e knew e Brian would be happy e e to marry her. (knew+NomCP; happy+NomCP)

5. I didn't know whether e to wake up and exercise or sleep in. (Know + NomCP)

6. It was e not too late for you to start a new life. (late+AdvCP)

9. They that e e work hard will often become successful. (That+restrictive relative clause; 'that' moves vacuously; Aux-V (intrasitive))

10. We e listen when pleasure e calls. (listen+AdvCP; 'when' doesn't move)

13. When my friends let me down, then my family will pick me up again. (fronted AdvCP; 'then' as AdvP, not conjunction; 'up' as adv., not verb particle)

14. A gym is e a place where people can keep in good shape e. (place+rel.cl, 'where' is fronted)

16. My Dad can run faster than your Dad e e . ('than' again; Dad+Aux+V)

17. The experimental plane e goes faster than a plane has ever traveled before. ('than' as head of CP, no 'e' in the CP)

19. They were e so exhausted that they could not walk another mile. (exhausted+ QualifyingCP or AdvCP, depending on your approach)

21. e e e e Rich to the point of embarrassment, Carnegie e decided e e to build public libraries e. (fronted AdvCP with be-raising; final e is original position of AdvCP

22. For us to be going there at this time of night would be foolish. (no e's in the sentence. Subject is a non-finite NomCP).

24. Brent 's college roommate asked him to go surfing with him.

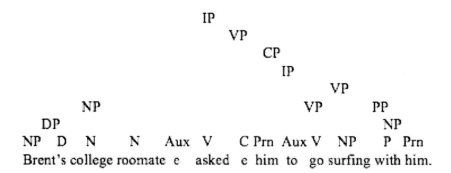

```
                              IP
                          VP
                             CP
                              IP
                                 VP
              NP                 VP     PP
          DP                            NP
      NP  D   N     N    Aux  V   C Prn Aux V  NP   P  Prn
      Brent's college roomate  e   asked  e  him to  go surfing with him.
```

The most interesting word in this sentence is 'surfing,' which looks like a gerund, but is here being treated as an NP. The phrase 'go +sport-ing' has been the object of much discussion. It seems to work well with intransitive verb-ing forms, so let's call it a VP. The main reason is that it acts like a noun for intransitive verbs, such as 'ride a horse,' and 'shoot skeet.' Instead of saying *'going riding horses/horseback,' we say 'go horseback riding,' where the N 'horseback' acts like a noun modifying another noun. The same is true of *'going shooting skeet,' which changes to 'going skeet shooting.' The word 'for' as lexicalized in the CP 'asked (for) him to go surfing...' sounds a little odd, but it doesn't seem to change the meaning, so there's not a good reason to consider the dependent clause an IP only. The CP is used nominally.

25. As a child, Brent had had to live with an aunt and uncle in their sea-side home.

```
              IP
                                       VP
                         VP
                          PP
                            NP              PP
        PP                   N               NP
         NP        Aux             CCP            NP
      P  D   N   NP Aux  Aux V  P   D   N Conj N  P D  N-N   N
      As a child, Bret had had to live with an aunt and uncle in their sea-side home.
```

The as-PP is connected to the top IP node directly, while the lower one connects with the subject NP, the Aux, and the highest VP. The form 'had to' looks very much like an infinitive, but it is not, as a strange lexicalization such as *'had for (him.self to live' makes clear. It is a type of substitute auxiliary with the same meaning as 'must.' It expands the limited number of verb forms for the meaning of 'must,' providing forms in all tenses and aspects. For example, where *'I will must' is impossible, 'I will have to' provides the needed form. The in-PP is functioning adverbially, modifying the verb 'live,' as is the with-PP. There is no dependent clause in this sentence, even though it looks like there might be. Since the as-PP has been fronted from the end of the sentence, this PS tree needs to be augmented by adding an empty category at the place the movement originated, as we saw elsewhere.

Answers to Chapter 9

Answers to Practice Diagramming Simple Sentence in Reed-Kellogg Style in 9.1.2

1. Sam's tennis is improving rapidly.

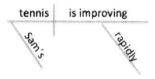

2. Our delighted host opened the champagne bottle very carefully.

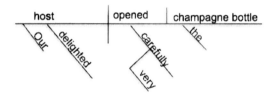

Answers to Practice Diagramming Prepositional Phrases in R-K

1. They are living in Phoenix.

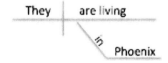

2. In March, many students have a week of vacation.

Answers to Practice with Subject Complements in R-K

1. The jacket is green.

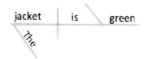

2. This is a green jacket.

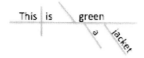

Answers to Practice with Transitive Verb in R-K

1. She has read her history assignment.

2. Would you put your shoes in the corner? (hint-make it a statement)

Answers to Practice with Indirect Objects in R-K

1. He is writing his niece a letter.

2. They gave the neighborhood children a warning about Halloween.

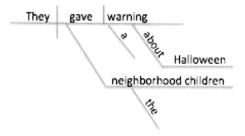

3. They will make the school new banners for the next track season.

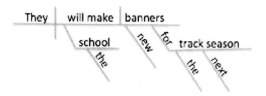

Answers to practice with complex transitive sentences in R-K

1. The populace elected her president.

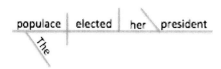

2. We never called him dishonest.

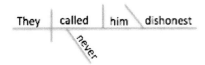

Answers to Practice with Coordinate Structures in R-K

1. They washed and dried the dishes.

2. The wheel and axel was invented millennia ago. (hint: a postposition!)

Answers to Practice with Prepositional Subject Complements

1. My friends are all in really good shape.

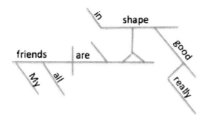

2. At this speed, we will be on time.

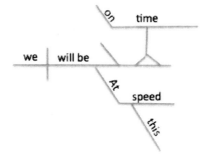

Answers to Practice with Nominal Clauses

2. Homer relates that it was ten days' sail from Ithaca to his next destination: the Isle of Aeolus, the king of the winds.

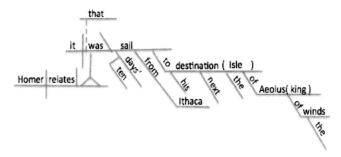

3. Odysseus was very grateful the king gave him a bag with all the winds in it except the one favorable one.

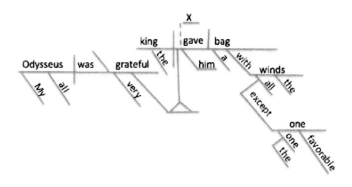

6. Odysseus next struggled on the Isle of the witch Circe for his crew to metamorphose back from pigs to men.

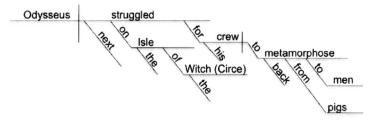

Answers to Practice with Gerunds in 9.2.4

1. We receive good by doing good.

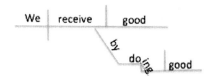

2. Buying and selling textbooks provides many with a living.

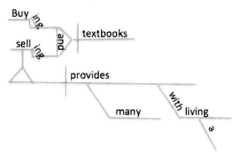

3. Visiting relatives can be very tiring

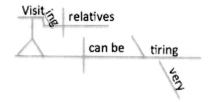

Answers to Practice Diagramming Participles in 9.2.6

2. Pushed by the crowd, the young demonstrator fell.

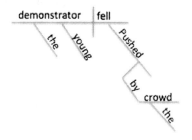

3. The students, realizing they could succeed, studied hard.

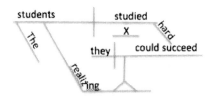

Answers to Practice with Subordinate and Relative Clauses

1. We listen when pleasure calls.

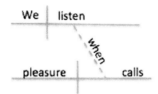

2. Because they were so excited, they missed the announcement.

6. I found the place to which you referred.

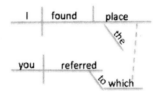

7. Those who play with tar will get stained

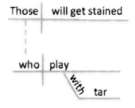

8. There is no logical reason why I should stay at home this evening.

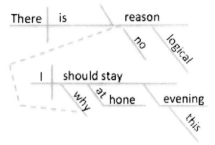

9. When my friends let me down, then my family will pick me up again.

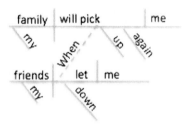

Answers to Practice Diagramming Clauses of Comparison in 9.4.1

3. The experimental plane goes faster than a plane has ever traveled before.

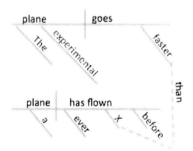

4. That's the fastest computer anyone has ever been built.

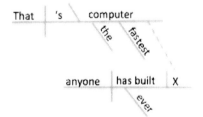

5. They were so exhausted that they could not walk another mile.

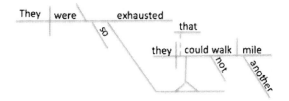

6. Our roommates thought that we were wise enough not to take such a risk.

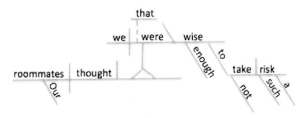

Answers to Summary Reed-Kellogg Diagraming Practice in 9.5.1

1. A bystander was amazed that things worked out. ('That' marks an adjective complement clause. Diagram the clause as if it were an appositive to the adjective). The main clause's subject is 'a bystander', verb 'was', then a slanted line for subject complement 'amazed'; the complement clause is on a stilt next to 'amazed' and its base has parentheses around it. CP subject: 'things', V: 'worked out'.

2. All the relatives knew they would be glad to get home.

Subject: 'all the relatives', V: knew, direct object clause on a stilt (without 'that') with its own subject 'they' V:'would be', subject complement 'glad', modifier below adjective (on a PP shape, as if 'to' were the preposition) 'to get' with another modifying PP shape below 'get': 'home' as the noun in a PP.

3. That they could arrive on time was now a certainty.

Subject nominal clause on a stilt with 'that' floating above the verb: subject 'they', V: could arrive, adverbial PP below V: 'on time.' Main clause V: 'was'

4. I wondered if/whether they would arrive on time

Similar to #2 above with 'if/whether they would arrive on time' as the direct object noun clause up on a stilt. The complementizer 'if/whether' floats above the direct object clause's v: 'would arrive.' The PP 'on time' is below 'would arrive.'

5. I didn't know whether to donate money to that campaign.

Similar to #4 above except that 'to donate' is on a PP shape with a direct object (half vertical line) for the verb's direct object 'money' and the PP 'to that campaign' is below the verb 'donate.' The main clause has 'n't' below the verb 'did know.'

6. It was not too late for you to start a new life.

Similar to #1 above in that 'for you to start a new life' is on a stilt to the right of the 'late.' The base of the stilt is in parentheses. 'For you' is on a PP shape which connects to a second PP shape containing 'to start.' Just like #5 above, the verb 'start' is followed by a direct object 'life' which has two modifiers 'a' and 'new.' The main clause is 'it was' followed by a slanting line for the subject complement 'late.' 'Was' is modified by 'not' and 'late' is by 'too.'

7. I am hoping you will come home soon.

Similar to #2 above with 'you will come home soon' as the direct object clause on a stilt following the main clause v: 'am hoping'. The dependent clause has subject: 'you', v: will come, which has two modifiers 'home' (on a PP shape as the noun), and 'soon' as an adverb.

8. I found the place to which you referred (Reed and Kellogg 96).

Main clause subject: 'I', v: 'found,' direct obj.: 'the place.' Relative clause is on a parallel sentence line (as yet unconnected) below the main clause: subj.: 'you', v: 'referred,' PP line modifying the verb 'to which.' A dotted line from 'place' goes down to touch the top of 'which'.

9. They that curry favor will be disappointed.

Main clause subj.: 'they', v: 'will be', subject complement (slanted line): 'disappointed.' Relative clause placement similar to #8 above: subj.: 'that', v: 'curry', direct object: 'favor.' A dotted line goes down from 'they' to 'that'.

10. We react when temptation rears its head. 'When…head' is an adverbial CP, with 'when' on the dotted line connecting the two main verbs.

11. He did what was considered right

Similar to #2 above. Main clause 'he did' with the verb followed by a direct object clause on a stilt: 'what was considered right', which is on a stilt after the half vertical line. Subj.: 'what', v: 'was considered' subject complement: 'right.'

12. This is the time when the election for president will be held.

'when …held' is a relative clause with 'when' as a modifier under 'held' and with a dotted line connecting 'when' to 'time'

13. When my gait slows down and my eyes dim, then I will need help from others. The 'When…dim' clause is compound with 'and' connecting the verbs 'slows' and 'dim.' As a whole, it is adverbial with 'when' on the dotted line between the main verbs slows/dim and 'will need'. 'From others' modifies 'help'. 'Then' modifies 'take.'

14. A school is an institution where students can be challenged and taught.

The clause 'where…taught' is similar to #12 above with 'where' modifying the compound verb 'challenged and taught' and a dotted line connecting 'where' to 'institution.'

15. My dad weighs less than your dad. Similar to section 9.4 #3 above. The phrase 'your dad X' represents 'weighs (a lot)' and 'than' is on a dotted line connecting 'less' to 'x'.

16. My Dad always eats faster than my Mom.. This is similar to #3 in section 9.4. above. 'Than your dad X' where 'x' represents the VP of the second clause. It has an 'x' modifying the VP representing 'fast.' The 'than' is on a dotted line connecting 'faster' with the 'x' modifying the second clause's VP.

17. The new oriber flies faster than any plane has ever flown. Similar to #3 is section 9.4 above. "X" modifies 'has flown.' 'than' is on a dotted line connecting 'faster' to the 'x'.

18. That's the fastest computer any company has ever built. 'any company … built X' is a relative clause with the 'x' as a direct object and a dotted line connecting the 'x' to 'computer.'

19. They were so exhausted that they could not swim another ten feet. 'that…feet' is a adverbial clause with 'that' on the dotted line connecting 'were' with 'swim.'

20. Our roommates thought that we were wise enough not to take such a risk. 'that…risk' is a nominal clause on a stilt as a direct object of 'thought'. 'Enough' modifies 'wise' and 'to take such a risk' uses the shape of a 'to'-prepositional modifier below 'wise' with 'not' modifying 'take' and 'such a risk' as the direct object of 'take.'

21. Rich to the point of embarrassment, Warren Buffet announced his support for a special tax on the wealthy. Here 'rich…embarrassment' is seen as an adjectival modifier of 'Warren Buffett.' 'to the point' is a PP that modifies 'rich' and 'of embarrassment' is a PP that modifies 'point.'

22. For us to stay at home when wild fires are approaching would be insane. This is similar to #24 is section 9.2.1 above.

23. Going anywhere safe would be wiser than staying here. The subject

of the main clause and the dependent 'than' clauses are both gerunds on broken lines up on a stilt. The stilt for 'staying here' is connected to an empty verb and predicate adjective (each marked with an 'X') representing 'would be wise.' 'Than' connects 'wiser' with the 'X' in the empty position for 'wise.'

Answers to Chapter 10

Answers to contrastive analysis practice (1) in 10.4.4

Choose 20 or so lines and set up a contrastive analysis of Chaucer's non-standard usage (according to present-day standards) and SAE.

Abbreviations:

      d.o.=direct object

      inf.=infinitive (of the verb)

      p.pt.=past participle

      pr.pt.= present participle

      subj. = subject

      sub.conj.=subordinating conjunction

N.B. Antiquated Middle English inflectional suffixes and the unidiomatic lexical items are replaced by modern ones in the middle column where Middle English syntactic features are isolated.

Middle English text	Middle English feature	American English form
	1. when that	1. when
WHEN that Aprilis, with	when+that	when (no 'that')
his showers swoot*,	2. showers sweet	2. sweet showers
*sweet	noun+adj	adj+noun
The drought of March	3. subj+ the drought has	3. subj+ has pierced the
hath pierced to the root,	pierced	drought
And bathed every vein in	d.o.+aux+verb	aux+verb+ d.o.
such licour,		
Of which virtue	4. of which virtue	4. by virtue of which the
engender'd is the flower;	engerdered is the flower	flower is engendered
When Zephyrus eke with	P+which NP+past	P+NP+P+which+be+p.pt.
his swoote breath	part.+be	

Inspired hath in every holt* and heath *grove, forest	5. When ... inspired has... Sub.conj. NP...p.pt+aux	
The tender croppes* and the younge sun *twigs, boughs		
Hath in the Ram <1> his halfe course y-run,	6. the young sun has in Aries his half course run	
And smalle fowles make melody,	subj+aux+PP+NP(do)+v; D+half+NP	
That sleepen all the night with open eye,		
(So pricketh them nature in their corages*); *hearts, inclinations	7. So influences them nature in their hearts 'So'+v+d.o.+subj+PP	
Then longe folk to go on pilgrimages,	8. Then long people to go on pilgrimages,	9. And some (go to) seek subj.(+go+ inf.) verb
And palmers <2> for to seeke strange strands,	'Then'+v+NP+inf	
To *ferne hallows couth* in sundry lands; *distant saints known*<3>		10. to Canterbury they go, to seek the holy blissful Martyr.
And specially, from every shire's end		e (for) +to V+ NP obj.
Of Engleland, to Canterbury they wend,		11. ... to seek the martyr, that has helped them
The holy blissful Martyr for to seek,		when they were sick. Rel.cl.: NP subj.rel.Prn +
That them hath holpen*, when that they were sick. *helped		aux.+ v + NP dir. obj.+CP (adv)['when that' – see above #1]
		12. It (so) happened that...
Befell that, in that season on a day,		
In Southwark at the Tabard <4> as I lay,		
Ready to wenden on my pilgrimage		
To Canterbury with devout corage,	13. At night was come into that hostelry a good	
At night was come into that hostelry	twenty-nine in a company of diverse	
Well nine and twenty in a company	people. PP(time)	
Of sundry folk, *by aventure y-fall *who had	+be(aux)+come+	

by chance fallen In fellowship*, and pilgrims were they all, into company.* <5> That toward Canterbury woulde ride. The chamber, and the stables were wide, And *well we weren eased at the best.* (*we were well provided) And shortly, when the sunne was to rest, with the best* So had I spoken with them every one, That I was of their fellowship anon, And made forword* early for to rise, *promise To take our way there as I you devise*. *describe, relate	PP(place)+subj 14. And pilgrims were they all. 'and' +NP+be+prn 15. that toward Canterbury would ride. 'that'+PP(place)+aux+v 16. And well we were provided at the best. 20. To make our way there as I you describe.	20. To make our way there as I will describe to you

Answers to Supplemental Contrastive Analysis Practice

Choose ten verses and analyze the differences between Wycliffe's translation and SAE. The following version is modernized to the extent of using more standard spelling, which allows us to focus on grammatical differences and not be too distracted by the choice of vocabulary items or the spelling conventions.

Middle English form	Middle English grammar	SAE grammar
[18] And some Epicureans, and Stoics, and philosophers disputed with him. And some said, What will this sower of words say? And others said, He seemeth to be a teller of new fiends; for he told to them Jesus, and the again-rising. [19] And they took and led him to Areopagus and said, May we know, what is this new doctrine, that is said of	1. What will this ... say? (modal aux +NP+V) 2. he told to them Jesus (Prn+V:told+PP I.O.+ NP D.O.) 3. they took and led him NP+V+ conj.+V + Prn	1. What is this ... saying?(prog.aux+NP+V) 2. he told them about J. (PRN+V told+NP I.O.+PP D.O.) 3. they (took him) [or] (led him) 4.

thee? ²⁰ For thou bringest in some new things to our ears; therefore we will know, what these things will be. ²¹ For all men of Athens and comelings harboured gave attention to none other thing, but either to say, either to hear, some new thing. ²² And Paul stood in the middle of Areopagus, and said, Men of Athens, by all things I see you as vain worshippers. ²³ For I passed, and saw your maumets, and found an altar, in which was written, To the unknown God. Therefore which thing ye unknowing worship, this thing I show to you. ²⁴ God that made the world and all things that be in it, this, for he is Lord of heaven and earth, dwelleth not in temples made with hand, ²⁵ neither is worshipped by man's hands, neither having need of any thing, for he giveth life to all men, and breathing, and all things; ²⁶ and made of one all the kind of men for to inhabit on all the face of the earth, determining times ordained, and terms of the dwelling of them, ²⁷ to seek God, if peradventure they feel him, either find, though he be not far from each of you. ²⁸ For in him we live, and move, and be. As also some of your poets said,	4. May we know, what is...? Y-n Q + direct Q 5. We will know... Prn+will+VP 6. 10. which thing you... which+thing+rel.cl. 11. unknowing 12. this thing I show to you 13. that be in it 19. the dwelling of them (NP+ of+ Prn) 20. we live,... and be.	5. 6. what+NP+are 7. visitors staying in town (Prep. V) 8. to no other thing 9. either...or 14. neither is worshiped... nor has... (correl. conj.)(tensed V) 16. to all men life, and breath, and all things 17. all the kinds (plural) 18. men to inhabit (trans. V)

| And we be also the kind of him. [29] Therefore since we be the kind of God, we shall not deem, that godly thing is like gold, and silver, either stone, either to graving of craft and thought of man.[b] [30] For God despiseth the times of this unknowing, and now showeth to men, that all every where do penance; [31] for that he hath ordained a day, in which he shall deem the world in equity, in a man in which he ordained, and gave faith to all men, and raised him from death. [32] And when they had heard the again-rising of dead men[c], some scorned, and some said, We shall hear thee again of this thing. [33] So Paul went out of the middle of them. [34] But some men drew to him, and believed. Among which Dionysius Areopagite was, and a woman, by name Damaris, and other men with them. | ('be' as intrans.) 21. we be … the kind (linking V) 22. the kind of him (~19) 26. among which … was | 23. masterful carving or human inventing 26. among whom was … |

Index/Glossary

Term	(page numbers)	Definition and/or Example

Absolute Phrase/Clause (132-3)   a phrase from which the complementizer or conjunction and the auxiliary/main verb 'be' has been deleted, such as 'The children waited, e1 their faces e2 e3 forlorn'

Abstract Noun (17, 19, 46-8 51, 67, 70)
a noun which can function as a singular subject without the determiner 'a,' such as 'honesty,' or 'patriotism'

Acc-ing gerund (139-40)   A 'verb+ing' form used nominally whose subject is in the accusative (=object) case (e.g., 'them'), such as 'Them coming home on time was really important.' The same as 'object-case gerund' (below).

Adjectival or Adjective Clause (106, 108, 117-8, 121, 132, 134, 198, 216)
Clause which modifies an NP

Adjectival(ly)   Functioning as an Adjective

Adjective Complement (78, 111-113, 124, 196, 211, 217)
a phrase that is required to complete a particular meaning of an adjective, such as 'sick of playing games'

Adjective Phrase (71, 74, 77-8, 121, 136, 204-6)
a phrase or constituent headed by an adjective; abbreviated AP

Adjective (102, 9-14, 17-22, 24-30, 38-40, 42, 44, 45, 48, 50, 57 59, 65-67, 71-5, 77-8, 8-, 85-6, 105, 120, 124-5, 137-8, 163, 166-7, 199, 201, 204-5, 213, 218)
an open lexical category used to modify nouns or noun phrases

Adjunct (29, 31, 104)   Technical term for optional modifiers

Adverbial Modifier (15, 18-19, 44, 76-7, 87, 102, 104, 140, 166-7, 190, 192-3, 196, 198, 200, 204, 221-2)
a phrase modifying an IP, AP, AdvP, or VP and which is usually characterized by having several possible positions in the clause

Adverbial or Adverb Clause (4, 76, 87, 107-113, 116, 118-21, 129, 132, 135, 137, 157, 169-71, 175-6, 181, 192-3, 198, 214)
Clauses that modify a verb, characterized by their ability to move within the sentence

Adverb(ial) Phrase (33, 76, 79)   a phrase or constituent headed by an adverb; abbreviated AdvP

Adverb (1-2, 4, 9-15, 17-19, 22-6, 28-9, 32-5, 38, 40-46, 55, 57, 59, 63-7, 73-4, 76-7, 79-81, 87-88, 100, 105, 107-9, 113,

116-7, 138, 140, 146, 149, 151, 154, 166, 179,
184, 113, 116-7, 138, 140, 146, 149, 151, 154,
166, 179, 184, 186, 190, 192, 198-9, 205, 208,
215, 217)
an open lexical category used to modify verbs,
or adjectives or their phrases, and sometimes
adverb phrases

Antecedent (52, 87, 154, 202)   The content word to which a pronoun refers.

AP (71, 77)   Adjective Phrase

Appositive (83-3, 105, 109-11, 113, 134, 198, 207-9)
an NP or CP which follows and modifies a
noun, adds information about it, and echos
the NP it's modifying, such as 'our biology
teacher Dr. Smith' or 'the message to leave
immediately'

Appositive Clause (110-1, 209)   a clause which immediately follows an NP
and restates what the NP is while adding a
little more informatio

Article (1, 12-14, 47-8, 67)   one of the words 'a,' 'an,' or 'the'

Attributive (10-13, 20-1, 38-40)   Naming an attribute i.e., "green" jacket,
where "green" is an attribute of "jacket". Also,
"green" precedes "jacket" and is then in an
attributive position relative to the noun
"jacket"

Attributive-only (38-39, 67)   Referring to the type of adjective that can
appear in front of the noun it is modifying but
not in the predicate of a linking verb.

Auxiliary (7, 29, 42, 61, 64-5, 67, 88-91, 93-4, 96, 99, 103-5, 107, 116, 118-9,
121, 124-5, 127-8, 130-3, 135, 137, 139-49,
151, 153, 157, 159-60, 166, 171, 173, 176-7,
180, 182-4, 189-90, 193, 210)
a closed lexical category that carries tense
(and number and person) information; the
head of an IP

Auxiliary Fronting (90-1, 96, 142, 144-6, 153, 182-4, 231)
The process of moving an auxiliary to
sentence-initial position in direct questions

Baa, Baa, Black Sheep Varieties (145-146)
Varieties of British English which allow the
main verb 'have' to be fronted in yes/no
questions, as in 'Have you any change?'

Bare Infinitive Form (128, 130-1, 180-1)
the uninflected form of a verb; technically an
infinitive ('to+base form of the verb') without
the word 'to'

Bare Infinitives (128, 130-1, 180-1)

    the dictionary form of a verb; technically the infinitive 'to+verb' without the 'to'

Base Form (127)   the uninflected form of a verb

Be-Raising (145-146, 183-4)   in English, the theoretically motivated movement of the main verb 'be' from the main verb position to the auxiliary position to explain why only this verb is fronted in yes/no questions.

Bivalent (30-1)   two values' in reference to verbs which can function in one of two sub-categories, such as transitive or intransitive

Cardinal Number (50, 65)   a word such as 'one,' 'two,' 'three,'...

Clause 3-5, 43, 49, 55, 58-61, 64-5, 74, 76, 81-82, 88, 95, 97, 99-100, 103-105, 107-135, 171-189, 208-219)

    a phrase with an auxiliary (visible or not) and a VP; the NP subject can be visible or not

Clitic (153)   a - usually contracted - form of a word that attaches to an adjacent (previous) word

Cliticize (94, 153, 182)   attach

Co-Indexing 105, 120, 122-3, 129-31, 135-6, 138)

    the process of using subscripts to identify two elements of the sentence as 1) having the same referent, or 2) the origin and the end-point of movement.

Comparative 10-15, 18, 25, 44-46, 50, 66, 228)

    Forms of adjectives ending in -er meaning 'more' or which use the words 'more' or 'less' for the same purpose.

Complement (noun) 27-32, 36, 38, 56-7, 59-60, 73-80, 82, 83-7, 89, 92-3, 97, 100, 102-3, 105, 108-13, 116, 124-5, 127-30, 134-5, 137, 154, 5, 165,7, 169, 171, 173, 175, 177, 185, 187, 188, 190-1, 198, 200-5, 197-8, 120-11, 217, 229, 231)

    a phrase that is required to complete the meaning of a larger phrase, e.g., 'living in Rome' is not the same as 'living.'

Complement (verb) (64-5)   to complete a grammatical unit

Complemented (38)   Technical term for completed grammatically

Complementizer (59-60, 64, 67, 76, 104-5, 107-8, 110-13, 115, 123, 127-8, 130, 132, 134-5, 137, 139, 140, 145, 169, 171, 176, 183, 190, 192, 208-10, 232)

Describes any of the three words that
introduce differing kinds of noun clauses
where the verb has a clause as its object or
complement: 1) 'that' when it introduces a
finite (tensed) clause 2) 'for' when it
introduces a full non-finite clause, or 3) 'if'
when it introduces an indirect question.

Complementizer Phrase (76, 104, 128, 145, 169, 183, 190)
a phrase in which an IP is embedded;
abbreviated CP

Complex Transitive Verb (27-8, 30-1, 34, 38, 67, 74, 105, 135, 161, 204-5)
a verb whose direct object has an AP or NP
complement, where the AP modifies the
direct object or the NP complement has the
same referent as the direct object

Conjunction (1-2, 5, 12, 18, 25, 43-4, 50, 58-61, 64-5, 67, 76-7, 96, 98-101, 104,
107, 109, 113, 116-7, 119-20, 124, 127-8,
132-4, 169, 173, 175, 205-6, 214-6, 224)
a closed lexical category that is used to
connect phrases. There are four types (67).

Connective (43)   another name for a conjunctive adverb, such
as 'however,' 'therefore,' or 'in fact.'

Constituency (97-8, 100)   The status of being a phrase

Constituent (69, 76, 89, 94, 127, 142, 151, 160, 189) the basic unit of a sentence,
synonymous with 'phrase'

Constituent Testing (69, 271)   Ways of testing to see if a certain string of
words make up a constituent or phrase

Correlative Conjunction (50, 59, 67, 98-9, 101)
both...and,' 'either... or,' 'whether... or,'
'neither... nor,' and 'not only, but also.'

Demonstrative Determiner (12, 48)   This, that, these, those, and yon

Demonstrative (12, 48)   one of the words 'this,' 'that,' 'these,' or 'those'

Dependent (subordinate) Clause (60, 76, 100, 104-5, 107-8, 110, 112-3, 121,
124-5, 127-8, 135-6, 140, 145, 156, 169-71,
174-5, 180-1, 183-4, 186, 188, 192, 199, 208,
214, 221-2)
a clause which cannot stand by itself as a
complete grammatical unit

Descriptive Grammar (4, 15-16)   Emphasizes that 'some ideas are expressed
this way' without making any judgment

Determiner (2, 12-14, 16, 19, 25, 47-50, 42-3, 56, 59, 64-5, 67-8, 71, 81, 83,
108-9, 117, 125-7, 139, 141, 146, 148-9, 166-
7, 177, 186, 201, 208)

a word or phrase used in the specifier postion of a noun phrase

Direct Object (27-30, 32-3, 73-4, 76-7, 89, 105, 111-2, 118, 123, 134-5, 137-8, 155, 158-60, 172, 176-7, 185, 187, 192, 198, 202, 204, 208-9, 211, 217, 229)
an NP or dependent clause which is required to complete the meaning of a verb (usually answers the question 'what' or 'who(m)'

Ditransitive Verb (31, 65, 74, 203) a verb which has both an indirect object (usually answering the question 'to whom' or 'for whom') and a direct object

Do Support (91) the use of the verb 'do' as an auxiliary in questions, negatives, and emphatic sentences

DRRRIIIPPP (55) Acronym for all ten types of pronouns: demonstrative, reciprocal, reflexive, relative, indefinite, intensive (or emphatic), interrogative, personal (subject or object), and possessive

Dummy Auxiliary (61, 67, 90-1, 94, 143, 160)
the use of the verb 'do' as an auxiliary in questions, negatives, and emphatic sentences

Dummy 'do' (61, 90-1, 144) the use of the verb 'do' as an auxiliary in questions, negatives, and emphatic sentences

Echo Questions (54, 142, 147-8, 153, 184)
question-like utterances of surprise that request the repetition of certain information, such as 'You ate what?'

Ellipsis (119) Another word for deletion or omission

Elliptical Clause (119) see reduced adverbial clause

Embedded (58, 69-71, 86, 101, 108, 131, 139-41, 149, 167, 174, 176, 183-4)
included inside something larger, such as a smaller phrase can be 'embedded' within a larger phrase

Empty Categories (65, 92, 94, 115-121, 124-6, 128-30, 132, 136-8, 140-4, 149, 151, 159-60, 163, 169, 173-76, 179-82, 184-89)
empty positions in the grammatical structure resulting from deletion or movement

Ex Cathedra (15) Latin for "from the chair" referring to papal authority to speak without error or rebuttal

Extraposition (154, 190-1) the movement of the subject, or part of one, toward the end of the sentence without the insertion of 'it' or 'there'

FANBOYS (58, 104) Acronym for simple coordinating conjunctions: 'for,' 'and,' 'nor,' 'but,' 'or,' 'yet,' or 'so'

Finite (61, 113, 116, 118)   referring to a clause whose verb carries tense
                                    information
Fronting (90-2, 94, 105, 118, 142, 144, 145-6, 148-9, 151, 153, 156-8, 182-4,
                                    186, 190, 192-3, 231)
                                    The process of moving a phrase to sentence-
                                    initial position
Gapping (116, 173-4)   deleting a portion of a (usually coordinate)
                                    clause
Gradable (39-40, 67, 73)   Refers to an adjective that has gradations and
                                    can, therefore, be modified by a qualifier,
                                    such as 'very'.
Grammarians, the (1-2, 10, 12-13, 25, 175)
                                    Eighteenth century language scholars who
                                    insisted on a "Latin treatment" of the English
                                    language
Head Noun (73, 81-2, 86, 108-9, 118, 125, 179, 214, 216)
                                    the NP which a relative clause is modifying
                                    or complementing
Head of a Phrase (92, 100)   The most important word in the phrase which
                                    other words in the phrase are complementing
                                    or modifying (or specifying).
Heavy Complement Shift (155, 190-1)
                                    the optional movement of part of a
                                    complement or direct object to sentence-final
                                    position
Homonyms 9, 30-2, 38)   two words that are spelled the same and
                                    pronounced the same, but which have
                                    different meanings and etymologies.
Homonymy (30-31)   the relation between homonyms (see
                                    'homonyms' above)
Indefinite Determiner (49-50, 53, 68)
                                    a word such as 'some,' 'any,' or 'every' when
                                    used as a determiner (in the specifier of NP
                                    position)
Indefinite Quantifier   a word such as half, many, few, several, all,
                                    and both when it's possible to stack them with
                                    a determiner, such as 'the.'
Indirect Object (27, 73, 105, 111, 158, 198, 203-4, 211)
                                    The NP (or CP) in a clause with a ditransitive
                                    verb which answers the question 'to whom'
                                    or 'for whom.'
Infinite (126)   not having tense or number

Infinitival Adjectival Clause (134) a clause which modifies a noun and whose
                                    auxiliary-main verb is in the form 'to+verb'
Infinitive (60-1, 64, 112, 125-8, 130-2, 134-6, 176, 180-1, 209-10, 227)
                                    The word 'to' followed by the base/dictionary
                                    form of a verb, such as 'to start'

Inflected Phrase (88, 95, 103, 127-8, 139)

> another word for main clause but also used for gerund clauses; abbreviated 'IP'

Inflection (11, 23-4, 64, 88, 90, 104, 143, 151, 290)

> Usually describing -er or -est endings for adjectives or adverbs, -s or 's endings for nouns, and –ed, -ing, -n, and –s endings for verbs

ing-of gerund (137)

> a verb-ing form followed by an 'of-PP' such as 'the reading of the book.' Syntactically it's a noun.

Intensifier/Qualifier (see Qualifier)

> an open lexical category used to modify adjective and adverb phrases; they have no comparatives and little or no stackability

Intensive/Emphatic Pronouns (54, 67)

> one of the words 'myself,' 'yourself,' 'himself,' 'herself,' 'itself,' 'ourselves,' 'yourselves,' or 'themselves,' when used similarly to an appositive for an NP

Interjection (1, 2, 205)

> an utterance such as 'wow!' which is not part of sentence structure

Interrogative Adverb (42-4, 55, 67, 146, 150, 208)

> one of the words 'where,' 'when,' 'how,' and 'why' when used in direct or indirect questions

Interrogative Determiner (48, 146, 150)

> the word 'whose' in a question where it precedes a noun.

Interrogative Pronoun (54-5, 146, 150)

> One of the words 'who' or 'what' is a question or an indirect question

Intransitive Verb (29-31, 74, 118, 127, 158, 213)

> a verb which does not have and does not require an NP object to function grammatically

Lexical Categories (9-14, 18-20, 22, 24, 25, 28, 44, 50, 63, 66, 67, 75, 77, 81, 92, 146, 163, 227, 246)

> the same as syntactic categories = grammatical categories = parts of speech

Lexical Gaps (99, 100)

> possible sound combinations which could be a word, but which have no meaning (yet), such as 'glink'

Linking Verb (11, 20, 24, 28-30, 38, 75, 105, 121, 134, 154, 158, 177, 201, 204, 246)

> A verb whose subject and NP complement have the same referent or whose AP complement modifies the subject; includes

'be,' 'seem,' 'become,' and some verbs of perception

Main (Independent) Clauses (167, 149, 151)
a clause which can stand by itself as a complete grammatical unit

Main-Verb Fronting (146, 151, 146) in Germanic languages, the movement of the main verb to sentence initial position for a yes/no question, as in 'Have you any change?' or to second position in a wh-question

Manner Adverbs (22, 25, 40-4, 67, 199)
The most common kind of adverbs which modify (describe) verbs

Mass noun (47)
a noun which normally has no plural form, such as 'furniture;' the same as 'non-count noun'

Modifier (73)
a phrase which adds information to another phrase, but which is not grammatically required to complete that phrase

Modify (22)
Describe, manner adverbs modify (describe) verbs

Movement (23, 33, 42, 90, 91, 94, 105, 118, 142-61, 181-90, 195,196, 219, 257, 265, 272)
the ability of some phrases to change location within the sentence

Node (165)
A juncture in a PS Tree

Nominal Absolute (132)
see Absolute Phrase/Clause

Nominal or Noun Clauses (82, 107, 110, 127, 198)
Clauses which have the same grammatical roles as NP's do.

Non-count noun (46, 47, 50, 243)
a noun which normally has no plural form, such as 'furniture;' the same as 'mass noun'

Non-Finite (60, 61, 112, 114, 116, 118, 119, 123, 125-35, 145, 149, 174-77, 180, 210, 229, 233, 264, 265)
not having an auxiliary or verb with tense information, such as an infinitive verb ('to go'), or a gerund or gerundive ('Surviving in the desert is a challenge.')

Non-Finite Nominal Clause (123, 134, 135, 176, 209, 210)
a non-finite clause whose auxiliary and main verb are not carrying tense information

Non-Gradable (39, 40, 73)   Refers to an adjective that has no gradations and cannot be modified by a qualifier, such as 'very'

Non-Restrictive Appositives (82, 209, 109 *)
          an appositive modifying an NP which is definite by itself, such as 'Mr. Smith, our neighbor' (where there is only one Mr. Smith)

Non-Restrictive Relative Clauses (109)
          Relative Clauses which are modifiers

Noun Complement (28, 30)   a phrase that is required to complete a particular meaning of an NP, such as 'the destruction of Rome'

Noun (4-20, 46-8)   an open lexical categoryusually having morphological plurals and possessives, and usually fitting the sentence "They have no ____."

NP (71)   Noun Phrase

Number (50, 51, 57, 65, 66, 85, 86, 87, 90, 94, 103, 116, 127, 144, 146, 159, 160)
          the grammatical distinction between singular and plural

Object (27-33, 47, 52, 54-5, 57, 59, 64-5, 67, 71-4, 76-7, 81, 89, 97, 105, 110-3, 115, 118, 123, 125, 127, 129, 134-5, 137-41, 155-6, 158-60, 171-2, 176-7, 185, 187, 192, 198, 200, 202-5, 207-9, 211, 213, 217, 229)
          the NP or dependent clause which is the complement of the head of another, larger phrase.

Object-case gerund A 'Verb+ing' (139)
          form used nominally. The subject of the verb is in the object case (e.g., 'him'), such as 'Him coming home on time was really important.' Also called 'acc-ing gerund'.

Object Pronoun (51, 55, 64, 65, 127, 129, 139, 159, 177, 187, 244)
          one of the words 'me,' 'you,' 'him,' 'her,' 'it,' 'us,' and 'them' when they serve as the object of a verb or preposition or as the subject of a non-finite clause

Obligatory Movement (142)   (syntactic) movement of a word or phrase that is obligatory for acceptable grammar

Open Categories (25, 45)   Lexical categories which are open in the sense that new words can always be added, borrowed, or created: nouns, verbs, adjectives, and adverbs

Ordinal Number (50)   a word such as' first', 'second,' 'third,'...

Participial Clause (119)	a clause which begins with either a present participle (ending in '-ing) or a past participle
Participial Phrase	another name for a participial clause
Past Participial Clause (119)	a clause which begins with a past participle
Past Participial Phrase	another name for a Past Participial Clause
Past Participle (7, 61, 89, 119-20, 158-60, 194)	a non-finite verb form usually ending in '-ed' or '-n'
(to) 'Pattern like' (12, 34, 50)	to belong to the same sequences of lexical a phrasal categories, such as " 'when' patterns like 'where.' "
Perfective Phrase (89)	a phrase beginning with a form of the aspectual auxiliary 'have' which has the main VP embedded within it; this results from a string of several auxiliaries
Personal Demonstrative (48)	one of the words 'we' or 'you' used as determiners, such as 'we students,' or 'you people.'
Phrasal Verb (34-8, 208)	A verb whose meaning has changed because it has combined with a verb particle and the meaning of the combination is not the same as the two individual meanings would indicate
Phrase Structure (69, 81, 95, 97, 104)	an analysis of the relationships of the words within a phrase and of phrases within larger phrases
Phrase Structure Tree (105, 162-197)	a graphic representation of the structure of a phrase in the generative approach to grammar
Possessive Adjectives (12)	a misnomer for 'possessive determiner) below
Possessive Determiners (12, 48, 67, 139, 231)	possessive adjectives", such as 'my' and 'your'
Possessive(-case) Gerund (139-141)	A 'Verb+ing' form where the subject of the verb is a possessive determiner (e.g., 'their') or a possessive noun (e.g., 'Tom's'), such as 'Their coming home on time was important.'
Possessive Noun (14, 17, 66, 81, 83-4, 141, 177, 201)	A noun with the possessive 's', as in "Luke's".
Possessive Pronoun (53, 55, 67, 231)	

one of the words mine, yours, his, hers, its, ours, or theirs

Poss-ing Gerund See 'possessive-case gerund' just above.

PP   Prepositional Phrase

PP Fronting (96, 156-7)   The process of moving a prepositional phrase to sentence-initial position

Predicate (31-2, 38 40, 64, 70, 73, 88, 90, 131, 133, 164-6, 171, 198)
                                the auxiliary and VP in a clause

Predicative (10-13, 27-29, 31, 38-40)
                                Refers to a position within a sentence's predicate

Predicative-only (11, 38-9, 67) Referring to the distribution of adjectives

Prepositional Object (72, 111, 138, 148, 192, 203, 208)
                                the NP (or CP) which follows a preposition

Prepositional Verb (27, 31-3, 34-8, 74, 158, 200)
                                a verb which needs a PP complement for a given meaning, such as 'living in LA'

Preposition (1-2, 6, 12, 17, 25, 27, 29, 31-8, 43, 47, 51, 53-4, 56-8, 64-7, 71-7, 97, 99, 102, 105, 110-11, 124-5, 134, 137-8, 148, 156-8, 166-7, 192, 200, 202-3, 206-11)
                                a lexical category including words such as 'by,' 'with,' 'along,' and dozens of others

Prescriptive Grammar   Emphasizes that 'some ideas should be written this way'

Present Participial Clause (119-20, 213)
                                a clause which begins with either a present participle (ending in '-ing)

Present Participial Phrase   another name for a Present Participial Clause

Present Participle (61, 119-20, 130, 133, 136, 177, 213)
                                a non-finite verb form ending in '-ing'

Progressive Phrase (7, 6, 88-9, 103, 140)
                                a phrase beginning with a form of the aspectual auxiliary 'be' which has the main VP embedded within it; this results from a string of several auxiliaries

Pronoun (7, 16-7, 25, 50-6, 59, 64-5, 67, 69-70, 81, 85-7, 101, 108-109, 113, 115, 123, 125,127-30, 139, 146, 148-9, 151, 154, 159-60, 177, 186-7, 214-5)
                                a lexical category that can replace and refer to an antecedent which is an NP

Qualifier (13-14, 19, 25, 39, 42, 44-6, 50, 63-4, 66-7, 75, 77, 79, 85, 118, 157-8, 175, 186, 199, 217, 237)

Subcategories (24, 47)   Sub-Categories refer to sub-categories of
                                     each lexical category ie: a verb sub-category

Subcategorize for (30)   a term used to describe the types of
                                     complements/objects that a verb requires,
                                     such as 'put' subcategorizes for an NP object
                                     and a PP complement
Subject (89, 103, 131)   the specifier of the main verb in a clause

Subject Pronoun (52, 54-5, 65, 123, 127-9,148, 160, 245)
                                     one of the words 'I,' 'you,' 'she,' 'he,' 'it,' 'we,'
                                     'they' when used as the subject of a clause.
Subject Relative Pronouns (148-9, 151, 186-8)
                                     what' and 'who' when use as the subject of a
                                     relative clause
Subordinating Conjunction (5, 43-4, 58, 60-1, 65, 67, 76, 100, 109, 113, 117,
                                     119-120, 127-8, 169, 214-15)
                                     a conjunction such as 'although,' 'while,' or
                                     'because,' which introduces a dependent
                                     clause. The clause will normally be movable
                                     within the sentence.
Superlative (10, 11-14, 44-46, 50, 66, 125, 217)
                                     Forms ending in -est meaning 'most,' which
                                     are also used for comparisons
Syntactic Movement (88, 90, 91, 94, 105, 118, 120, 132, 136, 142-161)
                                     movement of a word or phrase that is
                                     obligatory for acceptable grammar
Syntactic Testing (4, 14-19, 24, 32-39, 42, 44, 49-50, 66)
                                     Diagnostic tool used to determine the
                                     different types of: words, phrases, and clauses
Tense Hopping (90-1, 94, 116, 127, 143-4, 165, 173, 181-2)
                                     the movement of the tense (and number and
                                     person) information from the auxiliary to the
                                     main verb (in the simple present and past
                                     tenses)
Testing for Modifiers (165-7, 175, 178-9, 185, 187-8, 197)
                                     removing a phrase from within a larger
                                     phrase to see if it is required to complete the
                                     larger phrase grammatically or semantically
There Insertion (153)   a stylistic transformation where the word
                                     'there' is inserted into the NP-subject position,
                                     causing the NP-subject to move to the right of
                                     the verb
Third Person Singular (7, 14, 17, 90, 229)
                                     the information representing 'he,' 'she,' or 'it'

Trace (94, 142-144, 160)   an empty category left by a moved word or
                                     phrase

Transformation (62, 143-161) the effect of constituent/phrasal movement on a sentence

Transitive prepositional Verb (33, 203)

 a verb which has both a direct object and a PP complement (the most common example is 'put.')

Transitive Verb (28, 30-31) a verb which has an NP object

Unreduced Finite Adjective Clause (134)

 a relative clause or other adjective clause whose relative marker has not been deleted

Vacuous Movement (148-9, 151, 185-8, 272)

 the invisible movement of a subject relative pronoun from the specifier position of IP to the specifier position of CP to make all relative pronouns consistently CP structures

Vacuous Movement of Subject Relative Pronouns   (149, 151, 186-188)

 the invisible movement of a subject relative pronoun from the specifier position of IP to the specifier position of CP to make all relative pronouns consistently CP structures

Vacuous(ly) (148-9, 151, 185-8, 272)

 Invisible(y)

Verb Particle (2, 25, 34-36, 38, 67)

 a lexical item resembling an adverb or a preposition which has combined with a verb to create a verb with an idiomatic meaning

Verb Tense (6-7, 60-61) the distinction in English between present and past morphology of an auxiliary or verb

Verbless Clause (132 another name for Absolute Phrase/Clause

Verb (23-37, 67, 74-77, 204) an open lexical category with possible past and present participle forms

VP used Adjectivally (118, 124, 179, 239)

 a non-finite VP headed by an '-ing' verb form used attributively (before the noun)

'Wanna' Construction (142-3) a phonological elision of the two words 'want' and 'to'

Wh-Fronting (146, 149, 184, 186) The movement of the question words what, who(m), where, when, how, and why (and which+NP) to sentence-initial position in information questions

XP (59, 71-73) an abbreviation for a phrase of any category

References

Anonymous. "Churchill." Brainyquote.
    http://www.brainyquote.com/quotes/authors/w/winston_
    churchill_2.html#ixzz1eTiwlTj9. accessed 21 November 2011.
Anonymous. "Fairness" http://en.wikipedia.org/wiki/Justice. Accessed November
    2011.
Anonymous. Funniest Ambiguous Headlines. http://www.squidoo.com/funniest-
    headlines. Accessed August 2010.
Anonymous. List of English Prepositions. http://en.wikipedia.org/ wiki/ List_of_
    English_prepositions. Accessed August 2009.
Anonymous. "Preposition." ThinkExist.
    http://en.thinkexist.com/search/searchQuotation.
    asp?search=preposition. Accessed November 2011.
Aaron, Jane E. 2007. The Little, Brown Compact Handbook. New York: Pearson-
    Longman.
Bartlett, John, comp. 2000 Familiar Quotations, 10th ed, rev. and enl. By Nathan
    Haskell Dole. Boston: Little, Brown, 1919; Bartleby.com.
    www.bartleby.com/100/. 4 August 2008.
Benjamin, Arthur E. Nightly News with Brian William 21 November 2011.
    http://www.msnbc.msn.com/id/3032619/. Accessed 22 November 2011.
Bryson, Linda. "English Conjunctions." http://www2.gsu.edu /~wwwesl
    /egw/bryson.htm. 12 June 2009.
Burger, Henry. The Wordtree - a reverse dictionary. http://www.many-
    things.org/voa/wm/wm177.html; accessed 26 July 2008.
Butcher, S.H. and A. Lang. 1879. The Odyssey of Homer done into English
    prose. Preface to the 3nd Ed. London: MacMillan & Co.
    http://www.gutenberg.org/cache/epub/1728/pg1728.txt. Accessed Nov.
    2011.
Canary, Robert H. 2002. An Outline of Homer's Iliad. http://homepages.uwp.edu/
    canary/eng246/iliad.html. Accessed August 2009.
Chaucer, Geoffrey. The Canterbuty Tales. D. Laing Purves, Ed. Gutenberg
    Project text. Accessed 16 December 2011.
Clark, Mary M. 2003. The Structure of English for Readers, Writers and
    Teachers. Glen Allen, VA: College Publishing.
Conners, Robert J. and Andrea A. Lunsford. 1988. "Frequency of Formal Errors
    in Current College Writing, or Ma and Pa Kettle Do Research." College
    Composition and Communication, 39:4, 395-409. Dec 1988.
Contemporary English Version Bible. http://www.biblegateway.com/
    passage/?search=Acts%2021&version=CEV
Corbett, Edward P.J., 1987. Classical Rhetoric for the Modern Student. 3rd Ed.
    New York: Oxford UP.
Cowan, Ron. 2008. The Teacher's Grammar of English. New York: Cambridge
    University Press.
Crystal, David. The Cambridge Encyclopedia of Language. New York:
    Cambridge University Press. 1987
Curzan, Anne, and Michael Adams. 2006. How English Works: A Linguistic
    Introduction. New York: Pearson/Longman.

Hillocks, George, Jr. and Michael W. Smith. "Grammar and Usage." Handbook of Research on Teaching the English Language Arts." James Flood, Julie M. Jensen, Diane Lapp, and James R. Squire, eds. New York: Macmillan. 591- 603 at 598.

Hoffman, Melvin J. "Sentence diagramming: no unanimity among users." Academic Exchange Quarterly. Mar 2007.
http://www.thefreelibrary.com/
Sentence+diagramming:+no+unanimity+among+users-a0165912653.
Accessed August 2009.

Hunt, Kellogg W. 1970. Syntactic Maturity in Schoolchildren and Adults.Monographs of the Society for Research in Child Development, no. 134. Chicago, IL: University of Chicago Press.

Jung, Yeun-Jin. 2003. "Categories and Features in Gerundive Nominals." Studies in Generative Grammar. 13: 197-219 Seoul: Korean Generative Grammar Circle.

Lynch, Jack. "Prepositions." Guide to Grammar and Style.
http://andromeda.rutgers.edu/~jlynch/Writing/p.html#prepositions.   12 June 2009.

Klammer, Thomas P., Muriel R. Schultz, and Angela D. Volpe. 2007. Analyzing English Grammar. 5th Ed. New York: Pearson Longman.

MacQuade, Findlay. "Examining a Grammar Course: The Rationale and the Result." English Journal 69.7 October 1980: 26-30 at 29.

Maimon, Elaine P., Janice H. Peritz, Kathleen Blake Yancey. 2007. Boston: McGraw-Hill.

Pires, Acrisio. 2006. The minimalist syntax of defective domains: Gerunds and infinitives. Amsterdam: John Benjamins.

Radford, Andrew. 1988. Transformational Grammar: A First Course. Cambridge: Cambridge University Press.

Radford, Andrew. 1997. Syntactic theory and the structure of English: a minimalist approach. Cambridge: Cambridge University Press.

Reed, Alonzo and Brainerd Kellogg. 1880. Higher Lessons in English: A Work on English Grammar and Composition, in which the Science of the Language is made tributary to the Art of Expression. New York: Clark & Maynard.

Rickford, John. 1997. "Suite for Ebony and Phonics." Discover. Dec. 1997 82-87.

Siegel, Laura. 1998. Gerundive Nominals and The Role of Aspect. In Austin, J. and A. Lawson (Eds) The Proceedings of ESCOL '97. Ithaca: CLC Publications

Wycliffe Bible.
http://www.biblegateway.com/passage/?search=Acts%2010&version=WYC. Accessed August 2010.

CPSIA information can be obtained at www.ICGtesting.com
Printed in the USA
LVOW11s0331100115

422197LV00004B/143/P